Praise For *Gray Divorce*

"Gray divorce: blame the doctors for allowing people to live longer; blame the chemists with their little blue pills that allow for sexual rebirth; blame capitalism, which after all is a raging success that allows the privileged few to have serial marriages and divorces and pay for discarded wives, the children they put in boarding school, etc. But there it is—it's a reality of life and it's going to get worse or better depending upon which side of the age barrier you live. Dr. Jocelyn Elise Crowley has done a brilliant job describing the landscape of gray divorces. Celebrity divorces are described: they are, let us say, 'mature'—or at least fraying at the edges. She then goes into the statistics and demographics of divorces, and then personalizes it with interviews with everyday people. The bottom line is that these divorces are acceptable, alive, and well in America— and people who are bothered by them are just going to have to suck it up."

RAOUL FELDER, nationally and internationally recognized divorce and family lawyer, named one of America's 100 most powerful lawyers by *New York Law Journal*

"Research shows that gray divorces pose a significant health and financial risk for those couples who come apart later in life, as well as their family members. I know firsthand just how painful and devastating it can be. As a relationship expert and modern love doctor, I've worked with hundreds of couples that have experienced gray divorce. I believe *Gray Divorce* illuminates, through its stories and information, many of the reasons for this new phenomenon. It's my deepest wish that by understanding gray divorce, we can also create new ways to prevent the harm it can cause and promote healing for those who experience this life crisis."

DR. BRENDA WADE, author, psychologist, five-time national television host, and regular expert guest on *The Dr. Oz Show*

"Dr. Jocelyn Elise Crowley eloquently describes some of the intimate stories and causes behind gray divorce, a relatively new cultural phenomenon. As the author of *Your Best Age Is Now,* I was fascinated to learn some of the more intricate and in-depth reasons why some mid-lifers are motivated to make this marital choice. Dr. Crowley describes for her readers the more private portrait behind the often two-dimensional statistics described in the news. And in doing so, she provides a more relatable and empathic picture of the reasons behind this complex and difficult decision. Fortunately for us, her book reads more like a page-turning novel than a straight psychological textbook. Dr. Crowley's book is a must-read for anyone interested in the psychodyn⸱   ⸱ ⸱ ⸱ ⸱⸱⸱⸱⸱⸱ behind the midlife divorce and the real-life trials it can pos   ⸱s situation."

DR. ROBI LUDWIG, psychotl   1d author of *Your Best Age Is Now*

"Dr. Jocelyn Elise Crowley has written an incredibly insightful and engaging examination of the growing phenomenon of gray divorce. She is at the forefront of observing the trend that everyone will soon be talking about as it impacts more and more families. *Gray Divorce* excels in making us understand what makes long-term marriages fail, and the book can be reverse-engineered as a guide to making marriages work."

FRANCESCA HOGI, *Today Show* relationship expert, matchmaker, and love coach

"Gray divorce will only become more prevalent in the coming years, and our ability to understand—as well as help—the millions of people going through divorce at older ages depends on insightful social science research like that presented here by Dr. Jocelyn Elise Crowley. She uses compelling individual stories to show how the causes and consequences of gray divorce differ for women and men, and to build a case for personal and social intervention to help individuals and families in this situation. This is a valuable book about a subject of great—and growing—social importance."

PHILLIP N. COHEN, author of *Enduring Bonds: Families and Modern Inequality*

"We should all be incredibly grateful to Dr. Jocelyn Elise Crowley for her most important book. *Gray Divorce* is a must-read for everyone over 50 and everyone close to someone over 50, as well as for physicians, therapists, clergy, and others who work with them. Dr. Crowley has done us a great service by showing what's at stake, the losses, the gains, and the changes that come with a gray divorce. Millions are in that 'before it's too late' category of wondering if they should end their marriage now or hang in there for the duration. This book will help them feel they have a wise companion to help them through a most confusing and stressful period. My greatest admiration and gratitude go to Dr. Crowley for this book."

MIRA KIRSHENBAUM, Clinical Director of The Chestnut Hill Institute and author of *Too Good to Leave, Too Bad to Stay* and *I Love You but I Don't Trust You*

Gray Divorce

Gray Divorce

WHAT WE LOSE AND GAIN FROM
MID-LIFE SPLITS

Jocelyn Elise Crowley, PhD

UNIVERSITY OF CALIFORNIA PRESS

University of California Press, one of the most distinguished university presses in the United States, enriches lives around the world by advancing scholarship in the humanities, social sciences, and natural sciences. Its activities are supported by the UC Press Foundation and by philanthropic contributions from individuals and institutions. For more information, visit www.ucpress.edu.

University of California Press
Oakland, California

© 2018 by Jocelyn Elise Crowley

Library of Congress Cataloging-in-Publication Data

Names: Crowley, Jocelyn Elise, 1970- author.
Title: Gray divorce : what we lose and gain from mid-life splits / Jocelyn Elise Crowley.
Description: Oakland, California : University of California Press, [2018] | Includes bibliographical references and index. |
Identifiers: LCCN 2017025959 (print) | LCCN 2017028947 (ebook) | ISBN 9780520968110 (ebook) | ISBN 9780520295315 (cloth : alk. paper) | ISBN 9780520295322 (pbk : alk. paper)
Subjects: LCSH: Divorce—United States. | Older people—United States.
Classification: LCC HQ834 (ebook) | LCC HQ834 .c755 2018 (print) | DDC 306.89—dc23
LC record available at https://lccn.loc.gov/2017025959

Manufactured in the United States of America

27 26 25 24 23 22 21 20 19 18
10 9 8 7 6 5 4 3 2 1

In Loving Memory of Alan

Contents

Acknowledgments

I dread writing book acknowledgments because I know I will miss thanking people who were fundamental to the success of this project. To all of the folks I am now going to miss, thank you.

I am deeply grateful to my eighty interviewees who took time out of their busy lives to tell me their gray divorce stories. These were not always easy to tell, but they opened up to me in extraordinarily giving ways. I hope I have reflected their thoughts, emotions, and perspectives accurately.

In the development stages of the book, the Michael J. and Susan Angelides Public Policy Research Fund at the Edward J. Bloustein School of Planning and Public Policy supported the project financially. Stephanie Holcomb and Jessica Brand provided excellent research assistance, while Marc Weiner, with the assistance of Orin Puniello, devised and executed a recruitment strategy for the project that was seamless. Raymonde Pozzolano's transcription team was fabulous once again in moving the recorded voices of my interviewees onto paper.

At the University of California Press, Naomi Schneider served as an amazing guide through the publication process. I am truly grateful that she was a cheerleader for the book from its inception. The book would not be in its readable form without the incredible efforts of Tamie Parker

Song. I thank her for making my voice clearer and my arguments crisper. Thanks go to Robert Demke, PJHeim, and Francisco Reinking for assisting with all aspects of production. I also appreciate all of the help offered by Renee Donovan, Alex Dahne, and Chris Sosa Loomis in packaging this final product at the press. With her excellent partnership with the press, Isabella Michon continues to be the consummate professional in the field of book publicity.

My family and friends supported me throughout this entire journey. I am so grateful for their ongoing support. In particular I would like to thank Patricia Sheffield, Monica Crowley, Bill Siegel, Arlene Sheffield, Michael Hopp, M.B. Crowley, Susan and Stephen Braitman, Ellen Braitman, David Shapiro, Mark Braitman, Kathy Brister, John Spry, Amy Schapiro, Sandhya Higgins, Deborah Szillat, Suzanne Glaser, Maryann Barakso, Theresa Luhm, Elizabeth Wood, Oliver Zeff, Michelle Wilson, Laura Carucci, Susan Crawford Sullivan, Anne Marie Cammisa, Valerie Young, and the entire Pisapia family. Finally, my beautiful husband, Alan Colmes, did not live to see the end of this entire process, but I know he is still watching over me even as my heart is broken. This book is dedicated with the greatest possible love to his memory.

1 The Coming Tidal Wave of Gray Divorce

Melanie Griffith, 58 years old, divorced Antonio Banderas, 55 years old, after almost two decades of marriage. At the time of the divorce, the couple had one 18-year-old daughter named Stella. The official cause of the divorce as cited in their petition was irreconcilable differences, but there were also whispers of infidelity on Banderas's part. As per their divorce settlement, Banderas was able to retain the profits from some of his films, such as *The Mask of Zorro, Spy Kids,* and *Desperado.* However, the couple had to split money made in many of his other films, among which were *Shrek 2, Puss in Boots, Machete Kills,* and *Expendables 3.* They agreed to sell and divide the proceeds from their Los Angeles home, and Griffith, perhaps best known for her Golden Globe–winning performance in *Working Girl,* as well as her notable roles in *The Bonfire of the Vanities, Paradise,* and *Shining Through,* was able to keep their Aspen home. The court also had to divide their other major assets, including Pablo Picasso and Diego Rivera paintings. Finally, the court awarded Griffith with $65,000 per month in alimony. This was the second divorce for Banderas and the fourth for Griffith.

DIVORCE FINALIZED, JANUARY 2004—MARRIED FOR 20 YEARS

Blockbuster movie star Harrison Ford, 61 years old, divorced Melissa Mathison, 53 years old, after two decades of marriage. Harrison met Mathison while working on the movie *Apocalypse Now* in 1976. They had two children together, both of whom were teenagers when they decided to call it quits. The media reported that the cause of the divorce was Ford's promiscuous behavior. Gossip columnists noted that late in the marriage, Ford moved out of the couple's New York City apartment and started frequenting bars and strip clubs. Even though they tried to reconcile after a long period of tense relations, after a while both Ford and Mathison decided together that they had endured enough. Ford was best known for his featured roles in *Star Wars, Indiana Jones, Blade Runner,* and *The Fugitive.* Mathison was also significantly accomplished, writing with Steven Spielberg the screenplay for *E. T. the Extra-Terrestrial,* for which she received an Academy Award nomination. She also had screen writing credits for the films *The Black Stallion, The Escape Artist,* and *Twilight Zone: The Movie,* among others. Mathison reportedly received $90 million at the time of the divorce, as well as a percentage of future earnings from some of Ford's earlier movies. This was the second divorce for Ford and the first for Mathison.

DIVORCE FINALIZED, DECEMBER 2011—MARRIED FOR 31 YEARS

Mel Gibson, 55 years old, divorced his wife, Robyn Moore, 55 years old. They had had seven children and had been married for over three decades. At the time of the divorce, only one of their children was a minor. They originally had met when she was a dental nurse and he was a struggling actor in Australia. Later, Moore dedicated her life to raising their children, and the couple acquired enormous wealth through his films, such as the *Mad Max* and the *Lethal Weapon* series, *Braveheart,* and *The Passion of the Christ.* Gibson reportedly cited a lack of religious compatibility as the reason for his highly visible split; he was a devout Catholic, while she was an Episcopalian. But others attributed the breakdown to Gibson's alcoholism and his other erratic behavior. As part of the divorce settlement, the couple had to split their $850 million fortune, consisting not only of cash but also of significant real estate holdings in Australia, Fiji, California, and Costa Rica. This was a first divorce for both Gibson and Moore.

.   .   .   .   .

For a long time before their divorces, these well-known, A-list couples seemed to have "made it work" with their soul mates by their sides. They were the standout exceptions to almost all Hollywood marriages, which tend to end almost immediately after they begin. True, they had amassed extraordinary wealth and lived lifestyles that most people could only dream about. But they were over the age of 50, and it seemed as though they had settled into their marriages for the long run as they moved into mid-life with their beloved partners. So even though they were Hollywood marriages, they were "one of us," dedicated and devoted aging partners.

Then, suddenly, the cracks seemed to appear out of nowhere, and their marriages folded. The immediate public thirst for the details of their breakups was deep as both men and women all over the country asked, how could this be? This is not the way divorce is supposed to work! Divorce is painful enough the way it "normally" comes about, when the dreams of a young, in-love couple somehow run off course. But divorce in mid-life? That does not make any sense. What could make couples in this age group—and at this stage in their lives—go off the rails?

This is the mystery called gray divorce—defined as a divorce occurring at or after the age of 50. Many of these divorces take place after 20, 30, and even 40 years of marriage. They tend to shock the consciences, both near and far, of those who witness the implosion. The questions simply go on and on. Why would couples in mid-life want to make such a drastic change in their marital status? Haven't they seemed to deftly maneuver through the ups and downs of typical married life so far? Don't they care about the time that they have already invested in each other? Haven't they already successfully raised children to adulthood—or close to it—together? What could possibly go wrong at this stage in their lives? Aren't they with their soul mates by now?

These are the questions that drive this book. More specifically, this book aims to explore the dynamics surrounding an important societal trend that has been emerging across the American landscape in recent years: married couples splitting up when, by social convention and expectation, they should be planning and enjoying their retirement years together. The statistical forecasts for this aging Baby Boomer generation are dire. Almost everyone is aware that American society is aging. In 1990, as table 1 details, there were approximately 63.7 million Americans ages 50 and older. By 2010, the size of this population reached 99 million Americans. Meanwhile, as table 2 indicates, during the years 1990–2010, the divorce rate for all those aged 15 and higher dropped slightly from 19 to 17.9 divorces per 1,000 married persons. But the divorce rate for adults aged 50 and over moved in the opposite direction, doubling from 4.87 to 10.05. Put in other terms, this means that approximately one in four divorces in the United States is now "gray."

Numerically, this translates into about 643,152 older individuals obtaining a divorce in 2010 alone, as table 2 also illustrates.[1] More recent data show that the divorce rate for those aged 50 and over has remained stable into 2015, leading some to project that by 2030, 828,380 individuals will experience a gray divorce in that year alone.[2] Given current population growth trends, which predict that 158.5 million individuals aged 50 and older will be residing in the United States by 2050, this splitting-up trend implies that a growing percentage of both men and women will be living as divorced individuals in their mid-life years.[3] But will both sexes experience similar post–gray divorce lives? That is, will they have the same challenges and opportunities as they undergo these family transitions?

Simply put, the answer is an emphatic no. This book argues that there is a gray divorce penalty for both women and men divorcing at or after the age of 50, but the exact nature of the penalty is different for each sex. For women, we will see that it is an *economic* gray divorce penalty, and for men, a *social* divorce penalty.

Before exploring these penalties, we must first understand the emergence of gray divorce as a particularly recent phenomenon. More specifically, the explosion of gray divorce in contemporary America can be thought of as the combination of three macrolevel, societal trends, all interrelated. First and probably most important is the proliferation of a "divorce culture."[4] A country with a divorce culture has citizens with certain expectations about the likely rewards of marriage, and when these

Table 1 An Aging America

CURRENT AND PROJECTED POPULATION BY AGE GROUP, IN THOUSANDS

Population	1990	2000	2010	2020	2030	2040	2050	Percent Change in Population, 1990–2050 by Age Group
Total	**248,710**	**281,422**	**308,746**	**334,503**	**359,402**	**380,219**	**398,328**	**60.2**
Under 5	18,354	19,176	20,201	20,568	21,178	21,471	22,147	20.7
5 to 9	18,099	20,550	20,349	20,274	21,347	21,632	22,158	22.4
10 to 14	17,114	20,528	20,677	20,735	21,182	21,842	22,171	29.5
15 to 19	17,754	20,220	22,040	21,048	21,060	22,190	22,516	26.8
20 to 24	19,020	18,964	21,586	22,059	22,299	22,866	23,615	24.2
25 to 29	21,313	19,381	21,102	23,722	23,179	23,377	24,646	15.6
30 to 34	21,863	20,510	19,962	23,168	23,878	24,302	25,004	14.4
35 to 39	19,963	22,707	20,180	22,060	24,898	24,507	24,813	24.3
40 to 44	17,616	22,442	20,891	20,568	23,840	24,668	25,190	43.0
45 to 49	13,873	20,092	22,709	20,204	22,351	25,274	24,995	80.2
50 to 54	11,350	17,586	22,298	20,638	20,506	23,844	24,781	118.3
55 to 59	10,532	13,469	19,665	21,879	19,777	22,023	25,023	137.6
60 to 64	10,616	10,805	16,818	21,141	19,799	19,880	23,275	119.2
65 to 69	10,112	9,534	12,435	18,194	20,397	18,704	21,054	108.2
70 to 74	7,995	8,857	9,278	14,882	18,830	17,940	18,294	128.8
75 to 79	6,121	7,416	7,318	10,112	15,013	17,143	16,042	162.1
80 to 84	3,934	4,945	5,743	6,527	10,737	13,924	13,634	246.6
85 to 89	2,060	2,790	3,620	3,964	5,747	8,867	10,492	409.3
90 to 94	769	1,113	1448	2,024	2,464	4,320	5,951	673.9
95 and over	250	337	424	738	920	1447	2528	911.2
50 and over	**63,739**	**76,852**	**99,047**	**120,099**	**134,190**	**148,092**	**161,074**	**152.7**

SOURCES: 1990 Census of Population, General Population Characteristics, United States (1990 CP-1-1); US Census Bureau, Census 2000 Summary File 1 and 2010 Census Summary File 1; Projections of the Population by Sex and Age for the United States: 2015 to 2060 (NP2014-T9), table 9, US Census Bureau, Population Division. Release Date: December 2014.

NOTE: Column totals vary slightly due to rounding.

Table 2   The Gray Divorce Revolution

Year and Age Group	Number of Divorces per 1,000 Married Persons Ages 15+	Number of Persons Who Divorce	Percent Increase in the Number of People Who Divorce from 1990 to 2010
1990: All Ages: 15+	19.0	2,364,000	.2%
2010: All Ages: 15+	17.9	2,369,454	
1990: All Older Ages: 50+	4.87	206,207	211.9%
2010: All Older Ages: 50+	10.05	643,152	
1990: Ages 50–64	6.9	175,954	201.13%
2010: Ages 50–64	13.05	529,842	
1990: Ages 65+	1.79	30,053	277.03%
2010: Ages 65+	4.84	113,310	

SOURCES: Brown, Susan L., and I-Fen Lin. "The Gray Divorce Revolution: Rising Divorce among Middle-Aged and Older Adults, 1990–2010." *Journals of Gerontology Series B: Psychological Sciences and Social Sciences* 67, no. 6 (2012): 731–41; Clarke, Sally C., and National Center for Health Statistics. *Advance Report of Final Divorce Statistics, 1989 and 1990.* US Department of Health and Human Services National Center for Health Statistics, 1995; American Community Survey, various years.

expectations are not met, divorce becomes permissible. In the early part of the twentieth century, marriage involved a set of public obligations between couples. In particular, American marriages were partnerships that focused on pooling resources to provide children and other dependents with the tools deemed necessary to move them up the ladder of opportunity. The institution of marriage was also the bedrock of community life as families frequently looked to one another within their own neighborhoods for assistance in times of need.

Beginning in the second part of the twentieth century, Americans began seeing marriage through a different lens, the direct result of a seismic shift in individual priorities. Men and women had believed that living a satisfying life meant fulfilling the duties and obligations of the broader social world, a world where the values of mutual aid and cooperation were paramount. The personal revolution that took place mid-century, however, embodied a reorientation toward satisfaction with one's own life over communal duty. This did not mean that individuals no longer worried about the common good. It did mean, however, that both sexes started caring much more than ever before about their own individual well-being as they sought purposeful meaning in their lives.

This movement toward fulfilling personal goals had important consequences in the context of American marriage. As part of this revolution that emphasized self-satisfaction, men and women started to look at marriage as a site for their own inner growth. As a result, the formal commitment of marriage became a promise between both members of the couple to help each other meet individually based goals. In this new arrangement, the success of a marriage became measured by each person's level of contentment as part of a couple. If a certain baseline of happiness could not be obtained, either the husband or the wife now had the socially acceptable option of exiting the marriage through divorce. In other words, divorce became widely approved as a suitable termination of a contract between two people who were no longer happy together.[5]

The second factor propelling gray divorce has been the dramatic growth in life expectancy among Americans. According to the Centers for Disease Control and Prevention, in 1950, the average life expectancy of all Americans was 68.2 years.[6] Men lived until approximately 65.6 years, and women lived for about 71.1 years. By 2014, life expectancy had increased dramatically, to 78.8 years, on average, for all Americans. Men now live to 76.4 years, and women live approximately 81.2 years. As life expectancy continues to grow, the risk of losing a spouse to death decreases, while the risk of losing a spouse to divorce in later life increases. In addition, as the chance of divorce increases, a larger part of this older population has the potential to get remarried.[7] Indeed, table 3 illustrates the significant prevalence of remarriage in the United States today, with a substantial percentage of couples divorcing then remarrying twice, three times, or even more frequently. Americans who divorce in later years are not necessarily giving up on the institution of marriage; instead, in many cases, they are forming new marital units with other partners as they age.[8] Second, third, and even additional marriages are more likely to fail than first marriages; as the number of remarriages increases over time, we can potentially expect this trend to produce an increase in the number of older Americans experiencing a gray divorce as well.[9]

The third contributing factor to the rise in gray divorce has been the spread of no-fault divorce laws in the United States.[10] Throughout most of

Table 3   Marital History for People 15 Years and over by Age and Sex: 2008–2012

Characteristic	Total, 15 Years or Older	50–59 Years	60–69 Years	70 Years and Over
MALE				
Total	115,969,884	19,970,679	13,830,810	11,237,095
Percent				
Never Married	33.6	11.6	6.2	3.7
Ever Married	66.4	88.4	93.8	96.3
Married Once	49.9	60.5	60.3	69.4
Married Twice	13.0	21.6	24.4	20.4
Married Three Times or More	3.5	6.3	9.1	6.5
FEMALE				
Total	124,129,728	21,342,984	15,324,558	15,472,080
Percent				
Never Married	27.9	9.6	5.9	3.9
Ever Married	72.1	90.4	94.1	96.1
Married Once	54.5	61	64	74.1
Married Twice	14	22.3	22.4	17.3
Married Three Times or More	3.7	7	7.6	4.7

SOURCE: Lewis, Jamie M., and Rose M. Kreider. "Remarriage in the United States: American Community Survey Reports." 1–27: United States Census Bureau, 2015. Adapted from table 1.

American history, one party seeking a divorce had to establish "cause" for it to even be considered by the judicial system.[11] Commonly cited causes were cruelty, abandonment, or adultery. Establishing cause and assigning blame were particularly critical in divorce actions as they often dictated the terms of the settlement. For example, individuals who were proven as having committed adultery could receive a smaller percentage of the asset split as a penalty for their bad behavior. In addition, judges often determined the amount and duration of alimony awards based on who was at fault in causing the divorce. Because so much was at stake, each party to the divorce aimed to paint his or her spouse in the worst possible light, often fabricating charges along the way. These claims and counterclaims clogged up the judicial system with lies, delays, and character assassinations.

As a result, over time, observers of the court system started to advocate for cleaner and swifter procedures for divorce actions, whereby evidence of wrongdoing would not be important in establishing settlements. In this reformed system, the primary goal of the divorce process would be to separate the husband and wife as quickly and fairly as possible. Pursuant to these ends, in the 1970s and 1980s, reformers set into motion the no-fault divorce system, which does not mandate the assignment of blame for divorce actions.[12] The no-fault model quickly proliferated throughout most of the United States, although most states still permitted "cause-based" actions. Nevertheless, as a result of this no-fault revolution, divorce proceedings overall have become less investigatory and more private as the two members of the couple do not necessarily have to publicly lay out the reasons for their split. Overall, then, a growing divorce culture, the rise in life expectancy, and the emergence of no-fault laws created a fertile environment for the gray divorce phenomenon not only to take root but also to feverishly spread across the fifty states into the twenty-first century.

THE CONSEQUENCES OF GRAY DIVORCE

While there is no doubt that gray divorce is becoming a force to be reckoned with all over the United States, is it experienced in different ways by women and men? One way to think about the consequences of such a mid-life divorce is that a marital split represents a breakdown of a very important protective institution. Within the context of marriage, two people pool economic and social resources together in their interactions with the world. If one half of the couple is struggling for whatever reason in one of these areas, the other half can keep them both afloat until their problems are resolved. A divorce destroys this partnership, and now each individual must go it alone. When we think about the potential for post–gray divorce hardships, then, we must consider the distinct challenges facing single, mid-life women and single, mid-life men as they begin to restructure their new lives on their own.

First, let us consider economics. What is the relative financial position at mid-life for women and men? Undoubtedly, women have seen their economic power increase over time. The women's movement of the 1960s and 1970s helped them to use a singular voice in calling for greater financial equality with their male counterparts. As a result of their political efforts, women began to be more significant players in the paid labor market. In fact, over the course of the period 1975–2014, *all* women's labor force participation—from women 16 years old through women ages 75 and older—grew from 46.3% to 57%.[13] Of course, women below the typical retirement age have traditionally participated at much higher rates. In addition, it is important to note that it was not just women entering the labor force as single or married childless individuals. Women were also entering the labor force as mothers. In fact, mothers with children up to the age of 18 increased their labor force participation during this same time period from 47.4% to 70.8%.[14] In addition, excluding mothers of infants and toddlers who were more likely to be at home, mothers of children from the ages of six to 17 were most likely to participate in paid work over this period. Their labor force participation rate grew from 54.9% to 75.8%.[15]

Women also made inroads in terms of their earning power. While they still lagged behind their male counterparts in terms of total income, women became responsible for a greater share of their families' household earnings in the latter half of the twentieth century. More specifically, during the time period 1970–2013, wives moved from providing a median percentage of 26.6% of all household income to 37.3% of all household income.[16] Women were also successful in at least partially closing some of the pay gap with men. In 1979, they earned only 62.3% of male earnings, but by 2014, they made 82.5% of male earnings.[17] Over time, then, women have been advancing in the economic arena. Indeed, these two trends of increased labor force participation and higher earnings indicate that over time, women are more likely to be financially autonomous adults than they ever have been in the past. This also means that with their own occupational experiences and the ability to generate independent income, they increasingly have the capacity to leave unhappy marriages.[18]

However, women's gains have not been experienced uniformly, and some of their relative disadvantages compared to men only become more apparent as they age. For instance, married women are more likely than men to stay at home as homemakers, and this is especially true if the couple has children.[19] Some of these women remain at home for their entire marriage, leaving them without any easily marketable skill sets or retirement savings if they divorce in mid-life. Others reenter the labor market as their children grow older.[20] But, because these formerly employed women may have left the paid labor market at the height of their careers, they will likely earn less than similarly situated men when they return to jobs for which they are qualified. In addition, during their time away from paid employment, they are unlikely to be contributing to any type of retirement savings funds or to their social security accounts, further reducing their pool of future financial holdings. They are also unlikely to be able to catch up financially upon workforce reentry, no matter how hard they try, since women at this age have a good chance of facing significant age discrimination in finding, securing, and retaining employment.[21] And even if women work throughout their entire marriage, their lower wages relative to men will ultimately result in lower savings relative to men, and lower levels of social security benefits once they qualify.

Mid-life women also must face the realities of health care expenses and health insurance costs. In the United States, individuals can obtain privately sponsored health care insurance through their place of employment or through their spouses as dependents. If the latter is the case, prior to the passage of the Patient Protection and Affordable Care Act of 2010 (PPACA), a divorce meant that the half of the couple who was considered a dependent on the other spouse's health plan—typically the wife—could only receive temporary coverage through the Consolidated Omnibus Budget Reconciliation Act (COBRA). After this temporary coverage expired, these newly divorced individuals had to secure coverage either through their own employer if it were offered or through private purchase in the open market. These private plans were often especially costly, thus inhibiting enrollment. In addition, these plans might be unwilling to accept new applicants if those applicants had preexisting conditions. Fortunately, under the PPACA, there are new health insurance marketplaces promising lower rates, rules prohibiting discrimination based on sex and medical need, and tax credits and subsidies for those with low incomes to help them purchase insurance.

Besides private insurance, those experiencing a gray divorce will likely be eligible to receive Medicare for their health care needs, beginning at the age of 65. Medicare has several distinct parts, including coverage for hospital stays and doctor visits, but the program still leaves many of these costs to the individual, including prescription drugs.[22] It is also critical to note that Medicare does not cover nursing home stays beyond a limited time frame. If an individual has a low income, has few assets, and falls into one of a select set of eligible groups—parents and children with little means of support, people with disabilities, and the elderly—then he/she might qualify for the means-tested program Medicaid, which provides payments directly or indirectly to health care providers for these Americans' medical care, though it might not represent the highest quality of services.

Without a doubt, women facing a gray divorce are much more vulnerable than men confronting a gray divorce when it comes to health care costs and health insurance. Women under the Medicare-qualifying age of 65 are far more frequently dependent on their husbands' health insurance policies than vice versa. In fact, research has indicated that being a dependent on a husband's health insurance policy is a protective factor against a divorce.[23] This means that if women feel they must choose between adequate health care and an unhappy marriage, they are more likely to choose the unhappy marriage than women whose health care isn't dependent on their marriage. If women in this position do finally pursue a divorce, they lose their dependent coverage and must seek out a new insurance policy on their own.

At one end of the spectrum, such women might be fortunate enough to obtain employment-based coverage. However, others might not be able to find a job that offers such benefits. Many part-time and low-paying jobs that are female-dominated, for example, do not offer health benefits, and individual purchase of such policies might well be too expensive. At the opposite end of the spectrum, some women divorcing in mid-life might have such low incomes that they qualify for Medicaid.[24] In the middle of the spectrum, however, are the many people whose income is not high enough to afford private insurance, and is not low enough to qualify for Medicaid. Many of these Medicaid-ineligible divorced women become uninsured, often for long periods of time.[25] Moreover, the final impact of the PPACA on reducing insurance costs and thus bridging these insurance gaps is still unfolding.

Women over the age of 65 have Medicare coverage, but as described earlier, not every service is covered and premiums can be high. In addition, women are more likely than men to need long-term care, since they will outlive their male counterparts by an average of about five years.[26] Indeed, research demonstrates that women are more likely than men to enter a nursing home facility; they also tend to stay there longer than the opposite sex.[27] Recall, however, that Medicare does not cover nursing home stays beyond a short duration, and Medicaid steps in only after one's personal assets have been exhausted. To cover these costs, Americans are expected to purchase private, long-term health care insurance policies on their own. However, research has shown that a variety of factors prevent potential consumers from obtaining these long-term health care insurance plans.[28] Besides their incredibly high costs, consumers are doubtful about the fiscal viability of such plans. Companies come and go in this market as health care costs are increasingly volatile. There are also psychological barriers to making these purchases; weighing the pros and cons of long-term care forces people to think about the possibility of their own health deterioration, a subject many people want to avoid. As a result of these factors, only about 10% of American men and women over the age of 60 have such policies in place.[29]

While the harsh realities of economics tend to shape women's prospects as individuals after a gray divorce, social support is more likely to diminish for men after a gray divorce. The composition, breadth, and depth of men's friendships tend to be very different from women's friendships. Men are more likely to engage in activities with other men than to discuss their feelings.[30] If, then, they are facing a gray divorce, men are less likely to feel comfortable relaying their complex emotions to other men. In addition, married men often make and retain friendships with other coupled men in which the women in each couple are primarily responsible for making contact. In other words, the wives make plans, schedule events, and make phone calls on behalf of both halves of the couple, and the men assume the follower role. If there is a marital breakup, these friends have to decide which member of the divorcing couple—or both members of the couple—they are likely to support. If their consistent point of contact has been with the wives, they will be more likely to support and side with the wives after a breakup. Moreover, if their wives maintained the network of adult family relationships, men might lose these as well.

Relationships with children also change in the wake of a divorce.[31] In an intact, traditional family unit, mutual support between parents and children is commonplace. When children are young, parents are of course responsible for their overall care. As children age, parents move from providing basic needs, such as food, clothing, and shelter, to offering emotional and sometimes financial support. Yet the distribution of caregiving responsibilities between fathers and mothers is not equal. While fathers have increased the time that they spend taking care of their children over the past several decades, they still do much less of this work than mothers. Indeed, it is mothers who often have to struggle with balancing paid work and child care responsibilities.[32] Because of this more intensive time investment, children tend to establish stronger bonds with their mothers and less intense bonds with their fathers. If their parents divorce, children's attachments to their fathers may weaken even more, especially if these men become their noncustodial parents.[33]

Perhaps most noteworthy for the discussion here are the relationships that older divorcing men have with their adult or almost-adult children. Aging adults often need assistance with the tasks of daily living. For example, older adults require increasing levels of medical attention if they develop physical or mental health–related ailments. There are doctors' appointments to set up, drugs to administer, and health insurance claims to sort out. Aging adults also often require transportation, help with housing repairs, and companions for other errand-running activities. In married couples, partners typically care for each other. However, when couples experience a gray divorce, they immediately lose the care that they used to have from their former spouses.[34] To fill in this gap, divorcing mothers are often reliably helped by their adult children due to their strong, caregiving bonds and histories, but fathers might not be so lucky. At the time of a gray divorce, then, when aging fathers are most in need of various types of social support from their adult children, they might not be able to count on it.

·   ·   ·   ·   ·

Gray divorce, as has been highlighted here, is a complex, multifaceted process. It often affects mid-life men and women in very different ways. To understand these gender-based dynamics, I interviewed 40 men and 40 women who had experienced at least one gray divorce (divorce at or over the age of 50) in their lives. None of these individuals had been married to each other. All were heterosexual marriages, although gray divorce will likely emerge as a growing trend among gay and lesbian couples as they marry in greater numbers over time as well. These in-depth interviews took place over the phone from 2014 to 2015 and were typically one hour in length. I recruited these study participants using targeted advertising on Facebook.

It is important to emphasize, then, that all of these respondents self-selected into this study. Ultimately, the men and women who volunteered for participation tended to be more socioeconomically advantaged and white than a nationally representative sample of all individuals who have ever experienced a gray divorce.[35] This study, therefore, does not claim to speak for all Americans undergoing such a mid-life breakup. In many ways, in fact, because of their privileged socioeconomic status, these respondents are cushioned against some of the most severe consequences of mid-life divorce. Indeed, I broaden the discussion to the harsher penalties facing those from less-advantaged backgrounds in the conclusion of this book. Nevertheless, the lives of the central respondents captured here still provide us with rich detail and insight into the phenomenon of gray divorce as it is currently unfolding in the United States.

I also used an open-ended questionnaire—and never prompted potential answers—that enabled individuals to expand on any topic that they desired during the course of the interview. It is critical to note that all of their stories are told from their own point of view, with the biases emanating from lapses in memory, lack of information, and the desire to present socially desirable answers all potentially shaping their responses. In addition, and undoubtedly, their former partners, who are not interviewed in this book, might also contest parts or the entirety of their narratives. Nevertheless, the aim of this book is to present these respondents' voices as meaningful reflections on how they have processed their own personal gray divorces. The ultimate hope is to gain as much knowledge as possible about the multidimensional transition of gray divorce from these very personal reflections. Further information about the representativeness of the sample and the overall methods used in this study can be found in the data appendix.

As table 4 illustrates, the men and women who ended up participating in the study shared many similar characteristics. The average age of the

Table 4 Descriptive Statistics on Study Sample

Characteristic	Men	Women	Total
Average Age	58.5	59.2	58.8
Average Age of Ex-Spouse	54.4	59.0	56.7
Average Years Married before Gray Divorce	22.4	26.1	24.2
Average Number of Total Divorces	1.5	1.5	1.5
Average Years between Gray Divorce and Interview	2.1	2.7	2.4
Number of Respondents Who Lived Together before Marriage	21	25	46
Number of Respondents Who Initiated Divorce*	14	29	43
Number of Respondents with Biological/Adopted Children from This Marriage?	28	30	58
Average Number of Children from Focal Marriage	1.7	1.8	1.7
Number of Respondents Who Have Remarried	1	0	1
Number of Respondents Who Have Health Insurance Now	37	39	76
Number of Respondents Who Have Long-Term Care Insurance	1	5	6
Average Number of Persons in Household**	1.4	2.0	1.7
Political Party Identification***			
Republican	13	12	25
Democrat	10	15	25
Independent	5	5	10
Other	12	7	19
Average Household Income****	$99,036	$76,905	$88,402
Education			
Less Than High School	2	0	2
High School Diploma	3	4	7
Some College	7	8	15
Associate's Degree	1	5	6
Bachelor's Degree	10	16	26
Graduate or Professional Degree	17	7	24
Religion			
Roman Catholic	8	6	14
Non–Roman Catholic Christian	19	21	40
Jewish	2	5	7
Spiritual	7	4	11
None	3	4	7
Other	1	0	1
Race			
White	37	36	73
African-American	2	1	3
Hispanic	1	2	3
Native-American	0	1	1
TOTAL	40	40	80

NOTES: *Initiated Divorce: 2 men reported the divorce decision to be mutual. **Average Number of People in Household: 1 man reported this number as varying. ***Political Party Identification: 1 woman refused. ****Average Household Income: 3 women refused.

respondents was 58.8 years at the time of their interviews, and the average age of their ex-spouse was 56.7. Throughout this book, I will cite their ages as reported at the time of their interviews, not at the time of their divorces. The respondents represented in the study had been married for an average of 24.2 years before their gray divorce. Over the course of their lifetimes, respondents reported being married, on average, 1.5 times, and were interviewed about 2.4 years after their gray divorce. A little over half, 46 out of 80, had lived with their spouses before they got married. About half of the total sample initiated the divorce, with women more likely to do so than men. Approximately three-quarters of the total had biological or adopted children from their former marriages, with an average of about two. Only one man and no women had remarried after their gray divorce, but most respondents lived with at least one additional person, usually another family member, in their homes. Almost all respondents had health insurance at the time of their interviews, but only six had long-term health care insurance, with five being women. Most respondents were either Republicans or Democrats, with the remaining interviewees either claiming "other" party identifications or calling themselves "Independent." With respect to household income, these respondents were relatively advantaged; they made $88,402 on average, with male respondents reporting a much higher income than female respondents. They were also highly educated, with a total of 50 out of 80 of the interviewees having a bachelor's degree or a graduate or professional degree. In terms of religion, most were non–Roman Catholic Christian or Roman Catholic. Finally, 73 out of 80 of the respondents were white.

THE GRAY DIVORCE PENALTY

In developing the themes outlined earlier, this book argues that divorce in mid-life produces what I called a "gray divorce penalty." *The key point here is that women and men experience very different gray divorce penalties. Women face an economic gray divorce penalty.* For the reasons already briefly mentioned, as a result of their childbearing responsibilities and labor force participation patterns, as well as the structure of social policies in the United States, women are much more likely than men to struggle with financial problems if they divorce at or after the age of 50. But men do not emerge unscathed. *In particular, men face a social gray divorce penalty.* Again, as explained in the brief overview laid out earlier, men start out with weaker social networks before their divorces, and they suffer further friendship and adult family member relationship losses if they experience a marital breakup at or after the age of 50. They also face hardships because their adult children are less likely to offer them support in old age.

These gray divorce penalties are extremely difficult for the women and men who live through them. From the outside looking in, it is not easy to see a woman after a gray divorce worry about her long-term finances and ability—or inability—to retire. It is also disturbing to witness a man after a gray divorce deal with the emotional roller coaster of his life without a solid circle of friends, adult family members, or adult children offering support. But there are larger, macrolevel problems to consider as well. The impact of gray divorce extends well beyond the boundaries of the immediately affected couples into society at large.[36] For women, if they or their ex-husbands have had a work history, they will receive social security benefits, but this income might well not be enough to sustain them. Confronting the stark realities of deprivation or even poverty, these women might need to turn to the government for other types of income, food, or shelter needs. They also might require medical assistance in the form of Medicare or Medicaid. Costs for these programs are exploding at what many would argue is an unsustainable rate. The public economic expenses of gray divorce are thus clear. Taxpayers will be pressed to do more and more in response to women's economic vulnerability in the event of a gray divorce.

Men who lose social supports after a gray divorce can also impose significant costs on society. As men age, they may need a variety of services from friends, adult family members, and their adult children. This could involve a whole range of caregiving tasks, from help with basic chores such as paying bills to more complex duties, such as assistance with the activities of daily living. When these responsibilities are provided for by family members, they do not affect the public purse. However, if the links between older, divorcing men and their social networks weaken, they might find themselves nearly or even completely alone. They then might have to turn to publicly funded institutions for care, such as emergency rooms. In addition, if they require more intensive levels of long-term care, they might need to apply for Medicaid to cover the costs of nursing home stays if they deplete their own personal resources. In all of these cases, then, we can see that private, gray divorce penalties create public, gray divorce problems.

MOVING ON

The story of these Baby Boomers, of course, does not have to end there, with gray divorce penalties inflicting serious harm on both partners and society overall. In fact, for many individuals, just like the mid-life Hollywood couples we met at the beginning of this book who shocked us by splitting, seeking a gray divorce can open their lives to new worlds of hope. They can learn more about themselves as they build inspiring lives by themselves or with the companionship of new partners. They can, in essence, really start over after the age of 50.

The public costs of gray divorce are not inevitable and everlasting either. Poverty and overall economic strain among older women, and particularly those who are divorcing, can be prevented. Smart public policies in the areas of retirement income funding and health care reform can go far in meeting these needs. Similarly, socialization practices and cultural expectations around how men interact with their friends, family members, and adult children can change to strengthen these relationships. Support groups funded by a variety of sources can set men back on the course of personal growth and recovery. None of these goals is easy to achieve, but none is impossible either. This book ends with an aspirational road map for new beginnings for both couples and society at large facing the inevitability of gray divorce as it transforms social life across the United States.

2 Before the Gray Divorce

The difficulty I had with my . . . [ex-]wife was she didn't have [the] intellectual curiosity that I need. Um, she's bright enough. [But] she only got as far as an associate's degree. I've got four degrees; three master's and one BA, and we just never connected on that level. She criticized me for being a poor communicator, yet when I emailed her a paper or a research project or a questionnaire [that] I developed, . . . she took days to open it. Then when she opened it, I had to ask her what she thought. And she said, "I didn't understand it." And that was it. You know . . . I would have expected her to say, "Well, tell me a little bit more about it," [in] which [case] I could have presented [it] in a [different] way that would be of interest. So there were some real strains throughout that time.

—Mark, 67 years old, married for seven years

I initiated the divorce. And it was in response to a fairly long-standing problem with alcohol that my ex-husband had and still has . . . Our son was born in 1991 and we had our first round with a marriage counselor probably in 1994 . . . And then when our son was in probably seventh grade we had another huge blowout. I discovered a hotel receipt and went and counseled with our priest at that point. [The hotel receipt] was for the Oriental Fantasy suite at [this hotel] at 11:00 o'clock on a Tuesday morning and I'm quite certain I wasn't there at the time. (laughs) I can laugh about it now.

—Kathy, 53 years old, married for 25 years

．　　　．　　　．　　　．　　　．

Like all other types of divorce, gray divorce is rarely easy. In fact, for most couples it is extremely difficult. The case of Mark represents one important pattern for many experiencing a gray divorce—that in which two people grow apart who had at first seemed to have a lot in common. Mark had fallen for his wife quickly, and within a year of meeting her he proposed marriage on a romantic dinner cruise along the Seine in Paris. Initially, he loved being with his new wife. She was a great cook and, more importantly, had a wonderful sense of humor. He had a lot of fun with her throughout their time together. He appreciated her love for her family and the values that this love reflected. However, as the years went on, he could no longer handle the lack of intellectual stimulation in their relationship. He needed to be mentally challenged, and over time her inability to satisfy him in this way became too oppressive for him to continue. Though it was enormously painful, he felt the marriage had to end.

For others experiencing a gray divorce, there is a dramatic "moment of reckoning," such as that described by Kathy when she found the hotel receipt from her husband's extramarital dalliance. Prior to this discovery, the couple experienced a significant period of turmoil as she tried to deal with her husband's drinking problem. The couple even sought therapy to handle this serious addiction as they raised their only son. Although their marriage was riddled with cracks, Kathy reported that she was still willing to work on their union over the long run. What put her over the edge, however, was her husband's affair. No matter how she tried to understand and forgive his indiscretion, she could not get over it and so subsequently filed for divorce.

In many ways, both breakup stories represent common experiences of emotional upheaval that emerge when couples finally decide to go forward with their gray divorces. Both growing apart and sexual infidelity, as we shall see, play a pivotal role in many mid-life splits. Yet they are not the sole causes of all of these marital breakdowns; other factors are often at play. But before we move to map out the whole range of reasons *why* men and women divorce at or after the age of 50, it is important to know a little bit more about *who* is likely to divorce. While not everyone is immune from a split, not everyone is equally predisposed to breaking up either.

WHAT DO WE KNOW ABOUT THE PREDICTORS OF DIVORCE FOR YOUNGER COUPLES?

Certainly we have come to know quite a bit about the risk factors related to divorce, but it is important to point out that most of this research has been conducted among younger couples. With this critical caveat in mind, the first set of predictors has to do with an individual's sociodemographic character-istics. If a person marries as a teenager, is poor, is non-Catholic, experiences unemployment, has a low level of education, or grows up with parents who were not continuously married, that person is more likely to divorce than a person without these characteristics.[1] Notably, the effects of race have been less than clear-cut.[2] Some researchers have suggested that the tendency to divorce varies by racial group, while other studies have pointed to race as only making a difference in predicting divorce when it interacts with or is combined with other defining characteristics, such as level of education.[3]

One of the most important puzzles in terms of sociodemographic charac-teristics as predictors of divorce relates to women's financial prospects.[4] As discussed previously, women have been entering the labor market in greater numbers than ever before, and earning a larger share of their households' income. It is therefore possible that with these increased economic resources comes a new confidence to leave toxic marriages if these women so choose. Researchers have called this the "independence hypothesis." Interestingly, the evidence related to the independence hypothesis is complicated.[5]

The simplest way to look at this relationship is by studying changes in women's own personal income and their risk of divorce. However, this approach ignores women's reliance on their husbands' income or other sources of income in divorce decision-making; to address these issues, we might need to examine wives' contributions to total household earnings, looking for income interactions between partners or "divorce triggers" of set amounts of income contributed by each partner.[6] Others argue that rather than income, how much *time* a woman works is most important in affecting her propensity to divorce.[7] Still other research suggests that only when women *both* have below-average levels of marital satisfaction and are employed does paid work make a difference.[8] In this situation, when women have higher-than-average levels of marital satisfaction, employ-ment does not affect the initiation of divorce. But if these women have below-average levels of marital satisfaction *and* are employed for pay, they are more likely to divorce than women who are not satisfied in their marriages but are not employed. These findings suggest that the decision to divorce is not simply an economic one; it may be intertwined with assessments of marital quality as well. Another possible interpretation is that the causal direction of the independence hypothesis is reversed. That is, it is not women becoming more economically independent that emboldens them to leave unhappy marriages; rather, women start working more intensely in order to make it financially possible to leave their husbands.[9] From these different studies, then, we can see that the independence hypothesis debate is far from being settled.

Beyond sociodemographic factors, a second set of divorce predictors corresponds to a person's complex set of relationships with his/her partner. If an individual lives with this partner prior to marriage, has a premarital conception or a premarital birth, brings children from a previous union into the marriage, marries someone from a different race, is much older or has much more education than his/her partner, or is marrying for the second, third, or fourth time, that person is also more likely to experience a divorce than those without these characteristics.[10] Other research has explored couples' relating style as an important predictor of divorce.[11] These interactions can either be positive and reduce the probability of divorce, or be negative and increase the likelihood of divorce. Positive interactions may be those words and gestures that demonstrate forgiveness and sacrifice, for example.[12] These serve to strengthen marriages. On the other hand, couples with negative interactions in the form of conflict, domestic violence, or a weak commitment to marriage as an institution will be more likely to divorce than couples without these predictive factors.[13] Still other research has pointed to thoughts of marital dissolution as being correlated with divorce.[14] Extramarital sex is also a predictor of both poor relationship quality and divorce.[15]

WHAT DO WE KNOW ABOUT THE REASONS FOR DIVORCE OFFERED BY YOUNGER COUPLES?

Mapping out these predictors is clearly important in understanding the dynamics of divorce. But how do these couples that actually experience divorce—again, younger men and women upon whom the most numerous studies are based—describe *why* their marriages failed?[16] Before diving into these explanations, there are several key points to note. First, many of these studies simply ask husbands and wives for the reasons why they pursued a divorce without attributing responsibility. For example, a husband might report "infidelity" without clarifying whether it was his own or his wife's infidelity that caused the breakup. Second and most important are the gender-based differences and similarities that emerge for divorcing couples over time. Men and women have historically accounted for divorce in divergent ways, but more recently both genders have begun focusing on the importance of individualism within marriage as fundamental to their own personal happiness goals.[17] In other words, if their partnerships do not fulfill this goal of individual growth, both men and women are likely to move on.

One of the earliest studies examining the reasons offered for divorce took place in 1948; notably, it only sampled women. In this case, researchers asked 425 divorced women about the cause of their marital split.[18] Their top reasons all had to do with their husbands' bad behavior, including economic nonsupport; excessive authoritarianism; a combination of drinking, gambling, and involvement with other women; excessive drinking alone; and personality problems. In studies during the early 1960s, women reiterated some of these main concerns—but without attribution to either party—including mental cruelty, neglect of home and the children, financial problems, physical abuse, and drinking.[19] Interestingly, researchers started to note that the reasons offered for divorce were different for men. Men, for example, and again without attribution, agreed that mental cruelty and neglect of the home and children were important, but infidelity, sexual incompatibility, and in-law troubles were also significant causes of their marital split-ups.

In the 1960s and 1970s, women marched, protested, and demonstrated for equal rights, work opportunities, and freedom from the expectation of household and caregiving responsibilities. Notably, studies conducted in the 1970s and early 1980s on the explanations offered for divorce started to reflect these changes. Women, for example, and without attribution, continued to identify personality defects, home-life problems, authority issues, drinking, and infidelity as key reasons for their divorces; they also started to discuss communication issues and immaturity as central problems in driving their marital breakdowns. In addition, drawing from their experiences with the women's rights movement, they started to cite internal gender role conflicts as the cause of their divorces.[20] Men, for their part, echoed some of these same issues without attribution, such as personality conflicts, home-life problems, and communication troubles, as key reasons behind their divorces. Men also focused on their changing places within the family, such as joint conflict over gender roles and not being "sure" why the divorce happened. Some men explicitly listed women's desire for freedom, or women's "lib," as the reason behind their divorces, implying that women were troublemakers for entering the political arena, and that their families were now paying the price.[21]

As the country moved into the late 1980s and 1990s, the desire to have a new type of marriage model that emphasized the primacy of individualism and personal happiness started to emerge more strongly than ever before.[22] In this model, which had its origins in the mid-twentieth century, divorce may occur when either partner no longer feels that he or she has the ability to personally evolve in the marriage. Examples might include growing apart, having different values or lifestyles, and falling out of love. Any defect that interfered with these individually satisfying goals—in addition to the more typical conflicts over broader gender norms or negative behaviors—emerged as viable reasons for divorce. For example, and again without attribution, women pointed to infidelity, personality problems, incompatibility, and drinking/drug use as causing their divorces, but they also began to note growing apart as a key problem. At the same time, men agreed that incompatibility and infidelity were key reasons for their divorces, as well as a lack of communication and personality problems. But they, too, started to point to growing apart when they reflected on the causes of their divorces. Other research looking at these reasons for divorce in the 2000s noted that both men and women cited not being able to relate to each other about their evolving interests as another key point of discontent for splitting couples.[23]

Over the past several decades, then, younger individuals have offered changing rationales for seeking out a divorce. These explanations sometimes lacked attribution to either party but at other times could be ascertained via context. They also differed somewhat by sex. In the mid-twentieth century, women pointed to a lack of economic support as a key problem. Men, on the other hand, tended to cite sexual problems and issues with their in-laws as their main reasons for divorce. Changing gender roles, especially in the 1970s and 1980s, also caused couples to split.

As time moved on, both women and men started pointing to the need for strong communication practices and compatibility within their marriages as ways to prevent divorce. Most recently, they have cited their needs to meet individual fulfillment goals as critical in either keeping them together or driving them apart. Overall, then, there has been a gradual accumulation of reasons for divorce, with only a small set of explanations, such as economic nonsupport and problems with in-laws, reducing in importance. However, while certainly relevant in many ways, none of the studies mentioned earlier focused *solely* on the reasons why men and women might seek a divorce at age 50 or older. Instead, these studies reported the perceptions of mostly younger people in their twenties and thirties. The main question at issue here, then, is, do older couples have the same reasons for divorce as younger couples in modern America?

Unfortunately, there are only a handful of studies that focus on this older population, so what we know is limited. First, there are small sample studies. One research effort looked at the reasons for divorce among ten individuals aged 50 and above. This study noted that the following factors contributed to the divorce decision: flawed reasoning in initially marrying; personal baggage; physical/emotional abuse; communication problems; unbalanced roles; a change in interests; and long periods of unhappiness.[24] Another non-American study looked at 15 Israeli adults, ages 45 and up, and summarized the following factors as key in motivating a split: a lack of emotional mutuality and communication; the presence of long-term alternative sexual relationships; short-term affairs; and physical and emotional abuse.[25] In both cases, since the samples were so small, researchers did not divide the explanations by gender.

Second, there is one large-scale study conducted by the AARP (formerly the American Association of Retired Persons) in 2003. The AARP is the largest and most influential advocacy group for older Americans in the United States today, and this study is the broadest survey of mid-life divorce completed to date.[26] Using a random sample questionnaire, the

AARP captured the experiences of 1,148 older individuals in a mid-life divorce transition. This sample is slightly different than that considered in this book, in that it included all men and women ages 40–79 who had experienced a divorce in their forties, fifties, or sixties, whereas this book discusses only those who have undergone a divorce at age 50 or older. Nonetheless, there is still a considerable overlap in the population studied. What is interesting among these adults is that their top five explanations for parting ways with their spouses all involve marital deficiencies similar to their modern, younger counterparts.

Indeed, for men, the most commonly cited reason for divorce was that they simply fell out of love without a specific cause; their second most cited reason was a tie between sensing that they had different values and/ or lifestyles than their wives and cheating. These men pointed to verbal/ physical/emotional abuse as their third most commonly cited explanation for divorce. In fourth place, these men reported drug/alcohol abuse or refused to answer. Finally, they described falling in love with someone else as their explanation. Women reported many of the same reasons for divorce in the AARP study, but in a different order. First, they named verbal/physical/emotional abuse as the most common contributing factor in their divorce. Second, they cited drug/alcohol abuse and then, third, cheating as the driving reasons for divorce. Fourth, they pointed to different values/lifestyles as prompting them to divorce. Fifth, they asserted that they simply fell out of love and that this experience pushed them toward a divorce.

It is important to keep in mind, however, that as in many other studies, the reasons reported in the aggregate here could be attributable to either party. For example, a man could state that "cheating" was the central cause of his divorce, but either he or his wife could have engaged in the reported infidelity.[27] In addition, it is critical to note that these are closed-ended survey responses, meaning that respondents had to choose from a preselected set of options regarding the causes of their marital breakdowns. This particular method of obtaining information provides us with the breadth needed to learn about the reasons behind gray divorces, but it lacks the rich depth of a more narrative approach. In this book, I make forays into that depth, beginning the important work of permitting men and women to tell their breakup stories in their own voices, with all of the detail that they require to offer insight into the process of gray divorce as it is evolving in the United States today.

WHY DID YOU GET DIVORCED?

In order to better understand why men and women split up at or after the age of 50, the 80 interviewees in this book—40 men and 40 women—each described exactly why their marriages ended up failing. Note that both men and women could point to more than one cause in explaining their decision to divorce, and that for reasons where attribution was relevant, I asked respondents to assign responsibility accordingly.

Overall, both men and women tended to point to one another as causing the divorce (see table 5). This marks a departure from some of the previous research where attribution was unclear. In addition, just like the most recent studies on younger couples, we see some causes of divorce slip away over time. For example, we see infrequent references to factors such as economic nonsupport, lack of sex, problems with in-laws, or conflict over male and female gender roles as driving divorces, while other reasons have emerged to take their place. Indeed, throughout this chapter, we observe that men and women point to many of the same factors in causing divorce as younger couples point to, although the sexes rank them differently. These include growing apart, their partners' physical infidelity, and their partners' mental health problems. In terms of differences between the sexes, men cite financial problems and conflict over raising children, whereas women point to their husbands' pornography/alcohol/drug addictions and verbal/emotional abuse as critical reasons for their marital breakdowns. In all of these examples to follow, it is important to note that while their answers cite the specific reason under each category, they might also allude to other problems within their marriages (as stated earlier, respondents could mention multiple reasons for their divorce). In all cases, nonetheless, these explanations show that both sexes hold the standard of a strong and rewarding marriage as that to which they aspire. Each sex requires the other to behave in ways to fulfill these expectations, and if the partner will not or cannot, both husbands and wives move toward the divorce decision.

Table 5   Reasons for Gray Divorce

	40 Men	40 Women
Why Did You Get Divorced? (Ranked by Order of Mention)	1. We Grew Apart 2. Wives Engaged in Physical Cheating 3. Wives Had Financial Differences/Problems 4. Wives Had Mental Health Problems 5. Problems Related to Their Children	1. Husbands Engaged in Physical Cheating 2. Husbands Had Pornography/ Alcohol/Drug Addictions 3. Husbands Engaged in Verbal and Emotional Abuse 4. We Grew Apart 5. Husbands Had Mental Health Problems

Husbands Speak Out: We Grew Apart

By far, the most common reason that couples divorced according to the men in this study was that they simply grew apart. This happened for a wide variety of reasons. In some cases, there was one central issue that drove the couple in two separate directions. Dennis, a 59-year-old accountant, had been married to his stay-at-home wife, four years his junior, for 35 years. They had two boys and two girls, all of whom were now adults. For Dennis, the driving force behind their split was religion. About five years into their marriage, his wife became increasingly religious. At first, she just started to go to church more frequently, but over time she became a fundamentalist Christian who wanted her entire family to embrace her newfound beliefs as wholeheartedly as she did. Dennis was agnostic, and while initially he did not object to her new ways, over time he felt that her faith was intruding on too many aspects of their daily lives. For example, he noted that she started to control which friends and family members they could see, as well as the entertainment that they as a family could consume. All had to be vetted by her, and she only approved it if these activities supported her Christian beliefs.

During her process of religious transformation, Dennis noted, they as a couple grew increasingly distant. Interestingly, it was the traditional roles that his wife wanted to see implemented in her home that bothered Dennis most of all.

> She started [saying] that . . . my place [as the man] was [the] head of the family—that my word was the final word. I always viewed it as a partner-ship. You know, [she wanted me to be] responsible for making all major decisions in our family . . . she tried to convert me religiously, of course. She wanted me to be "the husband that God wanted me to be." . . . I just told her many times where she could stick God. I mean, it just got increasingly worse over time.

Dennis did not have a problem with his wife bringing the children to church, since he thought it gave them a good moral foundation for deci-sion-making in their lives. However, his wife's deference to him as "head of the household" became increasingly burdensome to him. He observed, "I didn't want it all to be about *my* decisions [in the family]. I viewed it as *our* decisions." After her transformation, however, they both found them-selves in a marriage that neither of them recognized anymore. Dennis did not want a divorce until the children were adults—and waited until the youngest was 18 years old—but later regretted this choice because he came to the realization that the children knew how unhappy he was during the entire marriage. Notably and somewhat ironically, his long hesitation in leaving resulted in his wife filing for divorce first.

Like Dennis, David also could point to a specific reason that his second marriage broke up. For Dennis, the main factor was religion. For David, 53 years old, it was the military life. David was on active duty in the Army for much of his marriage, which lasted over 15 years. He and his wife, 41 years old, had one son. While the couple struggled with debt issues, David maintained that it was primarily his physical absence from the marriage that precipitated its decline. He said that his wife, who worked as a legal administrative assistant, felt underappreciated over the course of their marriage. He also guessed that "she would add that she felt neglected and just basically that the connection there was severed. We didn't have that connection anymore."

David confessed that he held some responsibility for the loss of this marital bond. While he was deployed, he admitted, he did not call or email home daily. This lack of attention placed enormous stress on his relationship. But the tipping point, in his mind, was a choice that he made early on in their marriage having to do with buying a house next to her parents' home:

> Now that I look back on it, I kind of regret that I made that decision . . . Well, I just felt like she was more attached to her parents, and that was her support system . . . Rather than us relying on each other, she kind of more relied on her parents . . . I think it was a factor [in] our growing apart.

Indeed, when he came back home from one tour of duty and the Army wanted to move his home base in the United States, his wife said, "Well, go ahead. I'm not leaving." According to David, his wife had developed "comingled" bonds and emotions with her parents that were ultimately damaging to their marital relationship. Not surprisingly, she was the one who filed for divorce.

While Dennis cited his wife's religiosity as the primary wedge that split them apart, and David pointed to military life, others, like James, stated that he and his wife just started to have too many different opinions and points of view on everyday life. Noting that they were not "throwing pots and pans at each other, screaming and yelling," James and his wife decided that they would divorce when their three children (one girl and two boys) became adults, which happened 27 years after their marriage. James, 53 years old and an audit manager, was close in age to his wife, 50 years old, but gradually, over time, they diverged from each other in interests. For example, they disagreed over things like paying bills on time, which he wanted to do and she did not; they also differed on musical tastes. He "liked Led Zeppelin, Black Sabbath, Santana, Eric Clapton, and the Rolling Stones, and she liked Air Supply." Luckily, they did find some common ground in this area, as they were both fans of Elton John and Billy Joel.

But other areas of discord were much more serious. After their third child was born, his wife told him that she no longer wanted to have sex. According to James, she simply stated that she no longer enjoyed it. This was really troubling to him, and he completely shut down emotionally, vowing that he was not even going to try touching her. After coming to grips with this reality, he decided to focus his energies on the children.

Most guys would have just found a bunch of girlfriends and ran around, but I spent all [of] my extra time raising [our] children. I coached soccer, roller hockey, hardball, girls' softball, and six years of girls' cheerleading . . . Well, whatever my kids did, I got involved and I was around them, with them, near them, available to them through all [of] their formative years. One son also played ice hockey but I didn't coach ice hockey, [because] I can't ice skate (chuckling). So . . . whatever they did I was there and available for them. I helped with projects and homework and patched their boo-boos.

James made a point of noting that his wife was a good mother, but she was not involved in the children's outdoor activities. Instead, she helped them with their other needs, and the pair were very good parents in terms of their ability to work as a team. They just were no longer meant to be a couple, and eventually they mutually agreed to divorce.

Husbands Speak Out: Wives Engaged in Physical Cheating

Another very common reason given by men as to why they were involved in a gray divorce had to do with their spouses' cheating. Infidelity emerged in a variety of ways, but in each case it led to the ultimate demise of the marriage. Larry, for example, was a 57-year-old man with three teenage children. He was a wildly successful lawyer; his wife, 51 years old, was a distinguished scientist. He was in his second marriage of 17 years when he discovered his wife's infidelity.

In many ways, his wife's affair was a complete surprise. In 2012, he had been looking forward to a relaxing summer. Increasingly feeling the difficult emotional toll of caring for his elderly parents as their health started to decline, and desperate for relief, he was enthusiastic about bringing his children up to Maine to camp for the July and August months. After he dropped his children off, he thought that he and his wife would share a wonderful respite together, with few responsibilities to occupy their time.

I remember saying to myself, this is going to be a great summer. [We will be] kid-free for seven weeks. We can go away. We can go to the movies and go to dinner. [We can] have sex. [We can] walk around naked. It'll be a fabulous summer. And then that Sunday I'm in the room, in our bedroom, [and] my ex went to exercise or something. And I'm sort of a political junkie, and . . . the desktop computer in our room wasn't working, so I went to her laptop, which is next to her bed. That's how I found out that she had this relationship. It took me a day or two to process it, and then I confronted her.

On the laptop computer, he found what he called "junior high school love notes" between her and another scientist. After several days, he confronted her with his discovery in a local restaurant. He pointed out that they had a great life together, with three wonderful children, a nice home, and plenty of money, and he said that he would be willing to go to counseling to keep their marriage going. After only about two seconds, he reported, she declined the counseling offer. She was already moving on with her new man.

At first, Larry was in complete shock. He turned for advice to one of his friends whom he had met in law school. The friend explained that if his wife only grudgingly agreed to counseling, it might just simply delay the inevitable divorce. Moreover, if she was happy in this new relationship, it might make the divorce much easier for them both. This advice helped Larry significantly. Aided by his household income of $250,000 per year, Larry carefully thought about his next steps.

> You know, I'm a lawyer. I'm reasonably successful. I deal with stress on behalf of clients all the time. I handle big issues reasonably well. Sometimes I get rattled by tiny issues, but the big issues, I step up to the plate. Yeah, I'm sure I was in shock at the time, but, you know, I am a lawyer. So, I mean, I found a lawyer immediately.

Larry quickly filed for divorce. He also acknowledged that if this news had to be delivered to him, he was glad that his children were away at the time. Their summer at camp spared them, at least for a while, the immediacy of the family pain to come.

Sometimes men found out about their wives' affairs through second parties. Gregory, 67 years old, worked in quality assurance in a manufacturing plant. His third wife, who was 58 years old and to whom he had been married for 17 years, was a hairdresser. They did not have any children together. While at first they were happy, over time she started to engage in what he described as erratic and inexplicable behavior. For example, on various occasions she stopped coming home at night, saying that she was spending time with her girlfriends. One evening while she was away, he was driving home and received a birthday call from his wife's mother. It was, to say the least, a shocking conversation.

[My wife's mother] told me [that] her daughter had gone up to Gainesville. You know, Gainesville's about a one-hour drive and [her mother told me that she was] staying with some guy. Then that's when I got hurt; that's when it hurt right through my stomach. She was seeing someone. And so then [my wife's mother] started telling me [more] about [her daughter who] was married two times before me, too. Then she told me that she loved her daughter, but her daughter I guess cheated on all [of] her husbands. I didn't know that . . . After she cheated with other men, she [told me how her daughter] wrote letters to the men's wives to tell [them] and explained all the details of what they did. So I literally got sick to my stomach because I didn't know anything about my wife.

At this point during the call, Gregory had to pull his car over onto the side of the road because he was physically ill. He did not want the divorce, but he knew in his gut that he had to file. They continued to live together for a time, and he learned that she was dating an electrical engineer who made a decent amount of money. Gregory sadly recalled having to watch his wife get ready for dates with this other man before the divorce was finalized.

She was with this other guy for four days [and the rest of the time with me]. Sometimes she would come home and by law I [couldn't] do anything about it because [it was] her house. So a lot of times . . . we didn't fight. I just kept quiet and I respected her and I knew that she was seeing him. You know, she'd even get dressed early Sunday morning . . . [She] looked pretty and everything and I'd watch her just walk out. It hurt but I attributed it to my maturity. If I [were] young, I probably would've gone nuts, but at my matured age, I weathered through it. And I actually almost got used to it.

As much as he was pained by her cheating, Gregory maintained his composure as his divorce case was moving through the legal system. He never viewed his wife as a flawed cheater, but as an individual who was insecure and needed the acceptance of a series of men in her life as a way of dealing with this insecurity. Even as they parted ways when he filed for divorce, Gregory insisted that he wanted the best for her going forward.

Like Gregory, Donald, father of a 12-year-old girl and a 17-year-old boy, was not angry with his second wife after her infidelity. She filed for divorce after what she described as a long period of unhappiness with him. Donald was a truck driver and noted that marriages in his business face a lot of obstacles since there are long periods of time when husbands and wives do not see each other while the driver is on the road, and drivers' sleep schedules often vary, leading to further pressure on these couples' time together. But Donald had another problem. As a 52-year-old man, he was living with undiagnosed sleep apnea. When he finally went to the doctor for a sleep study, he discovered that he was waking up 77 times over a three- to four-hour time period. In addition to the challenges of working irregular hours, Donald was battling severe sleep deprivation.

In a way, Donald understood why his 41-year-old wife, who worked in the field of health insurance sales, strayed. He acknowledged that his wife had the very difficult job of keeping the house quiet during the day while he slept. And, due to his sleep problems, he admitted, he was not the most pleasant person to be around when he was awake.

> So anyway, she, because of a variety, not a variety, because of a barrage of different things that I had done, [wanted a divorce]. [These things were], you know, the belittling [of] her, the grouchiness all the time . . . [my] coming home at the end of the week and just being exhausted. [I also did not want] to do anything, just, you know, [wanted to] park myself on the sofa and watch TV . . . There is an age difference between her and me, and she decided to go find somebody younger, more energetic.

While sad about this situation, Donald assumed some responsibility for his wife's affair. Saying that "there were times I came home and might not have treated her exactly the way she wanted to be treated . . . and it's true, she put up with a lot," Donald did not fight her on the decision to file for divorce. Primarily he expressed remorse over not being kinder while at home and not seeking out medical attention for his sleep apnea until his marriage was irreparably damaged. They ended up divorcing after 18 years together.

Husbands Speak Out: Wives Had Financial Differences/Problems

Another set of men pointed to financial differences/problems that ended up terminating their marriages. At 62 years old, Douglas had been married to his wife for 34 years; she was 60. For him, there were multiple problems in their marriage that were exacerbated by severe financial stress. By way of background, they had very different personalities. Douglas was quiet and introspective, while his wife was outgoing, outspoken, and heavily involved in her interior design and home remodeling business. Over the course of their marriage, they had already weathered her affair with another man in the homebuilding industry, toughing it out in order to keep their family together, including their three children. But the relationship faced other types of obstacles. For example, Douglas stated that his wife often wondered out loud if he really loved her. Douglas maintained that he told her repeatedly that he loved her, but that did not seem to convince her that they were meant to be together.

When Douglas retired from an insurance claims adjusting company, he sold his shares and, unfortunately, according to him, "got into an enormous amount of litigation with my former partners over the value of the shares." With lawyer bills mounting, he noticed that his wife began to change in a number of ways. She altered her dressing style and started acting more open with everyone she met. It turned out that she had resumed her relationship with the homebuilder with whom she had previously had the affair. Douglas argued that she did this because she did not believe in fighting for money in the lawsuits like he did, and he believed the affair was a way for her to channel her energy more positively. Indeed, Douglas was candid about wanting to live a more affluent lifestyle, while his wife wanted to live in a simpler way:

> [One part of our city is] quite affluent and has come to denote a lifestyle. Kids go to private school. Parents live in big houses. You live in [a well-known] zip code . . . You go to a relatively limited number of churches. All [of] your children went to daycare or preschool at [a certain location] . . . [As] time went on . . . that was sort of the goal of my existence to some extent—to be, if not part of that community . . . to at least have the trappings of that community.

In reflecting on his wife's divorce filing, Douglas noted that she had grown up in that advantaged community, while he had not. Over time, she rebelled against her past. Their financial problems simply brought out in sharp relief the differences in their aspirations. The homebuilder with whom his wife reunited, according to Douglas, "was living a totally different life—low stress, less materialistic—and I think my wife in her counterculture sort of way embraced that."

Douglas and his wife faced significant financial stress, and they had divergent reactions to it. Douglas strongly wanted his money problems resolved with his bank account restored so that he could achieve a more lavish lifestyle. His wife reacted by going back to her previous lover, leading a simpler life, and ultimately filing for divorce.

As a very different example, Terry, 59 years old, and his wife, 58 years old, had financial fights over the course of their 27-year marriage, and these quarrels were primarily around how they used money in raising their two boys. His wife ultimately asked for the divorce, something Terry did not want. Initially, he believed that his marriage could be saved, despite their monetary disputes. Terry and his wife were both teachers when they were younger. But even though they shared this profession, they had very different financial values that they wanted to model for their sons. Terry explained this standoff in the following way:

> I wanted to instill a strong sense of responsibility and deferred gratification and she was almost in the polar opposite direction. Around that time, money started disappearing. I had credit card statements, including my own, hidden from me; the checkbook was kind of [hidden from me].

Over time, Terry ended up finding more and more receipts from purchases that were not made transparent to him at the time. For example, he discovered a receipt for a $900 pocketbook that one of his sons bought for his girlfriend. His attorney later described it to him as "financial cheating," and Terry found himself emotionally withdrawing from the marriage week by week.

When one of his sons went to college, problems over money only worsened.

> When [my son went away for school], there were multiple traffic offenses— moving violations—that were hidden from me. It concerned me because

> [those violations] definitely impact[ed] the insurance rates we were paying. And I would find these things out by intercepting the [mail]; when you have a traffic offense, you get 15 letters from lawyers saying, "Let me handle this." That's how I would find out about these things.

Probably the most damaging part of these disputes was that Terry did not believe his wife was simply covering up for the mistakes of his children. Instead, he felt that he was deliberately being misled by his wife and his sons, who were all unified against him.

> I believe to this day [that] it was an alliance. And it was well orchestrated. In all honesty, it was probably some of my more extreme reactions to these types of things being hidden from me that probably made them want to hide them even more.

Notably, Terry never described what his "more extreme reactions" were to his wife's behavior. He did point out that they both had accounting training before they pursued careers as teachers. In their early years together, Terry was responsible for making a budget that would help them reach their retirement goals. He reported that he was the one who handled the checks and the checkbook. However, when the couple started to have more disagreements about money, particularly around the children, Terry in essence gave up the fight. After years of battling each other, his wife finally filed for divorce. Terry sadly concluded, "I surrendered control of the family finances because the last decade or so I just didn't know what was happening. And I think I was just too afraid to ask." While he did not get into the specifics of "surrendering control" of the family's money, his resignation suggested defeat over who would ultimately manage their finances going forward.

Husbands Speak Out: Wives Had Mental Health Problems

The next most common reason cited by men as to why they experienced a gray divorce related to the mental health of their spouses. In some cases, husbands stated that a mental health illness had actually been documented by a doctor. In other cases, these men guessed that their spouses had some type of mental illness, such as anxiety and depression. The majority of men in both groups tended to note that these problems were not being successfully treated with psychotherapy or medications.

Michael, a 59-year-old lawyer, was in his third marriage. His wife, a registered nurse, was 49 years old. Michael acknowledged that his wife was sexually and physically abused as a child; she also had notably married at the early age of 16. Michael did not press her on the details of her past, but gradually throughout the course of their relatively short, four-year marriage became more inquisitive as her behavior with him become more erratic. At times she could be very kind to him, and at other points she could lash out and become very cruel.

He first learned from her directly that she had seen a psychiatrist and was diagnosed with posttraumatic stress disorder. But later, as she became more volatile at home, Michael decided to do a more intensive background check on her. Because of his profession, he had significant access to personal information contained in legal records. As he went through these files, he soon discovered to his horror that she had previously been arrested for prostitution.

> [Finding out] was tough, because it kind of fit in with her, you know, abuse pattern . . . She was abused by some men and abused by some stepfathers and stuff . . . I think it just made her kind of empty inside.

Digging deeper into these particular records, Michael learned that she had worked with a group of other women in a massage parlor. Luckily for her, the charges against her were dropped when she agreed to testify against the parlor owners. When Michael confronted her with this information, she completely denied participation in prostitution. She claimed that she was "just sleeping there [in the parlor] and they swept up everybody." The other massage parlor workers were only her associates when she needed them, and she claimed that she did not know about their illegal activities. Michael stated that he could accept a lot of legal infractions, but he simply could not move beyond this allegation of prostitution. In a sad and depressed state of mind, he finally decided to file for divorce.

Michael was clearly in a state of shock when he discovered his wife's past, a past that was most likely driven by her horrid history of abuse. Patrick, by contrast, had lived with his wife's depression for many years. He filed for divorce after 31 years of marriage and after rearing three daughters together. He had known his wife from a young age, and after he spent time in the Navy and she graduated from college, they married. She had an irregular work history, but was a private music teacher during the period of time that their marriage started to crumble. In Patrick's view, the couple was having clear communication problems primarily driven by his wife's clinical depression. For instance, he frequently found his wife at home, not attending to any of the household and child care needs of the family. He asked her to go to couples counseling, but she refused, saying that she did not have a problem. Meanwhile, Patrick grew increasingly frustrated at having to shoulder all of the work in the family.

> I came home one evening and the eldest daughter was in high school ... [She] was getting ready for a dance rehearsal and I walked in the door after ... a 10-hour day at work [as a quality engineer] ... [Right away I] got asked, "What's for dinner? Are you going to take [our daughter] to dance? [And what is she going] to eat because she hasn't eaten yet?" ... She was sitting in her chair doing her crochet or whatever and I just lost it. It was like ... "What have you been doing all day?" And she said, "Well, I gave a couple of piano lessons and I'm exhausted." I was like, "You're not doing anything." So all of the negotiation, the talking, and the working through things just kind of came to a head ... I said, "I can't do this anymore."

While he made himself clear that he strongly believed she needed to take additional steps to improve her outlook on life, Patrick reported that he reinforced his commitment to be there for her once again. He begged her to be more proactive with her mental health, saying, "I'm trying to make sure that I understand what you want."

Her depression manifested in a variety of ways. Because of her inactivity, according to him, she was close to weighing 300 pounds. Beyond increasingly relying on her husband to take care of everything in the house, she started to avoid social situations. Patrick planned all of his daughters' sweet 16 parties at their home, and at the start of each party his wife would go and hide in the bedroom to escape from interacting with anyone. One of the chief problems that Patrick recognized was that her current treatment for depression was not working. Earlier, she had sought out antidepressants from her general practitioner. When the specific pill that she was prescribed did not work, she did not go back to request a change. Moreover, much to Patrick's chagrin, she refused to see a psychiatrist with more experience in adjusting these types of medications.

Patrick argued that he was extremely patient with his wife's depression over the years. She responded to his entreaties to do more by insisting that "there is nothing wrong with me; I don't need to go see a counselor." But Patrick pushed her further. He stated that he understood that, due to their mental state, sometimes people with depression need more assistance in terms of comprehending their treatment options. He was willing to help her and be a true partner in this journey. But he kept pressing her and asking her, "When your medications don't change for . . . let's see, 1993 to 2003—ten years—and you don't change for ten years, don't you think it's time to figure [out] . . . something different?" He was clearly very frustrated. Over time, Patrick noted that he was more and more resentful of her behavior, and when she continued to argue that her medications were actually working well, Patrick recognized that the marriage was over. He was the one who filed for divorce.

Husbands Speak Out: Problems Related to Their Children

The final, smallest set of husbands described the cause of their divorces as starting with differences over how to raise their children. Timothy, 57 years old, was a systems analyst in a grocery store, while his wife, 50 years old, was a nurse. They had been married for 23 years and had one son. Timothy described his son as a special needs child, intellectually gifted with developmental and mental health issues. These issues included Asperger's Syndrome, bipolar disorder, and clinical depression with suicidal ideation. As a result of these problems, Timothy and his wife had to bring their son to psychiatric hospitals on a regular basis. Not surprisingly, tensions emerged with his wife over how to handle his son's challenges. Timothy was much more interested in pursuing a behavioral modification approach, while his wife wanted to accept their son's condition and the behavior that resulted as simply part of his nature as a human being.

Over time, Timothy's son's behavior became more and more volatile. He started walking out of school, and when he did attend, he got into

physical fights with other students. The couple began to argue more frequently about what to do.

> It was a compromising situation because we are both pretty smart. I mean,
> obviously I have a master's degree in finance and marketing. She has her . . .
> bachelor's in nursing but she also has a master's in management. So,
> you know, we're . . . smart people. We know how to deal with this but
> [we are] on different sides of the valley. [We are on] opposite sides of the
> river . . . Well, we tried to cooperate . . . I guess my point was, [my son's]
> got to take responsibility for his actions. [My wife], on the other hand,
> was [saying], you've got to be able to understand why he's doing this. Yes,
> I understand why he's doing that . . . And little by little, we're spreading
> apart.

As their son's behavior got worse, the couple agreed to separate for a short
time because they believed Timothy was the focal point of their son's
anger. However, while Timothy was living in his temporary apartment, his
son physically attacked his wife, ran away twice, and threatened to commit
suicide.

Timothy finally returned home, but tensions were still high. Although
their son was taking his medications, he was not getting better. One
day, the family's favorite college team was playing a football game.
Timothy had a superstitious practice, known by his son, in which he
felt that if he did not watch the game on television, his team would win.
When his team lost, Timothy's son accused him of secretly watching
the game on television in another room in the house; armed with this
suspicion, he then proceeded to physically attack Timothy. Timothy was
shocked.

> And the next thing I heard from my wife was, "Why didn't you spend more
> time with him during the summer?" . . . As I'm trying [to get him off of
> me], I'm sobbing at her, "Help me! He's punching me!" . . . I'm defending
> myself . . . I was astounded at what was going on, but the next thing I recall
> was he got a baseball bat and started to swing it . . . at me.

Timothy's wife increasingly blamed him for their son's aggressive behavior. After this alarming incident, she concluded that they could no longer
be together and demanded a divorce.

Now that we have heard the men's perspectives on the reasons for gray divorce, we turn to hear the women's stories. The reasons offered for a gray divorce by women are similar to those offered by men, and they also include new reasons. In order of prevalence, women named their husbands' sexual cheating, their husbands' pornography/alcohol/drug addictions, their husbands' verbal and emotional abuse, growing apart, and their husbands' mental health problems as the causes of their marital breakdowns.

Wives Speak Out: Husbands Engaged in Physical Cheating

Overwhelmingly, women cited physical cheating by their husbands as the most common cause of their divorces. Patricia, 58 years old, was a medical lab technician while her second husband, 37 years old, worked in a warehouse job. They had only been married for a short period of time when her husband got laid off and they were faced with mounting bills. He had become quite depressed as a result of his job loss and started spending more and more time at his best friend's house. In fact, they as a couple were quite close to his best friend and his best friend's wife. But this was quickly about to change.

> [His best male] friend came to my house on a Sunday . . . knocked at the door early on a Sunday . . . I didn't know where my husband was. He didn't come home. I knew that he had been at his friend's house, and I thought, well, maybe he stayed over. You know, they had a few beers and he decided to stay over which I never really felt comfortable with that either . . . But anyway, so this friend shows up at my house and his knuckles are all bloody . . . I just went, "Oh my God." And he goes, "Our marriages are over. I caught them together."

The best friend's hands were bloody because he had punched a wall when he caught the cheating couple in a sexual act. Astonishingly, once they were caught, the couple left for a hotel together. Later, Patricia found out that they wanted to move in with each other. Patricia was both shocked and devastated. However, after a period of time, the other couple reconciled, leaving Patricia's husband with no place to go.

As she thought about her husband and the havoc that he had wreaked on her family, Patricia still considered counseling as a potentially healing option. She wanted the family back together. But her husband did not have the same motivation to place her first in his life.

> I feel as though, you know, like an infidelity sometimes isn't enough [to break up a marriage]. You know, like they talk about . . . [it is] for better or for worse. But he talked about how he felt like he was really missing something by not being with her. That's what he wanted to do. And he constantly said that.

As she reflected on her options, Patricia decided to end their five-year marriage. She stated that she did not want to be number two in a man's life, or "the one that's [a] leftover." In her mind, her husband never seemed to get over the fact that he wanted to be with his best friend's wife and this was unacceptable to her over the long run.

Patricia discovered her husband's affair quite dramatically, when his best friend knocked on her door with bloody hands. Janet, 66 years old, found out about her husband's affair suddenly and without warning as well. She had been married once before; in her most recent marriage, she chose a man seven years younger with whom she felt she had a lot in common. Janet had worked a variety of jobs, including nursing, pharmaceutical sales, and teaching. Her husband had HVAC experience but wanted to make a living as a musician. One night, she thought he was acting strangely distant at home.

> I said, "What's going on?" I said, "Don't you want to be married anymore?" And he said, "I don't know." . . . I found out later [that] he was bringing [his girlfriend] out to the clubs where he was playing so that was another hit [to me]. So that was basically it. He said, "What shall we do?" I said, "You already made your choice." So he said, "I'm going to call my mother and go see if I can stay with her." All he really cared about was his musical equipment and getting that. He didn't even really [pack too much] . . . [He] just packed a little bag. He didn't even take his father's ashes, so it was a really [abrupt departure].

After some discussion, Janet found out that her husband had been having this affair for about six months. His new girlfriend was a band "groupie" and followed him around wherever he played. Everyone who knew the couple was shocked by his behavior. But Janet had another deep concern. She was worried about how his leaving would affect her two children from her previous marriage. Although her children were adults by the time her second marriage disintegrated, they had been quite young when their stepfather entered their lives. According to Janet, they loved their stepfather very much and his abandonment of their mother was truly disturbing.

Once he left, he did not make contact with Janet for one month. He finally returned home and they were able to spend some time processing what had happened in their marriage. She hoped that it was some type of mid-life crisis and that he would return permanently to the family home, but he never did. The affair was damaging to Janet on many levels. First of all, she loved him deeply, so it was sad and shocking that her husband replaced her with another woman. Second, because his HVAC work history was so erratic and he did not make much money as a musician, she had financially supported him throughout their marriage. This enabled him to pursue his career dreams, but cost her serious dollars and years of her life. She reported that after deep reflection, she faced no choice but to file for divorce.

Gail was another woman who experienced the pain of a cheating husband. A 67-year-old mother of four daughters, Gail received a call one night telling her that her 67-year-old husband was having an affair with his secretary. This was shocking to Gail, since her husband had suffered from sporadic impotence throughout their marriage. Indeed, prior to this revelation, their marriage of 41 years had been very rocky. Initially, after only five years of marriage, Gail's husband told her that he did not want to be married anymore. At that point, they already had three young daughters and she was pregnant with a fourth child. But it was not so much her husband's desire for divorce that rattled Gail to her core. Rather, she was harmed in a particularly cruel way by her husband's demands regarding her latest pregnancy.

> Then he came to me one night and he said . . . that I absolutely had to get an abortion. He [said] he wasn't going to be there one way or another, and that he wasn't going to support me. He felt like he should probably not be in our children's lives and so I had to get an abortion. So he took me to this [abortion facility], and I'm on the table crying. [Then] I got off the table and I said, "I can't do it." . . . We came home, and he kept telling me—badgering me—saying that I had to do it, so we went back the very next day and I did it. I held it against him our entire marriage.

Traumatized by this ordeal, Gail continued to face challenges with him after he chose to stay with her for the time being. At one point, distraught by his periodic impotence, her husband told her that he had gone to a sex therapist and wanted to work on his sexual problems. This action immediately signaled to Gail that he was probably having an affair and needed help performing. At that point, however, Gail was still aching to keep the marriage going and agreed to be his partner in his therapeutic exercises. After a short time, however, he eventually gave up on the therapy and Gail was at a loss as to where the marriage was going. She still felt upset by the abortion, and then used by him in sex therapy sessions that ultimately were unproductive for their future as a couple.

Yet Gail remained in the marriage for many additional years. She worked in the education field, while her husband had a lucrative job in the financial sector. She stated that in many ways, they "did . . . have a very good life. He made a good living, we had a lot of good friends, and we did a lot of family things" together. They ultimately did decide to have a fourth child, which she thought would bring them together.

However, when she had proof of this last affair with his secretary from the phone call she received, things disintegrated quickly. She confronted him with the charge, and he admitted that it was true. Due to his intermittent impotence problems, she was not sure whether he was having intercourse with her, but clearly his romantic affections were not contained within the marriage. At first, he stayed in the marital home, and Gail flailed about, still trying to make things work. She directly asked him to cut off all contact with his secretary, but he refused to do that. He came home later and later, and she reported repeatedly being alone, "sitting there with a cold dinner waiting for him and I'd say, 'Where were you?' And he was out with her. And I would start crying." Finally, after one month, he said that he could no longer see her cry, left, and officially filed for divorce.

Wives Speak Out: Husbands Had Pornography/
Alcohol/Drug Addictions

Unlike the men in this study, who did not list addiction as a principal cause of divorce, women experiencing a gray divorce next cited their husbands' addictions as a primary cause of their marital breakdowns. These addictions came in a variety of forms. For Brenda, 56 years old, it was her 53-year-old husband's Internet pornography addiction that doomed her marriage of 16 years. This was Brenda's third marriage and she desperately wanted it to succeed. However, one day she was looking through the history files on her computer and found numerous pornographic videos. She confronted her husband with this knowledge, and he admitted to viewing them. She explained to him that every time he looked at these images, she felt like he was cheating on her. He listened and vowed to be better, but eventually went back to the same behavior. She gave him an ultimatum, announcing that either he could get help for his addiction or the marriage was over.

Somewhat optimistically, he found a fellow member of the Hare Krishna faith, and spoke to him about his pornography addiction for a long time. Brenda hoped that through this spiritual counseling, her husband would be able to change his ways. Yet, even with religious intervention, Brenda noted that the addiction seemed to be getting worse. He was watching pornographic videos more frequently, and then feeling terrible about his actions, creating a negative feedback cycle in which it was difficult for him to be around her because he constantly was embarrassed by his problem.

Because she was also embarrassed by his addiction, Brenda felt extremely isolated and without support. She felt she could not speak to her friends or relatives about what she was going through in order to protect their privacy as a couple; she said that she "didn't want to 'out' him to our friends." As time passed on, the addiction continued. Brenda and her husband started sleeping in different bedrooms. They stopped communicating. With their relationship at a standstill, they finally discussed going their separate ways. Though they were both very sad about this outcome, Brenda concluded that divorce was the best possible choice in moving forward, and he concurred. Interestingly, the couple remained friends after the divorce as a sense of calm over the final resolution of the marriage emerged and peace finally took effect in their lives.

Beyond battling pornography addictions, other women who sought gray divorces pointed to their husbands' issues with alcohol as the main source of their divorces. Margaret, 56 years old, had been married to her husband, 55 years old, for 25 years. They worked together in the restaurant business, and she reported that she was always the more entrepreneurial, business-minded part of the team, whereas he was more design-focused. They owned restaurants in four different locations over the course of their union. In some of their ventures, they partnered with her sister, who was also business-oriented, and her sister's husband, an attorney. The main problem for the entire team came in the execution of their restaurant ideas. In Margaret's view, her husband loved the artistic part of planning new restaurant concepts since he was "very creative and very talented in the cooking industry, and loved being involved over the short term." After this initial stage of development, however, Margaret's husband lost interest and "kind of checked out."

One of the main contributing factors to his lack of motivation was alcoholism. Margaret explained that alcoholism is very common in the restaurant industry because alcohol is so readily available. Her husband also had a history of alcoholism in his family.

> [He would be] drinking in the morning. [He would be] drinking at work. [His] sleeping habits [were] very disturbing. [His] eating habits [were] disturbing. Again, this is a family business so . . . the family is very close. It's never been corporate. So [he would be] angry about my sister and me, who are very, very close. We're 11 months apart [in age] and we're like two peas in a pod. We've been in business forever . . . [He would say,] "You're married to your sister, not me."

Beyond his jealousy of her relationship with her sister, Margaret noted that their particular relationship history might have been a contributing factor to their demise. For years, they had been a carefree couple with no children to raise. They spent their twenties having fun and "resort hopping." In other words, without any serious responsibilities, they "had a fantastic life" in the beginning of their marriage. However, as they got older and Margaret had the opportunity to open restaurants near her sister, she increasingly noticed that her husband was unwilling, in her view, to grow up.

When the Great Recession of 2008 caused one of their newest restaurants to fail, Margaret wanted to get up, dust herself off, and move forward. Yet her husband seemed to be stuck in the past. He wanted to return to his free-spirited youth with no strings attached, and when she refused, he told her that she was ruining his life. Eventually, Margaret filed for divorce. When she did so, she already had a built-in system of emotional support. Tragically, her sister's husband had died one year prior to Margaret's decision to divorce, and after the death her sister had moved in with Margaret and her husband to regain her footing in the world. When Margaret's husband finally left the marital home, the two siblings could then lean on each other as they both worked to create new, independent futures without their spouses.

Probably the most devastating account of how addiction can ruin a marriage came from Ann, 56 years old, whose marriage ended after five years. Her husband, formerly in the armed services, was 53 years old and was addicted to both crack cocaine and crystal methamphetamine. When she met him, he was already an addict; however, he seemed to recognize the seriousness of his problem and was determined to do something about it. Initially, he sought in-patient treatment from the Veterans Administration. Ann recognized then that he was motivated to get clean, and once he finished the program, the couple got married and relocated away from the southwestern part of the country, where they had once lived.

They moved to a new city with the hope that the temptations of their old neighborhood would no longer haunt them. Unfortunately, with the Great Recession of 2008, they both lost their jobs; she was a manager at a drug store and he worked in the field of auto repairs. Then their house went into foreclosure, and their only option was to move back to their original hometown in the southwest, where they thought they could become employed once again. Unfortunately, returning home was a disaster for her husband; within a couple months he had reconnected with several of his old, drug-using friends. Ann discovered this problem immediately.

> [I knew he was using again by his] appearance, behavior, and, you know, rapid weight loss. I had taken on a job as an in-home caregiver and there was one week where, due to circumstances of the job, I could not come home . . . Within that one week that I was gone, he just had, like I said, a dramatic weight loss . . . And that's when it just kind of confirmed my suspicions.

Ann was devastated, but knew that there was not much she could do to help him with this problem.

Ann recognized that there was not much she could do to assist him because she herself was dealing with her own recovery from alcohol and cocaine abuse. She had firsthand knowledge that the desire to become sober must come from within. Many years prior to meeting this man, who was her fifth husband, Ann suffered a horrible tragedy. At the age of 22, she had two children, ages five and three, whom she left with a caregiver almost daily for about a year. The caretaker had a pool secured with a fence that contained a padlock. One day after unlocking the fence, the caretaker briefly went inside to go to the bathroom, and by the time she came back out, both children were drowning at the bottom of the pool. The caretaker, a nurse by training, attempted CPR, but could not resuscitate the children.

The death of her children was too much for Ann to bear, and she turned to alcohol and cocaine. Drugs felt like her only option, as other methods of coping had failed. For example, she tried to speak to a counselor at her local church, but the counselor would end up crying after each session. The overwhelming devastation proved to be too great for even the counselor to provide a positive therapeutic outcome. Ann also suffered from incredible internal conflict because she had taken these two children away from their physically violent biological father. She had left "New Orleans due to their father [being] extremely abusive to me and . . . extremely violent as well . . . So I left a violent place to get away . . . I kind of felt like I left that abusive situation to make a better life and then here they died anyway."

After she used alcohol and cocaine for a while, she realized that she was not going to wake up one day with her children by her side. In other words, self-medication simply was not going to change what happened. So she decided to get sober, and she was able to stay sober. Even though she herself was able to stay sober, she extended understanding toward drug users, saying, "That's probably where I was sympathetic to my [last ex-husband] because I knew how powerful it was. You know, if you've never done drugs, or never experienced that, it's hard to understand the power and the pull of it." Yet, Ann wanted a different life for herself, and so when her latest husband refused treatment again, she filed for divorce.

Wives Speak Out: Husbands Engaged in Verbal
and Emotional Abuse

Men and women differed in another way as they discussed the reasons
their marriages ended. Unlike men, women cited various types of verbal
and emotional abuse by their ex-partners as leading them to the decision
to divorce. Cheryl, 68 years old, had been married to her husband, 64
years old, for 32 years. Looking back on her life with her spouse, she said
she should have known that the relationship was not going to work from
the beginning.

> I'm going to tell you about our wedding night. We got married and drove to
> New Orleans. When we got there, he got out of the car to go get the keys for
> the room. [When] he came back, he threw the keys at me and told me to
> bring in the suitcases because he was tired ... So I'm in my "going away
> outfit" and shoes [with high] heels carrying in suitcases ... That kind of
> explains the rest of the marriage.

Cheryl noted that this was not how the couple interacted prior to getting
married, so at first she just hoped that her husband was not thinking
clearly. She loved him, and during the first part of their marriage they had
a boy and a girl. She was a stay-at-home mother while he was a supervi-
sory auditor with the federal government, so while they were not rich, they
were comfortable.

Over the years, however, Cheryl noted that his behavior was increasingly erratic and abusive on many levels. For example, when the children
were young, they went to Disney World as a family. However, once they
arrived, he refused to leave the motel room for several days. She and the
children expressed confusion over this seemingly arbitrary decision. But
she also began to notice that this emotionally abusive "withholding" tendency was becoming a pattern. Cheryl clearly felt that the dynamic
between them was "always hand out the carrot, pull it back, hand out the
carrot, pull it back. If I was happy, he was sad. If I was sad, he was happy."
As another example of his withholding behavior, Cheryl described how
hurt she was every holiday season when he would ask what she wanted so
that their children would have something to give to her. She would in turn
ask him what he wanted so that she could purchase the gifts that would

also come from the children. Yet each year he would receive the gifts that he wanted and there would be nothing for her.

Beyond these individual incidents of emotional abuse, he was verbally abusive. The most disturbing area of nearly constant verbal abuse involved Cheryl's relationship with one of her children, who was born with birth defects. She was the primary caregiver for this child, but her husband would never acknowledge or be grateful for her efforts. Within the context of their marriage, she stated that her "role was to be his scapegoat. Everything that went wrong [with this child] was my fault and he appreciated absolutely nothing that I did. To hear him tell it, he did it all . . . You would think he raised her . . . [and that] I didn't have a thing to do with it." After so many years of abuse, Cheryl expressed relief when she finally decided to file for divorce. Even though it was a long marriage that she felt had such promise, "The peace of not having him in my life was so much worth it."

Another woman who was the victim of significant emotional and verbal abuse from her 61-year-old husband was Nancy, who was 54 years old. This was Nancy's third marriage, and it lasted for four years and did not produce any biological or adopted children. She did have two teenaged girls from her second marriage, a marriage that was not successful because, she felt, that particular husband was immature, irresponsible, and not a good provider. Nancy was therefore attracted to her new husband because he seemed to be extremely self-reliant. That outward composure, however, as she was soon to find out, was really simply disguising an obsessive and controlling personality. According to Nancy, "He just wanted to control certain aspects of my life, like how I raised my kids and . . . what I did with my money, even before we were married. He was always giving me unsolicited advice and then if I didn't take the advice, he would get mad at me."

What really put Nancy over the edge was how he started to monitor her daughters' behavior. He constantly told Nancy that she was not doing a good job raising them, that the children were undisciplined, and that she was an overall bad role model for them. As a result of this constant barrage of negativity, the children became very fearful of their stepfather. Nancy offered many examples of how his strict, authoritarian parenting style had devastating consequences for their family. For example, one of her daughters wanted a pet snake. Her husband immediately objected, saying that there would be no snakes in his house. But Nancy had other plans.

> I said [to myself], well, you know what? It's my house, too. I want to get a snake. So I had to sneak around . . . I found myself constantly lying to him just so there wouldn't be arguments . . . So I'll tell you what, the funny thing . . . about the snake story [is that] I bought it anyway and he never went in my daughter's room. I was like, okay, I can get her the snake and we'll hide the snake because he never went into her room. Well, one day, I go down there and I say, "Come on, it's time to have dinner" and she's playing with the snake. The snake gets away from her and climbs into an office chair between the seat cushion and the molding for the cushion. So the two of us are trying to take this chair apart to get the snake out and he's coming down the stairs [saying], "Where are you?" And we're like, oh my God, what are we going to do? We got the snake out luckily and threw it into the snake tank and covered it with a blanket.

This example was only a mild form of control that Nancy's new husband tried to impose on the family. His behavior toward the three of them became more serious, objectionable, and outrageous over time.

One repeated cause of concern was the way he treated Nancy's younger daughter. Nancy described this child as very overweight and discussed how she had been trying to kindly help redirect her food choices toward healthier options. Yet her husband never believed that Nancy was doing enough in this area of parenting. He told her repeatedly that she needed to control what her daughter was eating 100% of the time. When he finally had enough with his wife's "failures" in this area, he took matters into his own hands.

> He actually put a lock on our refrigerator so [that] she couldn't get into the refrigerator. And I said to him . . . at the time I said to him . . . "This is the kind of stuff [that] you read about in books where somebody hides someone underneath his bed in a cage—that kind of thing." Very controlling.

This was not the end of her husband's disturbing actions. When he drank, he became even more verbally abusive to her and her daughters. Nancy would try to go to another room and put earplugs into her ears so that she would not have to hear him, but he would follow her around and "sit about an inch from my ear and scream at me. He would call me these names and [say], 'your daughters are worthless pieces of shit, blah, blah, blah.'" Over time, as the abuse increased in intensity, Nancy decided she could no longer have her daughters exposed to his mistreatment. She also wanted her daughters to respect her as a mother—so, finally, she gave him an ultimatum. She told him that if he called her one more name, she would file for divorce. After one final, particularly vitriolic encounter with him, she made good on her word and immediately told him that she was suing for divorce.

Wives Speak Out: We Grew Apart

Additionally, like some men in this study, several women cited growing apart as a reason for their gray divorces. Theresa, 51 years old, had recently divorced her husband, 52 years old. Their divorce was not caused by any dramatic circumstances but rather by a divergence in their life desires. They had a teenaged daughter, and throughout most of her daughter's life, Theresa was a stay-at-home mother. Her husband worked in the field of computer sales, which required that he travel extensively. For the limited time that he was at home, he did not have a strong interest in any family-oriented activities. For example, he would not attend their daughter's school-based events but instead would stay at home and read the newspaper.

This disturbed Theresa in a variety of ways. Prior to having her daughter, Theresa had made good money as an administrative assistant. The couple had discussed their postbaby plans, which involved Theresa and her husband both returning to work part-time in order to share child care responsibilities. However, during her maternity leave, Theresa's husband obtained a much higher paying full-time job. They decided as a team that she would stay at home, but she soon missed the rewards of working for pay. She also felt extremely socially isolated, without any close friends and family members nearby, and her husband's lack of participation in family life only made their circumstances worse. Theresa suggested couples therapy, but her husband denied that there was any problem in their relationship.

Tensions gradually worsened to Theresa's final breaking point:

> It was progressing over time but it got to the point where my daughter was
> old enough that I started realizing that she was spending all [of] her time in
> her room. He was spending all [of] his time in the living room. I was spend-
> ing most of my time sitting in the dining room . . . The house was quiet all
> [of] the time and we were all miserable. I kept trying to explain to him and
> point out to him that this was not healthy for any of us. [I would say that]
> this was miserable, we were all miserable, and he said, "What do you mean?
> What are you talking about? I don't understand. What do you think is
> wrong?"

With his inability to acknowledge their lack of family cohesion, Theresa
gave him an ultimatum. She told him that he needed to pay more attention
to his family and become more involved in home life. She also emphasized
that if things did not improve, she was going to take action toward ending
the marriage. When he did not put any more effort into addressing their
issues, Theresa hired an attorney to pursue the divorce. She noted that he
probably did not believe that she would actually go so far and do this, but
there was no going backward in her mind. The marriage was over.

Pamela, like Theresa, also discussed the process of growing apart that
served to unravel her marriage. The couple had lived on the east coast for
a long time while she was finishing her nursing degree training. They then
decided that they wanted to live in the southwest, so they purchased a new
home there. Pamela, 68 years old at the time of her interview, had a husband twelve years her senior. Together they had successfully raised three
daughters. But there was tension in the marriage. She noted that she was
much more ambitious than her husband in terms of her career. As an
example, her husband once relocated out to their new home for one year
on his own while Pamela finished her career in school nursing. Once there,
he was only able to obtain part-time employment in a retail setting and
was spending his money quite frivolously in her view.

> [Once I moved out to our new house and joined him], I began to question
> some of his decision-making and realized that he was overliving his income.
> I was continuing to support him and I supported a daughter on the east
> coast with her mortgage. Then I was working all the time as a nurse, having

retired from a full-time job in the school system on the east coast . . . I think with my asking so many questions and causing him some discomfort, he decided that he wanted to be independent of me.

Another strain on the marriage was that his sister had come to live with them on two separate occasions. Pamela supported her financially during the first visit, but told her husband that he needed to financially support her during the next visit. He viewed this statement as challenging to him and perhaps hurt his pride in the process. It was then that he decided to file for a divorce and he told her directly how he felt: "I just fell out of love and this is what I want: peace, quiet, and contentment."

In many ways, his decision to go forward and file for divorce was extremely painful. Pamela believed that by educating him about his spending habits, he would change and not decide to part ways. But during their 44 years together as husband and wife, she also recognized that there were cracks in their marriage. While she was the stable earner in the relationship, he was much more of a risk-taker. He would engage in a variety of business ventures, but none of them actually paid off. Pamela also discovered that at one point he had a girlfriend during their marriage, so they went to counseling and ultimately renewed their vows to each other. Although at the time they recommitted themselves to the marriage, the affair was still a significant strain on their relationship.

They also had cultural differences that she suspected might be keeping them apart; he was a Korean immigrant while she was white and born in the United States. These differences, she suspected, might have led to divergent views on the proper roles of men and women in marriage. In the end, all of the pieces of this marriage could not be glued back together again into one more harmonious whole, and she had to deal with the fact that he no longer loved her. Divorce, at this point, was inevitable.

Wives Speak Out: Husbands Had Mental Health Problems

Finally, the smallest set of wives divorced their husbands in mid-life due to their partners' mental health problems. Joan and her husband, both 53 years old, had been married for 34 years. They had four children very early in their marriage, which, Joan explained, made them immediately into coparents instead of what they should have been first and foremost: partners. One of the biggest strains on their marriage with this large family was their financial situation. Joan maintained that her husband had severe anxiety issues that led him to be extremely controlling. He worked in the hospitality industry, but was also a pastor, a job that paid him a small sum of money as well. He felt that pastoring was his true calling and loved that the congregation looked up to him. While he held this leadership position, he insisted that Joan do everything he said so that she would not outshine him, which included only taking low-paying jobs. She described herself as revolving through a series of retail, hospital, restaurant, and teaching positions that made little income when she really needed to earn a lot more to support her large family.

While Joan indicated that she loved her husband throughout their marriage, his anxiety-driven controlling ways put significant strain on them as a couple. She said that at home, it was "his way" only, and there was no compromising on important issues affecting the family. She pursued individual therapy to help her cope, but their attempts at couples counseling repeatedly failed. He would attend the sessions, but he would simply not be open to hearing her point of view. According to Joan, his own perceived self-importance was only made worse by his pastor job, where he liked having his "ego stroked" in particular by female congregants. Joan reported that she knew that he "talked to them about me and played the woe-is-me card" to them, a fact that continuously diminished her self-worth.

Joan admitted that her behavior in the marriage was not always impeccable. She had a one-night stand at one point that she deeply regretted. But she was desperate for attention and found herself without a voice in her own marriage. Her husband would hound her at home repeatedly until she agreed with him on some point, and this made her feel emotionally crushed. She also had no one in whom to confide about her predicament, since, as the pastor's wife, he expected her to behave in a certain way and not complain. She sadly stated, "I had to be what he wanted me to be and I wasn't allowed to be my own person. So I had no outlet, I had no friends to talk to [about my daily problems]."

Although she was not sure about the origins of his anxiety, Joan was certain that on some level, he was threatened by her because she was a strong person. She successfully ran the household on a "shoestring" budget, and even effectively homeschooled her children for a period of time. They finally began discussing the possibility of divorce when their youngest child was 14, but it took 10 years for him to finally agree that they were not going to make it as a couple. It was only then that he filed for divorce.

.   .   .   .   .

As this chapter has illustrated, men and women experiencing a gray divorce do not take the decision to split lightly. They are not Baby Boomers who wake up one day and decide to spread their wings on their own. Instead, like their younger counterparts, these couples each desire a successful marriage. While there were some differences between the sexes in the specific reasons offered for pursuing a gray divorce, more importantly there were similarities in that each sex wanted the other to behave enthusiastically as part of a loving, unified couple. When this bar was not met, couples moved toward divorce. And as we shall see next, once the decision to divorce is made, men and women experience very different gray divorce penalties in the areas of finances and relationships.

3 Shortchanged

THE ECONOMIC GRAY DIVORCE PENALTY

I'm one of the individuals [who] benefits from the pensions that a lot of companies don't have today . . . My wife only got [one-half of that pension] for the 17 years that we were together . . . She doesn't get any percentage . . . of the pension that I accumulated on my own before that. And we started [another retirement savings fund] while we were married, and she got one-half of that, which is only right, because whatever came out of my paycheck, . . . half belongs to her.

—Gregory, 67 years old, married for 17 years

If it were just for [what I have financially saved to support myself after the divorce], I would say [that] I would probably be terrified [about my future]. There's probably no possible way that I could keep a roof over my head with just social security. And the school system [where I work now] pays so poorly. I mean it's ridiculous . . . I am very lucky in that my parents were very, very good financial savers and investors. They are retired and living very comfortably, and they are kind enough to help my sister and me every year. They send us a very nice check and it enables us to continue putting away for our retirement and fix the house a little bit, that kind of thing . . . It's very generous and my father and mother assure me every year that [I] can count on this. [The check is] coming every November; [they] will send it, so [I] know it's coming.

—Theresa, 51 years old, married for 20 years

·　　·　　·　　·　　·

As we have seen, there are multiple paths that couples travel on their way to a gray divorce. These paths can be very painful, especially for adults who are in the middle of their lives and who have frequently spent many years together. Once at least one member of the couple decides to pursue a divorce, both husband and wife must unlink many parts of their lives, one of the most difficult being their financial holdings. This can be an extremely complicated uncoupling, and as such, the discussion presented here only highlights the major features of the division process. One of the most significant aspects of this process is that it can lead to inequitable results between the sexes. This is the first gray divorce penalty—the economic penalty—and the one experienced much more harshly by women than by men.

This point can be quickly made by looking at the cases of Gregory and Theresa, both of whose divorces were described here and in an earlier chapter. Gregory worked in the field of quality assurance in a manufacturing plant. He was married to his third wife, a hair stylist, for 17 years. Gregory had access to a traditional pension plan that paid him a monthly, guaranteed income for as long as he managed to live, a type of pension plan now quite rare in the American economy. It used to be more common, though, particularly in male-dominated industries. Gregory also had additional savings in another retirement fund. Upon divorce, he only had to share the part of his pension that he had earned while he was married. The part that he had accumulated while he was single was his alone. And while he had to split the second retirement savings fund with his wife, Gregory optimistically noted that he was fully financially secure for the years to come.

In contrast, Theresa had spent most of her 20-year marriage as a stay-at-home mother while her husband worked in the field of computer sales. They had one daughter together, and while Theresa found motherhood rewarding, she missed many aspects of her former life as an administrative assistant, including financial independence. Luckily for Theresa, her parents were financially knowledgeable and helped her buy bonds and other types of savings accounts over the course of her life. Most importantly, after her divorce, Theresa had parents who were actually writing her checks to cover her living expenses every year. She stoically observed that without this help, she would not be able to cover her major bills, as she had only a poorly paying secretarial job in the school system. The cost of living, and ultimately retiring, was simply too high.

Gregory and Theresa faced new financial realities after their gray divorces. And as this chapter will show, men and women often must confront different concerns as they relate to money management once they are single again. But before delving into their very personal stories, it is first important to understand how assets, liabilities, income streams, and health care costs are divided in typical divorce scenarios across the United States.

RULES OF ENGAGEMENT

Put bluntly, divorce forces both halves of a couple to reexamine their financial lives.[1] One of the first tasks that must be undertaken in the case of a gray divorce is to divide assets that are marital property (also called community or joint property) from assets that are separate property (also known as sole or nonmarital property).[2] Marital property is all property that was amassed by either half of the couple during the marriage. Separate property, on the other hand, is composed of all assets that each half of the couple brought into the marriage or obtained as a result of a gift or inheritance. In the case of gray divorce, marital property is that which must be divided in some way between the couple, whereas separate property is usually retained by the person who acquired it. In general, states divide marital property either equally—right down the middle— or "equitably." "Equitably" does not necessarily mean a 50/50 split. Instead, judges have the right to consider a variety of factors that will impose some sense of fairness between the couple. These factors might include who was responsible for causing the divorce (fault), potential incomes of each party, the health of each half of the couple, and other related, financial variables.

MAJOR PROPERTY: ASSETS AND LIABILITIES

Since separate property distribution tends to be relatively straightforward, most discussion and debate involve the allocation of marital property. For many middle-class families, the most valuable asset couples tend to own together is the family home. A home is also often an emotional asset, as couples have valuable memories attached to it. Nonetheless, its monetary value must be assessed and divided in the majority of gray divorce cases. Couples can follow a number of different routes with respect to splitting this asset. One half of the couple can buy the other out in terms of ownership, and continue to live in the home. Alternatively, the couple can agree to place the house on the market immediately and split the proceeds once it is sold. A final option is continuing joint ownership until a later date, when the partner who remained in the house sells it and pays the other half of the couple his/her fair share. Cars, which typically represent another set of important material assets for middle-class families, can be divided in similar ways, although, in practicality, usually each half of the couple agrees on simply assuming responsibility for one of the two automobiles that were held in the marriage.

Of course, financially secure couples experiencing gray divorce may have other significant assets to divide, such as mutual funds, investment trusts, checking and savings accounts, certificates of deposits, stocks, bonds, and the value of any other saving vehicles. These may be divided equally or equitably, as each judge sees fit. For those wealthier couples facing a gray divorce, other key assets that are likely to face division are Individual Retirement Accounts, or IRAs.[3] IRAs are accounts for saving money within the realm of earnings-linked retirement programs. There are limitations on how much money can be saved each year, and individuals face penalties if they make any withdrawals before the age of 59½ years. The two main types are traditional IRAs and Roth IRAs. Traditional IRAs use tax-deferred contributions to grow in size, with taxes only paid on increases in value (earnings and gains) when the funds are accessed upon retirement. After the age of 70½, individuals must start taking minimum distributions. Roth IRAs, on the other hand, utilize contributions that have already been taxed and earnings accumulate until they are distributed tax-free upon retirement. Savings can continue throughout one's lifetime, as there is no mandatory withdrawal age. To participate in a Roth IRA, however, one must meet certain income-eligibility guidelines. Both types of IRAs are subject to division in a gray divorce.

Some couples might also have significant assets or holdings that are not easily split, such as term life insurance and permanent life insurance. The value of these items, as well as the designated beneficiaries, must be decided at the time of divorce. The same is true regarding annuities, which pay a benefit to an individual for a fixed or an indefinite period of time until death. To preserve the greatest value, a divorce decree will often mandate a specific allocation at the time when they become due. Other critical assets that might require the help of the court to divide include land and personal property such as pets, club memberships, military benefits, and intellectual property. These latter items can often prove to be contentious in nature during a divorce, especially if they have sentimental meaning or are difficult to value.

Just like assets, debts need to be addressed in the case of a gray divorce as well. However, it is important to note that debts are not as easily assigned as assets. Even if the divorce decree states that one member of the couple must pay off a specific debt—and indemnify the other part of the couple as to his/her full responsibility—lenders and creditors do not normally sign on to this settlement. Therefore, in certain cases, lenders and creditors may pursue either party after a divorce if an obligation is not paid. This becomes an even more complicated matter because some states regard all debts incurred during the marriage to be part of the marital estate, regardless of who actually signed the original loan application. In addition, other states allow creditors to seize assets from the marriage in order to pay off debts incurred by one spouse even *before* the couple became married. Ideally, all debts would be retired at the time of the divorce, but this may not be possible. If there is significant debt from the marriage that cannot be paid off, bankruptcy might be the only option going forward for the couple.[4]

Finally, it is important to note that in many cases, federal income taxes operate the same way as debts. Even if a divorce decree determines that one party is responsible for paying back taxes, this settlement is not binding on the range of actions available to the Internal Revenue Service (IRS). Moreover, audits that hold both parties responsible for taxes can occur for up to three years after a particular filing date, or long after a family court may have granted a divorce. As in the case of other debts, couples can pursue settlements that explicitly state who is responsible for all of the taxes, and indemnify the other party from further responsibility. In these situations, if the assigned party does not pay, and the IRS pursues the indemnified half of the couple, this innocent party can then sue his or her ex-partner for all outlays made to fulfill these obligations. Of course, litigation can be both lengthy and costly, making IRS debts notoriously difficult to both resolve and retire.

Given the discussion so far, who has the greater financial burden after a gray divorce? That is, do men or women pay the higher economic gray divorce penalty? On its surface, the division of assets and liabilities does not seem to provide a clear-cut advantage to one spouse over another, but upon further inspection, the likelihood is high that women generally end up shortchanged. States with equal or 50/50 distribution rules set the clock back to the same starting point for each half of the couple, but if men have better income prospects going into the future due to work experiences and stronger educational backgrounds, they also have the ability to move forward financially at a faster rate than their female counterparts. In other states, where equitable distribution laws rule, judges have wide latitude to determine what is fair. Some judges who understand the realities of the disadvantages faced by women in the paid labor market (due to lower earnings, time out of the workforce, etc.) may compensate them by giving them additional benefits in assets and fewer debts. Other judges, who view women as relatively equal in terms of future potential earning power, might engage in fewer financially compensatory actions. Overall, the limited research that exists on this type of wealth division—assets minus liabilities—for individuals in mid-life suggests that on average women suffer a substantially greater economic gray divorce penalty than men.[5]

INCOME STREAMS

In addition to splitting the major assets and liabilities described earlier, many couples experiencing a gray divorce might need to divide income streams that used to be jointly held or were presumed to be jointly held. These streams are extremely important in that they have the ability to keep both men and women not only financially comfortable in the later years of their lives in the best-case scenario, but above the poverty line in the worst-case scenario. The first type of income stream is alimony, also known as spousal support. Most commonly, this represents income transfers from husbands, typically the higher-wage earners during the marriage, to wives, typically the lower-income earners during the marriage.

Granted from the nineteenth century to the present day, alimony represents a way for mostly women to sustain themselves financially after their marriages have ended.[6] Although state legislatures define permissible forms of alimony, judges have significant discretion in awarding it, if at all, and also have wide latitude in terms of justifying guidelines for its implementation.[7] Factors individual judges can consider are many, and can include the length of the marriage, the earning power and health of each party, the guilt of each party in causing the divorce, and time spent out of the workforce to raise children.

Judges also retain substantial power over the type of alimony awarded.[8] *Pendente lite* alimony refers to temporary support while a divorce is pending, and rehabilitative alimony assists one partner, usually the wife, in gaining education and employment skills over a short period of time so that she can become self-sufficient. Lump sum alimony is a onetime payment between partners to equalize contributions made to the common good of the marriage, such as money spent on the education or training of the husband. Reimbursement alimony is similar to lump sum payments but involves payments spread out over a longer period of time. Long-term or permanent alimony can also be awarded when the capacity of one partner to sustain a particular standard of living cannot be reached using other methods. These longer-term forms of alimony are important in cases where women in particular have taken long periods of time out of the labor market to raise children or to care for other dependents.

While these types of payments are important forms of income, particularly for women, judges might be viewing them as less appropriate than in the past. This is because, first, the rise in no-fault divorce rather than divorce by cause, such as cruelty or adultery, means that fewer alimony awards are dispensed as a form of punishment against the person who caused the divorce.[9] Second, women have pursued jobs in greater numbers than ever before, potentially leading judges to believe that women can and should take care of themselves economically. Third, in recent years, men have organized themselves into alimony reform groups across numerous states. They have lobbied state legislatures to reduce these obligations and have even achieved some legal changes, especially in the area of ending long-term or permanent alimony.[10]

Alimony income streams can have very different impacts on men and women. In a small number of cases, men might suffer greater consequences, especially if the alimony that they are charged with paying is exorbitant or is awarded over their lifetime. These obligations can prevent men from retiring or otherwise reduce their standard of living in relation to that of their ex-wives. However, in the years to come, women are much more likely to pay an economic gray divorce penalty with respect to alimony than men. Recall that judges have discretion over whether alimony is paid at all. While there were approximately 344,000 awards for women and 22,000 awards for men in 2013, this represents a notable downward trend from earlier years (see table 6). Without the protection of alimony, women who stayed at home to raise their children for either part or all of their lives will become especially economically vulnerable after a gray divorce.

The second most important income stream subject to division is social security. Social security is payments based on contributions that a wage earner gives the federal government in the form of a payroll tax while working. Both employers and employees contribute 6.2% of the employees' earnings up to a certain amount per year in these taxes. In order to ultimately qualify for benefits, a worker has to earn 40 credits, with each credit equaling a set amount of earnings. A person can earn up to four credits per year. Once a worker reaches a retirement age, at the earliest at age 62 but more commonly 65 or 67, he or she can start collecting monthly social security benefits. The benefits distributed are progressive in that they give a higher rate of return to lower earners; benefits are also adjusted for inflation. Central to the discussion here, the social security program calculates benefits using a formula based on the 35 years of highest taxable income. In a nutshell, earnings drive later benefits. As such, it is critical to note that if an individual spends time out of the paid labor market for any reason, social security enters zeros into the equation for determining benefits for those years.

Judges do not divide social security benefits down the middle as a pooled resource in cases of divorce. Instead, the rules of the program itself outline benefit options if a marriage breaks down. Recognizing that divorced couples were once an economic unit, the program provides these now separated individuals with benefits based on their own earnings or their

Table 6   Number of Alimony Recipients in the United States by Sex

YEAR	MEN Number of Recipients	WOMEN Number of Recipients
1994	8,000	416,000
1995	10,000	453,000
1996	1,000	476,000
1997	16,000	393,000
1998	7,000	417,000
1999	16,000	446,000
2000	10,000	438,000
2001	4,000	449,000
2002	14,000	400,000
2003	21,000	380,000
2004	18,000	487,000
2005	11,000	403,000
2006	13,000	382,000
2007	11,000	401,000
2008	13,000	417,000
2009	30,000	320,000
2010	11,000	384,000
2011	18,000	403,000
2012	23,000	361,000
2013	22,000	344,000

SOURCE: US Census Bureau, Current Population Survey, Annual Social and Economic Supplement, Various Years.

NOTE: The occurrence of male alimony recipients is a relatively rare event so the variability in these numbers is largely the result of small sample sizes.

ex-spouses' earnings. In the latter case, each half of the couple has the ability to draw upon "derivative benefits" based on their ex-spouses' benefit levels. Several criteria have to be met for this to be an option. These include the following rules: (1) couples must have been married for at least ten years, with the higher earners currently entitled to benefits; (2) the lower-wage earners must be applying for social security benefits and at least 62 years old and unmarried; (3) the lower-wage earners' benefits based on their own work records would be less than one-half of the higher earners' benefits. In these cases, the social security program awards derivative benefits equal to one-half of the higher-wage earners' benefits. If the higher earners die, then the lower-earning spouses can apply for survivors' benefits, which are 100% of their ex-spouses' benefits.[11] However, the lower earners cannot tap derivative benefits if they remarry.

The rules that govern social security benefits disadvantage women in many ways in comparison with men because of their unique relationship with the paid labor market.[12] First, although women have been participating in the labor market at growing rates, they still lag behind men for a variety of reasons, most often due to caregiving responsibilities. In 2014, women had a labor force participation rate of 57.0%, while men had a rate of 69.2%.[13] In addition, labor force participation rates mask differences between those who work full-time and those who work part-time; the Bureau of Labor Statistics considers both sets of workers as participating in paid work even though they log extremely disparate hours, with women more likely to be part-time earners. Also recall that zeros get entered into the social security benefit formula for every year a person does not engage in paid work. This is much more likely to happen for women, as they are the primary caregivers for children and aging parents. Another way social security benefits disadvantage women has to do with the fact that women continue to earn less than their male counterparts. Recall that in 2014, women working full-time had median earnings that were 82.5% of male median earnings.[14] Finally, occupational segregation depresses women's earnings overall. While some professional and managerial occupations have become more integrated over time, women still work disproportionately in sales and service jobs with low wages and few benefits.

In addition to the income streams of alimony and social security, a retirement plan is another stream of revenue for some higher-earning couples. There are two main types of retirement plans offered by employers to male and female employees—defined-benefit plans and defined-contribution plans—both of which are potentially divisible at the time of a divorce. Historically, employers funded defined-benefit plans, also known as traditional pension plans, in male-dominated industries such as transportation, manufacturing, and communications, as well as in some government-related jobs. In these plans, after each worker retires, he or she receives a monthly retirement payment for the rest of his/her life based on earnings and years of service; this is also called an annuity. It is important to note that employees must be working for an employer for a significant period of time in order to be vested, or eligible for benefits. In addition, defined-benefit programs are generally not portable or accessible prior to retirement. In many cases, only one-half of the divorcing couple has a defined-benefit plan. As a result, in terms of division rules, the person with the defined-benefit plan can either pay off his/her ex-spouse with a lump sum or agree that the nonparticipating spouse will receive a share of these benefits later when the participant retires. In these cases, participants must develop what is known as a qualified domestic relations order, or QDRO. This QDRO spells out the terms of the distribution plan and becomes part of the official divorce settlement. The Pension Protection Act of 2006 enables members of a divorcing couple to return to court to obtain a QDRO if one was not issued in the original judgment.

It is important to note that defined-contribution plans are now emerging as the most common form of retirement accounts in the United States today and have in many cases replaced defined-benefit plans.[15] Under these programs, each employee puts a certain percentage of his/her wages into an account during the work year, and the employer may contribute as well. Employees then choose to deposit these monies into a select set of stock and bond accounts. The most common form of a defined-contribution plan is the 401(k) for corporate employees and the 403(b) for nonprofit and educational workers. In many ways, defined-contribution plans place the risk of establishing a secure retirement income on employees rather than on employers, as is the case in defined-benefit plans.[16] This is true for a number of reasons. First, employees need to make enough money to contribute to the plan, as well as avoid borrowing from the funds for emergencies, since such actions come with high financial penalties. Second, employees are relying on the stock and bond markets to increase over the long run, but cannot control these macrolevel forces. Third, unlike defined-benefit annuities, workers can potentially outlive savings that are held in defined-contribution plans.

Interestingly, over time, some data suggest that in the overall population, men and women from 1998 to 2012 have roughly equivalent rates of access to any type of retirement plan (such as defined-benefit plans, defined-contribution plans, and IRAs). For example, in 1998, about 60 percent of men and 60 percent of women were offered such types of plans, and of those offered 46 percent of men and 41 percent of women actually participated. By 2012, about 60 percent of men and 63 percent of women were offered such types of plans, and of those offered 46 percent of men and 46 percent of women actually participated.[17]

Retirement offerings and participation rates are one piece of the puzzle, yet they tell us nothing about the amount of money contributed by each sex into the plans. While many workers may funnel some of their income to defined-contribution plans when they are offered, divorced women in particular are much less likely to use them as significant savings vehicles because of multiple, competing demands on their earnings.[18] Wage discrimination and lower levels of education attainment are among the multiple factors that affect the amount of money women can contribute to these accounts. In addition, research has shown that women tend to invest more conservatively than men; less investment, of course, restricts postretirement income.[19] In these ways, then, divorced women at or over the age of 50 face an illusion of equality in that they are being offered retirement plans like their male counterparts, but are much less likely to sustain or grow them over the long run due to their much more limited or constrained financial circumstances. Also importantly, upon a divorce there are no similar requirements regarding the division of defined-contribution plans as there are related to defined-benefit plans (such as outlined in a QDRO). With more and more workers having access only to defined-contribution plans, women's economic position after a gray divorce only runs the risk of becoming more uncertain.

Finally, faced with unstable income streams in later life in the areas of alimony, social security, and retirement benefits, women may attempt to seek out additional employment prospects for steady earnings in their sixties and beyond. Indeed, research shows that there are important differences between married women and divorced women in that the latter are much more likely to work in their retirement years.[20] However, changing skill needs and limited educational backgrounds may prove prohibitive for these older, divorced women as they try to obtain meaningful and financially rewarding work.[21] Adding to the difficulty is the serious problem of age discrimination by employers.[22] Employers frequently see older workers as too expensive to pay, too expensive to train, and too expensive to retain. This means that women who want to increase their incomes in later life through employment might find it difficult to do so, despite their strongest efforts. In the area of all income streams, then, women on average pay a higher economic gray divorce penalty than men.

HEALTH CARE AND HEALTH INSURANCE

In addition to income needs, another serious financial concern for those experiencing a gray divorce is health care and health insurance. For those under the age of 65, health insurance in the United States is still highly linked to employment and marriage. In 2015, about 57.5 million out of the approximately 98 total million women living in the United States ages 19–64 (59%) had employment-based coverage.[23] However, in many cases, this was not coverage through their own employment, but rather coverage that they received as a qualifying dependent of their spouses. Only 35% of working age women are insured through their own job, versus 44% of men, and women are more likely to be on a policy as a dependent, at 24%, versus 16% for men. In addition, women working in low-wage jobs or working part-time are much less likely to be offered employer-sponsored health plans than women with higher-wage jobs or those working full-time.

While very low-income women can apply for the means-tested health insurance program, Medicaid, millions of women fall through the cracks of coverage. The high cost of private insurance and the strict income rules governing Medicaid are responsible for most of these gaps. As described earlier, the Patient Protection and Affordable Care Act of 2010 (PPACA) attempted to address some of these problems by offering individuals the opportunity to buy their own insurance in newly created, state-based health insurance marketplaces. The PPACA also offered tax credits and subsidies to purchase insurance for people living on lower incomes, and encouraged states to broaden eligibility for their Medicaid programs by raising income thresholds for participation.[24] Yet, despite these reforms, in 2015 there were approximately 24.3 million nonelderly uninsured adults, with almost half being women.[25]

Fortunately, most American women become eligible for Medicare at age 65.[26] In 2015, approximately 55.5 million Americans received at least some health care coverage through the Medicare program; over half were women.[27] Medicare has evolved since it first began in 1965 in many ways that benefit women. When it initially started operating, the program focused on hospital stays and not on preventative care or prescription drug coverage. It took decades for Medicare to include what are now considered to be essential services. For example, it was not until 1990 that the program covered Pap smears; routine mammograms qualified as reimbursable services beginning in 1991.[28] However, until recently women were still responsible for 20% of these expenses, as well as other tests that were specific to female health concerns. To address these financially related barriers to care, the passage of the PPACA put an end to any cost sharing for these tests, and offered women annual visits with medical professionals to devise suitable and individualized health plans.

Nonetheless, there are still significant gaping holes in coverage. Medicare does not pay for hearing aids, dental care, and eyeglasses. Cost-sharing continues for many other services, which include deductibles in 2017 of $1,316 for 60-day benefit periods involving inpatient hospital care (with no monthly premiums for most, but coinsurance of $329 per day for hospital days 61 to 90 and $658 per day on hospital day 91 and beyond), annual deductibles of $183 for doctors' visits (with monthly premiums of $134 per month, but adjusted for income, with most paying $109 per month; after the deductible is met, then an additional 20% of all Medicare-approved costs), and not more than $400 in deductibles for prescription plans (plus premiums, coinsurance, and copayments that vary by plan).[29] Individuals are responsible for all of these copayments or coinsurance fees when seeing a doctor or obtaining prescription drugs.[30] There are also no limits on Medicare out-of-pocket spending, or costs for which an individual can still be held privately responsible.

Just like women under the age of 65, women over the age of 65 are also disadvantaged relative to men in the area of health care expenditures. Because of the aforementioned gaps in complete coverage, the fact that they live longer than men, and the nature of their illnesses, women tend to spend much more on out-of-pocket health care costs than men. In 2012, women ages 65 to 84 paid $52.3 million on out-of-pocket medical goods and services, versus $41.8 million for men in the same age group.[31] What happens when individuals cannot afford supplementary insurance or do not have the ability to pay for these out-of-pocket expenses? This is where Medicaid steps in to provide additional assistance. Medicaid pays for costs that Medicare does not cover and even extends benefits in certain states by providing assistance for vision, dental, and hearing aids. Medicaid is especially important for Black and Hispanic women, who have lower incomes compared to whites (especially the whites who volunteered to participate in this study of gray divorce), in obtaining critical medical care. Individuals who qualify for Medicare and Medicaid, approximately 11 million in 2014, are known as "dually eligible enrollees," and not surprisingly, women represented approximately 66% of the 6.4 million dually eligible enrollees ages 65 and older.[32]

In addition, long-term care assistance, as discussed earlier, is not covered by any type of traditional insurance, yet it is critical for women, who live longer than men. There are private plans available, but not many people take advantage of this option.[33] Part of the reason that few Americans hold these policies is that they are extremely expensive, costing on average for a single man and a single woman, both age 55, about $1,050 and $1,500 per year for a mid-level plan in 2017.[34] Given these hard financial realities, most women in their older years rely on unpaid caregivers for their health-related needs. When this option is not available or appropriate, there are other solutions. These can involve community-based, home-based, or institutionally based care. Yet all of this care is extremely expensive. In 2016, the median annual cost of adult day care within the community was $17,680; home health aide services cost approximately $46,332; and nursing home care with a private room was $92,378 per year.[35]

Long-term care costs can be devastating to women when they are most vulnerable. For those without long-term care insurance, Medicare only covers a select number of services, often within a designated time limit. Then, only when these otherwise uninsured women have spent down their life savings do they qualify for Medicaid to help with long-term costs; even then they typically have to pay part of their social security benefits as "copays" for this care. The hard reality is that due to the current structure of the health care system in the United States, many women will spend the last years of their lives in financially challenging circumstances and even poverty. Health care is thus the final area where women pay a higher economic gray divorce penalty than men.

WHAT ARE YOUR FINANCIAL CONCERNS?

Individual holdings of assets and liabilities, income streams, and health insurance portfolios coalesce in various forms in the lives of those experiencing a gray divorce to produce either a climate of financial security or a climate of financial worry. The research presented thus far suggests that men are more likely to be financially secure, and women are more likely to feel financially worried after a gray divorce, given the economic facts on the ground. In fact, the AARP survey of individuals experiencing a gray divorce conducted in 2003 notes that women are four times as likely as men to be afraid of being financially destitute after splitting up with their spouses.[36]

Recall, however, that the sample of men and women in this book is relatively financially advantaged. Therefore, it is not surprising that when asked about these potential concerns, a plurality of each sex stated that they were not worried about their postretirement economic well-being. Yet, even so, the story is more complex. As we will see, the interviews demonstrate that there were still important differences between the sexes as they framed their perceptions of financial security (see table 7). While some men reported successfully keeping their ex-partners "away from" what they viewed as their own retirement accounts from a defensive posture, other men were much more often involved in "proactively managing" their financial futures. They were risk-takers, happy with continued employment, and tenacious in packaging solid income streams for their benefit going forward. In addition, due to their long work histories in particular industries, they often had access to defined-benefit or traditional pension plans that bolstered their financial strength. In terms of health care, recall that, as table 4 in chapter 1 illustrated, 37 out of 40 of the men reported having traditional health care insurance, but only one out of 40 men had a long-term health care insurance policy in place. The most common reason men cited for why they did not have a long-term care policy was simply that they had not given it any thought, and if they did think they might need coverage, it was much too early in their lives to consider purchasing it. This is consistent with their overall approach to financial security, in which ruminating over future speed bumps was simply not a part of their mind set.

There were many women who also stated that they were financially secure in their retirements. Like the men, some women reported success in

Table 7   Financial Worries from a Gray Divorce

	40 Men	40 Women
Financial Concerns (Ranked by Order of Mention)	1. No Worries (Keeping Ex-Partners away from Retirement Savings) and Proactive Money Management Strategies: —*Risk-Taking* —*Excited to Voluntarily Continue Working* —*Putting Together Solid Income Streams*	1. No Worries (Keeping Ex-Partners away from Retirement Savings) and Reactive Money Management Strategies: —*Leading Minimalist Lifestyles* —*Depending on Relatives* 2. Need to Continue Working

keeping their ex-partners "away" from their retirement incomes as their key financial maintenance strategy. But, unlike the men, other women reported being financially secure through "reactive" rather than "proactive" plans, meaning they decreased spending on themselves or relied on others to support them. More specifically, some engaged in leading minimalist lifestyles or becoming thriftier in terms of consumption. Other women depended on the wealth of their relatives as their means of assuring a secure retirement. Moreover, because of their more sporadic work histories, most often due to childrearing responsibilities, these women often did not have traditional, defined-benefit pension plans or high levels of savings in their IRAs or defined-contribution 401(k)s. Finally, an important subset of women *did* report significant financial worries that made them believe that they would have to work until they died. These women tended to discuss their lack of financial security in catastrophic terms.

Differences between men and women also emerged in the health care arena. Again, table 4 in chapter 1 indicates that most women, like the men, were protected by having traditional health care insurance (39 out of 40 women). Similar to the men as well, having long-term health care insurance was rare (five out of 40 women). Interestingly, however, when they were asked why they did not have a long-term care health insurance policy, the most common reason offered by these women was that it was simply too expensive or they had too much debt. In other words, instead of not having it because they did not worry about the future or thought it was too early to consider it, these women, unlike the men, *had* thought about it and concluded that they could not afford it. The small number of women *with* long-term health care policies also had thought about it, and were in exceptional circumstances that enabled them to buy it. If these were the circumstances facing the more relatively financially well-off women in this study, it is not a stretch to imagine that poorer women would face even more obstacles in economically sustaining themselves. In terms of concerns over money overall, then, as we shall see, women were much more likely to face a higher economic gray divorce penalty than men.

Husbands Speak Out: Proactively Managing Their Secure Financial Future

Money simply was not an issue for most men interviewed here. In many cases, they argued that their amassed retirement income was theirs alone and should not be subject to division in their divorce. John, 54 years old and a computer technician, had been married to his wife, 52 years old, for 27 years. Their marriage had fallen apart as both he and she stopped communicating effectively, even to the point where they were barely speaking to each other. After they agreed to divorce, he described the asset division process as quite easy. He stated that his wife had no interest in alimony and that once they went into mediation, the couple moved quickly through all of the required steps of financial decision-making. They each retained a vehicle as part of the settlement, which only left the house and their retirement accounts in play.

At that point, John dug his heels into the sand and told his wife that she could have the house, but that in no way was she going to get part of his retirement accounts, which included both a defined-benefit plan from a past job and a defined-contribution plan from his current job. He knew the value of these income streams—especially the defined-benefit plan—and he believed himself to be within his rights in keeping her "away" from them.

I worked for another major company you may have heard of . . . for twenty-seven years until it decided it no longer needed my services. Well, after twenty-seven years . . . it's one of the few companies that still uses the "p" word, pension . . . And when this whole thing came about, my first comment to her was, "You can have the house, [but] keep your hands off my retirement [accounts]."

His wife agreed to this settlement, according to John, because there were many other pieces of their financial holdings that would be allocated in her favor. They had three children, including one daughter who was under 21, for whom he continued to pay both child support and health insurance premiums. John also noted that his wife had received substantial inheritances from both a neighbor and her mother. Since he was still young, John aimed to continue working at a salary of approximately $50,000 per year, during which time he would regularly contribute money into his retirement savings account and receive health insurance from his employer. He also did not worry about purchasing long-term health care insurance, speculating that the "government will take care of me" if he needed that type of medical assistance down the road.

Scott, who had recently ended a three-year marriage at age 65, similarly boasted of his desire and ability to keep his wife, 68 years old, "away" from his defined-benefit pension plan, but he also had other proactive financial strategies up his sleeve. He had been in the high-tech optics business, temporarily retired, and then returned to part-time work in the field of solar panel sales. His wife was now retired, but had previously worked as a manager of a real estate agency. At the end of their marriage, which in his perspective was caused by his wife's verbal abuse, they had, Scott stated, the standard items to divide, such as cars, a motorcycle, and a house. They did not consider alimony at all since the marriage was so short, and they both proceeded through the divorce process without an attorney, dividing their assets relatively amicably.

In their negotiations, Scott made it clear at "the time that we sat down to talk [that] . . . nothing [related to my retirement income] is in play." They pursued a no-fault divorce, whereby they paid $70, sent in their papers to the court, and met with the judge to say that they had successfully distributed their assets between them. Scott maintained that because his wife had her own retirement savings, he believed that it was fair for them to simply go their own ways. He reported a steady income of $116,000 per year, and noted that he was willing to be a risk-taker and gamble some extra money in the stock market. In fact, after learning how to sell stocks short, he made a significant amount of money. He also collected a significant survivor's benefit from Canada due to the death of his first wife. This, in combination with other income in the form of his social security benefits, made him feel extremely financially secure. In addition, he had Medicare to cover his health needs and some health benefits from his new part-time job, and he had not bought a long-term health care insurance policy. He said that even after witnessing the costs associated with putting both of his parents in nursing homes, the possibility of his needing this type of care did not "scare me but I haven't really researched anything either." In the short term, at least, he found his health care needs adequately covered.

Steven was another wealthy man who had no concerns about his financial well-being after his divorce. He simply loved his job so much that he could not envision leaving it; this was his proactive financial management strategy. In fact, he was a successful insurance salesperson in Minnesota who made approximately $250,000 per year at the age of 53. He had been married to his wife, age 50, for 27 years, and she worked with him in the insurance business. He was in charge of sales and she ran the back office.

> [While I was married], we had a nice income. We had a nice lifestyle. We had a second home in Utah. We figured out in the early 2000s how to work remotely. We put everything on the cloud before it was the cloud.

Cracks in the marriage started to appear when they had differing ideas about what would constitute a satisfying life going forward.

> So she wanted to scale all of that back. [Her idea was to] figure out what a basic acceptable income is and . . . just work for that. [She wanted to] . . . quit trying to make more money. And I'm like, "No." The beautiful thing about the insurance business is [that] you control your time and you control your income. If you're not happy with your income, go sell something. If you're happy with your income, take a vacation. Well, she wanted to scale it

back and spend more time at church and doing ministry-related things. I wanted to spend the same amount of time doing business and recreational things.

To fulfill his goals, he began traveling to Alaska, where he grew up and found that he could relax. He also rented a place in South Dakota where he could pheasant hunt for two months per year, fulfilling another one of his passions. Eventually, his strong love for skiing in the mountains of Colorado and other places in the Rockies prompted him to leave his primary home in Minnesota for longer and longer periods during the year.

These differences eventually frayed their marriage. They also fought over how to instill personal money management responsibility in their children, and Steven admitted to an extramarital affair that took place while the couple was apart. At this point, the marriage was unsalvageable. Like Scott, Steven and his wife did not obtain legal advice at the time of the divorce, as they were able to come up with a financial agreement on their own and both thought lawyers were too expensive. They divided their insurance business equally, they sold their Utah home, and his wife took possession of the Minnesota home. Alimony was not an issue for them since, according to Steven, they had worked as a team in their insurance business. At the time of the divorce, while not having a defined-benefit plan, Steven did have an IRA and a 401(k) in his current position. His wife only had an IRA, but Steven insisted that she felt fairly compensated by other assets she received as part of the divorce settlement. He stated that he had no fears whatsoever about his financial future because he loved his job and the lifestyle it permitted him to live. He had traditional health care insurance, but did not have long-term health care insurance. At this point in his life, he really had not given a long-term health care policy significant thought. However, he did note that he was planning to buy a long-term care policy in the near future, as he believed that he could afford it and that it would be a wise economic decision.

Brian, 57 years old, was an example of another man who felt financially secure after his gray divorce. He was proactive and tenacious in putting a package of multiple income streams together—independent of his wife—to make him comfortable in his retirement years. Brian had divorced his wife after 24 years together. Initially, they had shared many common interests while she was in the Navy and he was a Department of Defense contractor working for a series of private companies. However, as their marriage progressed, she developed a serious alcohol problem. Another significant strain on the marriage was that in his capacity as a contractor with the Department of Defense, he had to take a job that placed the couple in England for over 20 years. His wife stayed at home raising their three children for a significant percentage of this time, and then took on a variety of part-time jobs as the children grew up. After Brian's stint in England, an employer sent him to work in Guam. Meanwhile, his wife longed to go back to the United States, so they agreed that they would buy a house in Minnesota and she would relocate without him until he could be transferred. In all of these jobs, he acquired a traditional pension plan as well as a 401(k).

During the course of these transitions, his wife successfully completed an alcohol rehabilitation program. As a result of this treatment, according to Brian, his wife also developed a new personality and no longer wanted to be married. After their decision to divorce, he maintained that his wife, at 62 years old with no alimony, would be financially secure in the future because she was receiving some financial support from the Navy as well as social security benefits based on his income. In the divorce settlement, she also received their Minnesota home as well as a small lake property. However, she had no other retirement income and Brian wanted to protect his own future income streams.

While he was not represented by an attorney during the divorce, she did hire a lawyer who fought him for half of his 401(k). Nonetheless, Brian was very smart about putting a package of income streams together for himself that would enable him to reach his retirement goals. Some of his income was out of his control; around the time of the divorce, Brian began collecting disability payments after he went into kidney failure. But while he ultimately had to give his wife part of his 401(k), he was able to fully retain the entirety of his traditional, defined-benefit plan. He received Medicare as a result of his disability status, and had not purchased any expensive long-term health care insurance, which he felt he did not need. Overall, Brian reported being fully confident that he had assembled multiple monetary income streams effectively and that his overall financial future would be extremely bright. As it stood now, even though he was retired, he earned approximately $60,000 per year.

Wives Speak Out: Reactively Managing Their Secure Financial Future

There were many wives who experienced a gray divorce who, like their male counterparts, reported very few worries about their financial futures. For some, just like the men, this meant keeping their spouses "away" from the retirement income that they felt they had earned on their own. However, in most other cases, these women stated that they would be secure going forward because of their own personal financial strategies, which were much more "reactive" or self-limiting than the men's "proactive" strategies. These techniques involved reducing spending or drawing upon the help of family members to sustain them.

Denise was one of the most successful women in this study in advocating on behalf of her financial future and making sure that her husband was kept "away" from her retirement income. She was 61 years old and her husband was 67 years old. They had been married for 42 years, during which time she had a lucrative career as a technician at a nuclear power plant. He had a much more erratic work history, employed at times as a carpenter and as a handyman. After she decided to divorce her husband due to his cheating and emotional and verbal abuse, she immediately went to an attorney for representation, and he did not.

> Okay, this is what I told my attorney. I'm fully employed and I have a 401(k). Our house is paid for, and he draws social security. Give him the house, let me keep my 401(k). I can start over, [but] he can't . . . [Ultimately when I made this offer, he wrote back and said to my attorney, with whom he accused me of having a romantic relationship], "You and your money-hungry girlfriend can have this house; I don't want anything they ever gave me"—"they" meaning me and [our two] boys—and "I'm leaving it. She can have it."

Denise thought that she was being "Christian" by offering him the house in the first place, but he was so upset by the divorce that he did not engage in any type of negotiations with her.

The final divorce settlement, therefore, heavily favored Denise. She received the home, since he rejected it. But most importantly to Denise, she had language placed into the agreement that enabled her to keep all of her retirement income while he would retain his retirement income, which was nothing. She insisted that while she tried to help him by initially suggesting that he take the house, she lost patience with him over time and would not do more for him. For example, she said that at one point late in the negotiations, his only desire was that she buy him a new car, but she refused. In making this decision, she reasoned that she knew he was not destitute because he had been part of a successful class-action lawsuit involving exposure to asbestos. She only wanted a secure retirement, and although she did not have a defined-benefit pension plan, her 401(k) account was substantial. She also had traditional health insurance but noted that she could not afford long-term health care insurance at her stage in life. With the significant contributions of one of her son's family with whom she lived, she reported an annual household income of close to $250,000.

Other women declared that they would be financially secure in their retirements, but only by maintaining a more minimalist lifestyle. This was a more self-limiting or reactive strategy to protecting retirement income rather than the more proactive strategy employed by many of the men in this study. For instance, Beverly, 64 years old, had been in a marriage of 24 years that ended when her 57-year-old husband refused to seek treatment for his addiction to gay pornography. Although they tried to work out the relationship in counseling, he was not able or willing to stop his destructive behavior. At the time of her divorce, her work history provided some insight into her retirement resources. Before having her two children, a son and a daughter, Beverly was a computer trainer. Later on, and for most of their marriage, she had been a stay-at-home mother. Once her children were older, she reentered the paid workforce. Beverly had held numerous jobs, including employment at an afterschool program for kids and then at a fitness center; over the last ten years she had happily worked at a hospital as a secretary.

Beverly's husband had a more erratic career as a computer technician. She noted that after witnessing the attacks of September 11 on television, her husband never fully recovered emotionally, stating that "after that [tragedy] his work started failing where he wasn't getting very good reviews and he basically wasn't working. He would, you know, sleep all day and get up at night." When they decided to part ways, they were in very different bargaining positions. He had amassed a significant retirement portfolio from his previous jobs, while she had very little due to time spent at home and the low-paying nature of her positions. With the assistance of attorneys, however, they divided most of their assets evenly: the cars, his retirement portfolio, and other belongings. Beverly ended up buying him out of his share of the house as well and, in doing so, secured a significant asset.

> We had our divorce finalized during the time that the housing market wasn't that great . . . We [could have kept] the house pretty much the way it was until at some point we would sell the house and divide it at that point. But I did not want to do that with him. I wanted to close that book now . . . And so I kind of pressured him, I think, to not do that option. And I think he needed the money then, [with his] not having a job. So it wasn't like I had to work real hard to pressure him to make that change, to make that agreement. But I think he is aware that I have sold the house. He is [also] aware that . . . my son and I have bought a house together . . . It's a house that is a multifamily home so he has his living space and I have my living space. My ex-husband is aware of that and . . . that it's in a better area . . . I'm sure he must get the idea that I made a significant amount of money on that house sale and that he may regret that decision back then.

After the divorce and the sale of the house, Beverly was able to start putting money away for her own retirement into both IRAs and a 403(b) from her job. In addition, she eventually took advantage of a voluntary retirement incentive program whereby she could retire and then be paid full salary for six more months. Overall, she thought she was in a good position financially, but she also expressed how she had to change her spending habits in the process of mapping out her financial future. She stated that she simply was not "spending as much as I used to when I was working." And even though she planned on receiving social security soon, this additional income would not give her complete peace of mind. Instead, she had to rely on lifestyle simplification strategies to help sustain her going forward. On this point, she noted that by the time she would start to receive social security, "I won't have huge amounts of money, but I am a minimalist, I think, and so I will be quite happy." She also reported that she had traditional health care insurance through the PPACA, but could not afford a long-term health care insurance policy right now. She concluded her assessment of her finances by stating that with strict monetary discipline, she would have a solid economic future with about $50,000 in income per year.

Janet echoed Beverly's view that she was going to be financially secure after her divorce, but only if she behaved in conservative ways when it came to spending. As described in an earlier chapter, Janet decided to get divorced from her husband when she found out that he was having an affair. Financially, she had always outearned her husband of 13 years. He worked in the field of HVAC and taught HVAC classes for a living as well, but his true passion was his music. Meanwhile, she had held multiple, well-paying jobs. At first she taught elementary school, but later became a registered nurse. After this occupational transition, she worked in a maternity center and then in the field of hospital quality assurance. Later she moved on to employment at various pharmaceutical companies doing research as well as conducting audits related to clinical trials.

Overall, Janet's divorce was extremely stressful. She went through three attorneys before finding the best representation for her. Making matters worse, her husband hired an aggressive lawyer who immediately started filing paperwork related to securing alimony for him. At first, the emotional weight of the divorce crushed Janet. She sadly recalled, "I would shake and just fall apart. It was really bad; it was [bad] every day." Her doctor prescribed medication to help her deal with the stress of the divorce, which was then compounded by the unforeseen death of her sister. The former couple finally came up with a settlement whereby she would keep her main home, and they would divide the value of their second, beach home. He would also receive a percentage of her retirement benefits from her IRA and 401(k) account. She ended up giving him a total of $200,000 as his final, lump-sum settlement for all of these assets. Unsurprisingly, according to Janet, her husband immediately spent all of the money, exactly the opposite type of behavior Janet valued at this point in her life.

I [am financially secure because at first I] continued working and put a lot away. I'm very thrifty and the house [at the beach], you know, if I ever had to sell [it, would be worth a lot] ... And I'm selling the other house [that] I owned before we got married ... So he gave up all of that. He gave up all [of] his rights to anything else. So I have saved and I have invested and I'm doing okay ... [In addition], I have social security and two small [retirement funds], but I [also] bought an annuity that I will start taking in January.

Like Beverly, Janet was very secure in terms of her retirement, even as she was making only $35,000 per year after her divorce. She reached her goals, as Beverly did, by being as thrifty as possible in her day-to-day life. She had traditional health care and was also one of the few individuals who reported purchasing long-term health care insurance to take care of her future medical expenses; her field of employment had given her an opportunity to buy such a policy at an extremely reasonable rate, and therefore her case was largely exceptional given her means.

Finally, and unlike men in this study, there were women experiencing a gray divorce who reported being financially secure but only within the safety net of their families' financial assistance. This was also a reactive strategy in that it did not involve active engagement with financial planning, but rather passivity in terms of having the good fortune of being able to access family-based resources. Catherine, who like her husband was 66 years old, had been married for 41 years. She was one of very few people in this study who did not know why she got divorced beyond her husband suddenly telling her he wanted out of the marriage. She worked in research administration at the university level, while her husband was a professor and then was employed in the field of educational management. She reported that she was "furious" at the time that her husband told her the marriage was over. She went into automatic pilot mode upon his sudden announcement and simply started tagging the objects in the house that she wanted after they split up.

As they moved toward a divorce, both Catherine and her husband hired attorneys. According to Catherine, alimony was not an issue since they made approximately the same income. They each kept a car, various personal assets, and half of their savings account. Catherine was not interested in retaining the house, so she asked for half of its value instead. She also reported having a 401(k) that would be a good source of income going forward. She added that her financial security also came from another source: her family.

> I am [fine], you know, but I have family money . . . I have family money so I don't need to worry about it . . . I mean, I try to take care of myself and not rely on that but it's there . . . [The money is from] several different sources [and is] . . . certainly more than enough.

While she did not elaborate, Catherine remarked that her husband had less financial security than she did. Still earning $150,000 per year in her job, Catherine also had both health insurance and a rare long-term health care insurance policy. She did not describe how she was able to purchase this policy; her family's resources may have played a role. Overall, though, it was clear that she had multiple mechanisms in place to protect her financial future.

Wives Speak Out: Need to Work to Secure Their Financial Future

Both men and women in this study most commonly anticipated futures that held significant financial security. This is not surprising, as the sample overall was a relatively advantaged group. However, while most men planned their stability around proactive strategies that could maximize their lifestyles, most women relied on more reactive strategies that achieved security by reducing spending and relying on family money. In addition, however, and unlike any of the men, there was a second set of women who described futures where they would not be financially secure at all. These women all argued that only by maintaining a foot in the paid labor market without any possibility for retirement would they be able to sustain themselves over the long run.

Janice, 61 years old, was a director of a nonprofit organization when she divorced her husband, who was also 61 years old and a highly paid IT consultant. They had been married for 36 years. She described her marriage as ending because the couple grew apart in their interests. This happened for three primary reasons. First, she was very active and social, while over time he became more of an introvert. Second, she continued to pursue her education while married, eventually obtaining three degrees, but never felt supported by him in what she viewed as important self-development. Third, she suspected that he was having an affair.

Initially, they went to mediation to reach a fair divorce settlement, but she soon found out through his employer that he was not being forthcoming about his total compensation package. After receiving this information, she told him that she would only consider mediation again when he was honest about his complete earnings and benefit package. Since they could not agree to mediate any further at that point, they remained separated for 12 years before she finally decided to file for a formal divorce. During this time, they came up with an arrangement for him to see his two daughters consistently, as well as a financial agreement in which he provided her with money on a regular basis to pay household bills.

Janice did have somewhat of an erratic work pattern, but that was partially due to her desire—with her husband's blessing—to stay at home with their two girls when they were young. Right before she had her children, she worked for retail store developers. Then she took about seven years off to raise her children. Once the girls were in school, she returned to work in a variety of jobs before obtaining her present position in a nonprofit organization. All of these changes, she said, "hurt me financially and professionally." Meanwhile, her husband remained steadily employed in the same field for years, enabling him to move up the corporate ladder at a rapid rate. Once they decided to officially divorce, they had many assets to divide. This included a marital home in both of their names, four cars (three of which were in his name), a boat, and other possessions that he sold prior to the divorce. Her attorney advised her to put the marital home in her name only, and then sell it immediately. This would enable her to buy a smaller, more affordable townhome.

Despite this action, Janice remained unstable financially. Most distressing to her was the division of income streams that had to be determined at the time of the divorce. It was her strong belief that the "partner who gives up a career path or interrupts [his or her] career path is the one [who] gets the short end of the stick in all of this stuff." The first piece of devastating news that she received was when her attorney told her that she would not be able to obtain any alimony from her husband because she had proven herself to be capable of supporting herself during their

12-year separation. The second piece of bad news that she received related to how she had to fight to get her share of the couple's retirement savings.

> That was the hard thing. Because when we were working, his company matched [his retirement] contributions. So . . . I fully trusted this man from the time we started dating until we were separated. I trusted him. I took money from my work . . . and put it into his IRA because his company matched it. So I had a very small IRA under $10,000 which was already in my name before we got married . . . I had to give him half of that during the divorce process. And he fought in the court system, [saying] that he refused to give me half of . . . his IRA . . . When we first started the proceedings, he was willing to give me 20% or 22% . . . And my attorney laughed and said, "No. Come back with a better offer." And then we ended up having to get the judge involved and then two attorneys and the judge kind of negotiated back and forth. And ultimately I ended up at 47%.

Yet, due to the significant assets that he sold prior to the divorce and his relatively strong earning potential, Janice's husband was going to be in a much better position monetarily than she was going forward. Although she had health insurance in her job, she stated that she could not afford to buy long-term health care insurance and was concerned about the effects of her financial situation on her girls.

> I have thought about [needing a nursing home] and it's frightening to me . . . Very seldom in my life have I had this panic attack about the future. That makes me panic because I don't have the money now to get insurance . . . for nursing home care . . . I'm so afraid. I am afraid that my daughters will feel [that] they have to assume some responsibility and because I had children later in life, they're early in their . . . career paths. I don't want them to take a break in what they are doing in their lives to worry about me.

Janet sadly summarized her situation by stating that she would "have to work until the day I die."

In addition to the economic consequences of moving into and out of the labor market due to child care responsibilities, another type of problem experienced by women involves their overrepresentation in jobs with low wages. This can also force women into working far into their supposed retirement years. Connie, 61 years old, was married to her husband, 65 years old, for nine years. Although she did not have any children from this last, third marriage, she did have six children from her previous relationships. In fact, her youngest daughter was still in elementary school when Connie married this last time. When this daughter became a teenager, she told her mother that her latest husband—the child's stepfather—had sexually molested her. Connie was shocked, disgusted, and outraged. The couple immediately separated as the police and child protective services became involved.

For a long time, Connie was a Head Start preschool teacher, which paid her a modest salary. When Head Start started experiencing declining enrollments, she lost her job. She attended a retraining program in her state to become a licensed, certified nursing assistant. During her training, she had to put in significant time at a nursing home, which required a high level of physical exertion. At her age, this was very difficult. Fortunately, once she obtained her degree, she secured a nighttime, private-duty nursing job that was much less strenuous in nature. This work was steady, but still very low paying. Her last husband had also held a series of jobs in his lifetime. He worked for a while as a computer programmer and then as an automobile buyer. According to Connie, he lost many jobs in these fields over time as companies laid off workers. When he finally decided to retire from full-time employment, he secured a part-time position at the United States Postal Service for some extra income.

When she filed for divorce, they both shared the same attorney to save money. The issue of alimony did not come up at all because Connie wanted to completely sever ties with him as soon as possible due to the child molestation charges. There was not much property to divide between them either.

Oh, this is so sad. Actually we had lost his home that he owned coming into the marriage; that's where we lived at first. We lost that to foreclosure because of his job issues. I still owned my family farm where I'm living right now, so that belonged to me . . . When the divorce occurred, he had no property, he had no vehicle, [and] I had two vehicles in my name. I let him use one for a couple of months until he did get another vehicle. So basically we just divided up things . . . and he had his brother come with the U-Haul. We packed his stuff up and shipped him out.

Connie was very fearful as she pondered her economic future. During her tenure as a Head Start teacher, she had saved some money, but in the wake of her divorce, she had quickly spent it all.

> I had an investment fund and at the time that I lost my teaching job, I had cashed that in and paid off the mortgage of the home that I am living in now. And I had no other [savings]. I [also] didn't have any health care for a couple of years either by the way . . . I just now qualified for Medicaid . . . [I am very worried] because I'll be 62 in July . . . If I take my retirement this summer at 62, I get a whopping $695 a month [in social security], which means that I will have to continue to work until I can't, obviously.

While she was a teacher in Head Start, she never made more than $24,000 per year. Because she also took time out of the paid labor market to raise her children, her social security benefits were also going to be extremely small, as she noted. In her new job as a nurse, she made even less money. In fact, Connie now reported earning $22,000 per year, earnings so low that they entitled her to Medicaid benefits. With this as her current economic reality, long-term health care insurance was simply off the table. Most importantly, as she summarized her future, Connie could not foresee a time when she would be able to retire.

Taking time off to raise children and working low-paying jobs were clearly important factors that shaped the bleak economic futures of many women going through a gray divorce. As a result of these circumstances, they reported the need to work well into their retirement years. Another set of women, however, faced a different challenge that necessitated that they continue to work into their old age. This involved trusting their husbands to handle their finances and then having their husbands abuse that trust. For example, Carolyn and her husband had two children and were married for 30 years; she was 66 years old and he was 65. She stated that she was not quite sure why he wanted to get a divorce, but at the end of their three decades together he declared that he wanted to be "free" and "single" once again.

Before getting married, Carolyn was an executive assistant. She then gave birth to her children and wanted to be accessible to them when they were not in school. With this goal in mind, she became a teaching assistant for special education students. Her husband worked in construction for a period of time after serving in Vietnam. He ultimately received disability after a work accident, as well as from a diagnosis of posttraumatic stress disorder from his time in the military. The disability was retroactively applied once he qualified, and at one point he received a lump-sum check for $103,000 for past months of eligible benefits. Carolyn thought that they were going to use the money to do some home renovations and also to buy two new vehicles. Shortly after they bought the cars, however, her husband filed for divorce, and she discovered something very troubling about the $103,000.

> I don't know what I expected in [our savings account] after the vehicles [were purchased]. Maybe like $50,000 or something? . . . [But] he apparently took that money out of there with the idea of getting a divorce . . . He didn't spend it down. He just took it out of there, [with] checks made out to him to cash [for] $5,000 at a time . . . But that's how he took that money out of there . . . Checks [were] made out to himself at $5,000 at a time and out of $103,000, there was $1,300 left.

Carolyn was shocked, then, not only by her husband's desire for a divorce, but also about the missing money. They each hired an attorney in order to proceed to a final settlement.

Carolyn requested alimony immediately and her husband initially refused. However, she was steadfast in this demand because she was earning so little as a teaching assistant. Ultimately, he agreed to pay her $1,500 per month for five years. She left her teaching job and took on two new jobs in a nursing home that, when combined, earned her more money. She worked in the medical records department as well as in the reception area of the nursing home. She also tutored in a private educational setting, and served as a hostess in a local sports arena so that she could pay all of her bills.

In the divorce settlement, she received one car with an outstanding loan, and he kept the other car. Using her small IRA that she developed from her modest jobs, Carolyn could buy him out of the house. She wanted to keep it because she felt that her children had a strong attachment to it. After cashing out the IRA, however, she reported "worrying about money all the time." She made ends meet through her four jobs, small pension from teaching, and social security benefits. With her grandson working and living with her now, she reported having a total household income of $35,000 per year. Ironically, even though she worked in a nursing home and had traditional health care insurance, she said that she could not even imagine having long-term health care insurance; it was frankly well beyond her reach. She was also resigned to the fact that retirement was simply not going to be in her near future.

.   .   .   .   .

A gray divorce signals the end of an important, romantic relationship between two mature adults. Emotions can be very raw, because two lives that have been highly intertwined are now set on new paths to move in separate directions. Undoubtedly, untangling the finances between these two parties unleashes additional stress upon them. But this pain is not evenly distributed. Women pay a much higher *economic* gray divorce penalty than men for the variety of reasons outlined earlier. They suffer disproportionately in the area of receiving their fair share of marital assets and debts, securing stable income streams, and protecting their health and well-being. Yet a divorce involves much more than the often-heated division of money. A marital breakdown in mid-life also has an impact on the nature, composition, and depth of each partner's social relationships. And it is in this arena, as we shall see next, that men are much more likely to pay a higher *social* gray divorce penalty than women.

4 People Who Need People

THE SOCIAL GRAY DIVORCE PENALTY

Oh, there's a time of the year [that is very hard]—my birthday is relatively close to Father's Day and our anniversary was right around there. Then there's Fourth of July and I usually find myself alone . . . That's crushing every year. And so that's really difficult for me. And then I guess the other thing is that now when I go back to Phoenix [where I used to live with my family], I just don't feel like that is home anymore. And I feel somewhat uncomfortable around my friends . . . I don't have . . . a real place to hang out with the kids and [my ex-wife's] not going to participate in helping me with that in any sort of meaningful way. So, I don't know. I guess those are the things about just being alone a lot. The holidays are difficult and not feeling as, you know, connected in a place that I lived for 30 years.

—Frank, 56 years old, married for 22 years

Let's see, now my daughter was married, [and] she had two kids [at the time of the divorce] . . . And I do remember that [with my] two kids—I don't know who called who— probably my daughter called my son [to tell him about the divorce]. He was away at college . . . They just talked all night. Now exactly what they talked about, I don't know. Obviously [they talked about] our situation but I don't know specifically what they said. Neither one ever really mentioned it, but they were angry at their father and they 100% stood behind me because he basically ruined me financially. So both kids were behind me, as was my family and his family as well.

—Carolyn, 66 years old, married for 30 years

.   .   .   .   .

As we have seen, at age 50 or older, women splitting up from their husbands are more likely than men to pay a higher *economic* gray divorce penalty. However, women are not the only ones who suffer from the consequences of gray divorce. A gray divorce not only splits couples' material assets, but also can shatter their interpersonal networks of support. In this area, men are more likely than women to pay a higher *social* gray divorce penalty.

The difference in gray divorce's social cost for men and women can be easily seen when we compare the cases of Frank and Carolyn. Frank described the end of his marriage as one of a gradual decrease in mutual interests. The couple also experienced significant financial stress as his wife, in his view, constantly spent too much money on things that they could not afford. After they divorced, Frank's parents continued to be a strong source of support for him, but he lost many of his friends to his former wife. Frank also had to contend with changing relationships involving his two sons, who were teenagers at the time of the divorce. While they were both saddened by their parents' breakup, the younger one became closer to his father over time. The older son, however, remained "kind of quiet around people and . . . not as close [to me]." Frank observed that this older son seemed lost as he was "trying to figure out life at this point." In a number of different ways, then, the divorce was a shock to Frank's social system—a shock that he was still adjusting to several years after it became final.

In contrast, Carolyn had a much stronger network of support in place after her divorce. As described in an earlier chapter, after 30 years of marriage and two children, Carolyn's husband announced that he wanted to be free and single once again. He ended up stealing thousands of dollars from a joint bank account before the divorce was finalized, prompting Carolyn to work four different jobs to support herself. In response to their father's actions, Carolyn's adult children rallied to her side. And although Carolyn's mother was suffering from Alzheimer's disease at the time, she still recognized the significance of the divorce, and cried out of love for Carolyn when she told her what was happening.

For his part, Carolyn's father said that he felt "guilty" that he did not protect his daughter from the evils inflicted on her by her former husband, and promised to do everything in his power to help. Carolyn also reported strong relationships with her former husband's family, in particular his niece and his brother. They continued to include her in social events and actually saw her more frequently than when she was married. In Carolyn's view, even his own relatives recognized that her former husband had acted dishonorably, and they wanted to sustain their relationship with her over the long run, even after the divorce.

Frank's feelings of being cut off from the most important relationships in his life are emblematic of many men's journeys through the most diffi-cult parts of their gray divorces. And while women like Carolyn have social challenges as well, women tend to have deeper networks of support to carry them through these life transitions. In this chapter, we will examine the way postdivorce relationships tend to work differently for men and women.

RELATIONSHIPS WITH FRIENDS AND ADULT FAMILY MEMBERS

Fundamental to the emotional health of all individuals are the relation-ships that they establish with friends and adult family members over their lives. Women and men tend to differ in the types of close relationships that they have as they progress through their mid-life years.[1] During this period of time, older women often find themselves undergoing a variety of physical and relational changes such as menopause, the departure of their children from their homes, and the aging and ultimate death of their par-ents. In response to these changes, women tend to lean heavily on others, including friends and adult family members, to help relieve their emotional burdens. While electronic media such as email and Internet chatrooms can provide women with some of the support that they need, they also tend to have at their disposal strong, close, and, most importantly, real-life social networks of mostly other women to help sustain themselves and carry them forward.[2]

Older men likewise face physical changes at this point in their lives, as well as the loss of their children as dependents and the declining health of their parents. However, there is an important distinction between the sexes. Mid-life men tend to have significantly smaller social networks of both friends and adult family members than women.[3] In addition, the nature of these relationships tends to be different than those held by women. On this point, society places significant pressure on men—particularly younger men—to have relationships that are based on commonly shared activities, rather than emotional intimacy.[4] For example, younger men tend to interact with other men largely as members of the same clubs, social groups, or athletic teams. Men in these cases identify with one another due to a commonly shared enterprise rather than mutual and vested interdependence.[5] This is not to say that men cannot have deep friendships that are similar to those held by women. In fact, as men age, many can and do have voluntary relationships with other men as friends or adult family members that involve multifaceted commitments and strong interpersonal ties. Indeed, sharing, caring, and trust can be the hallmarks of all of these relationships.[6] However, generally speaking, many male relationships tend to lack the emotional grounding that is fundamental to the foundation of most female social networks.

When couples across the age spectrum marry, their networks of relationships often change.[7] While single, each part of the couple maintains his/her own friends. However, after marriage, relationships with other couples come to be important as well. These joint relationships with other couples serve many purposes, such as bouncing things off each other as mutual sounding boards, sharing activity-based partnerships, and enlisting each other as emotional helpers. Couple friendships with other couples can promote a stable social structure around which newly married couples can grow as a team. Indeed, research suggests that this couple-based interdependence directly relates to many different measures of marital quality, such as overall happiness, high levels of intimacy, and healthy communication skills like effective problem solving.[8]

When men and women divorce, however, their relationships with both individuals and other couples change as well.[9] With respect to relationships with individual friends and adult family members, divorce can prompt a significant reevaluation of who is part of one's inner circle and who is out. This is in part due to the varying levels of support desired or received by each half of the couple as they move through this difficult transition.[10] As we've seen, men in general have fewer friends and adult family member allies than women after a divorce.[11] Older men in particular often have fewer strong friends than women before the divorce and the marital breakdown simply leaves them further isolated. Further, older women often encourage their husbands to pursue individually based friendships and contacts with adult family members during the marriage, but once the marriage ends, men no longer have this external prompt to be socially outgoing. Aging men also may rely on their wives as a primary source of emotional sustenance and interpersonal motivation, and become somewhat lost when their marriage ends.[12] Conversely, women overall and those in mid-life in particular frequently acquire larger numbers of friends as a result of a tumultuous divorce transition as they proactively seek out broader forms of social support.[13] Moreover, women often have stronger links with adult family members than men after a divorce. This is because women tend to be the ones who do the "kinkeeper" work during the marriage, and these systems of family support are thus already strongly in place for them when they are looking for assistance.[14]

It is also important to note that previously married couples across a wide age spectrum have a much more difficult time maintaining friendships with intact couples after they divorce.[15] Why might this be the case? One possibility is that they may have only engaged in "paired couple" activities while they were all married, such that when one couple breaks up, the friendships no longer make sense. The intact couple might also completely disengage from the friendship for fear of alienating each individual within the divorcing couple. Intact couples might also disagree with the behavior of one or both parties to the divorce, and therefore want to aggressively cut ties altogether. Yet all might not be lost. To the extent that relationships with an intact couple are maintained, a divorced man often is able to remain friends with the male part of the couple while a divorced woman might be more likely to remain friends with the female half of the couple.[16] However, even within this pattern, sustaining these types of linkages can be very stressful for all involved parties, primarily due to perceptions and misperceptions about true loyalties over the long run.

RELATIONSHIPS WITH CHILDREN

In addition to changing relationships with friends and adult family members, men and women experiencing gray divorce also have to manage their interactions with their children, if they have any.[17] Due to their own age, the majority of men and women going through a gray divorce have adult rather than minor children. This fact, however, does not lessen the amount of stress that both parents face when they move toward a breakup. And while no parent looks forward to losing ties with his/her offspring, the potential for harm is again not equally distributed between men and women. More specifically, just as in the case of relationships with friends and adult family members, older men pay a higher social divorce penalty with respect to maintaining healthy bonds with their children than women.

To understand these dynamics, we must first acknowledge that the mostly young adults who are the children of parents experiencing a gray divorce are going through specific transitions in their own lives that are very different from the circumstances facing minor children.[18] For one thing, these children still may be relying on their parents for help with paying for college tuition, or they may be just starting out in the workforce by taking entry-level, low-paying jobs. In either case, they may be somewhat dependent on their parents for monetary assistance, even as they are moving in the direction of economic independence. Secondly, these relatively young, adult children are maturing out of the more self-oriented stages of adolescence toward responsible adulthood when they should be able to more holistically respond to the needs of others, including their parents. And then also, at this point in their children's development, parents begin communicating with them as the adults whom they are becoming. This means more free-flowing, bidirectional conversations that no longer have to be filtered for age-appropriate ears. Overall, then, these mostly adult children of parents experiencing a gray divorce are likely to react in very different ways than younger children whose parents are breaking up.

For many adult children, their parents' decision to divorce is not surprising. They may have witnessed problems in their parents' marriages for years, and may even be relieved that their mothers and fathers are finally doing something positive in their lives by splitting.[19] Yet, for other adult children of a gray divorce, hearing about their parents' intention to break up can be devastating.[20] They may feel "in the middle" of their parents' decision to part ways, especially when they are asked to mediate over the inevitable disputes to follow.[21] They also may have to hear stories about their parents' flawed thoughts, actions, and belief systems that are difficult to process. Their parents' divorce, then, may place these adult children in new and potentially uncomfortable familial roles as their fathers' and mothers' lives are being reconstituted.[22]

From the perspective of the parents, on the other hand, gray divorce brings a different set of concerns, worries that affect fathers and mothers in distinct ways. In considering a gray divorce, men are more likely than women to fear complete abandonment by their adult children.[23] Indeed, these fears are not unfounded.[24] Parents rightly perceive that adult children can have a wide array of reactions to a gray divorce, many of which can be negative.[25] For numerous reasons, however, adult children tend to direct their negative responses much more at fathers than at mothers. The first explanation for this gender difference is that even though they have increased their participation in the paid labor market over time, women still do the majority of carework with respect to raising their children.[26] This can lead children to develop strong maternal alliances, even as they get older. A second possible explanation for their inclination toward greater maternal sympathy is that socialization processes enable more women than men to freely express to their children their emotions about a disturbing event like a divorce. This communication then serves to generate stronger bonds between them and their adult children.

Men's weakened relationships with their adult children after a gray divorce play out in a variety of interactional arenas. For example, divorced fathers have less weekly contact with their adult children as compared with stably married men; in addition, adult children are less likely to coreside with their divorced fathers than with stably married men.[27] If these fathers remarry, adult-child relationships can be even worse if fathers "swap" their old families for their new families, although this effect is likely to be weakened when the youngest child in the first family is already at least age 18 at the time of the divorce.[28] In addition, father-daughter relationships might be particularly subject to strain after a gray divorce.[29] Indeed, research has demonstrated that both the quality and quantity of contact in father-daughter relationships are more adversely affected after a divorce than any of the other relationships involved.[30] This may be because daughters are more likely to identify with their mothers at this stage in their lives.

The consequences of losing their adult children for older divorcing men not only serve to harm them emotionally, but also can wreak havoc with their material well-being in their older years. Typically as parents age, they switch care-related roles with their children. That is, they used to take care of their children's needs when they were babies, but in later life their adult children will begin to take care of them. If fathers' relationships with their adult children have suffered as a result of their gray divorce, they will be less likely to receive this type of personal and material assistance.[31] Indeed, research suggests that support supplied from adult children in the form of household assistance, practical advice, and emotional aid diminishes dramatically for fathers in comparison to mothers after a gray divorce.

The number of face-to-face and phone contacts disproportionately decreases for fathers as compared with mothers as well.[32] This can be especially devastating if these aging fathers have mental and physical limitations and have not remarried with new spouses upon whom to rely for help.[33] In this vacuum of assistance, fathers experiencing a gray divorce may have no other choice than to turn to more institutional forms of care in their later years. This type of care, especially high-quality care, is of course more expensive and resource-intensive than family care, and thus is out of the reach of many men.

So how did the men and women in this study experience social support changes after their gray divorces? First we consider relationships with friends and adult family members, and then we turn to their interactions with their mostly adult children.

SOCIAL SUPPORT: RELATIONSHIPS WITH FRIENDS AND ADULT FAMILY MEMBERS AFTER A GRAY DIVORCE

Without a doubt, social support during and after a gray divorce is extremely important to the health and well-being of those going through this transition. Of course, the first key source of support can come from friends and adult family members, both of whom can offer emotional and practical assistance. As discussed earlier, however, research suggests that men might have fewer and weaker forms of these types of social support than women. The causes of these gender differences are complex, but most likely relate to male patterns of relationships that emerge due to a variety of cultural and socialization practices.

In the research conducted here, gender differences also emerged, with men experiencing significant disadvantages in the nature of the social supports that they received in comparison with women. With respect to relationships with friends and adult family members, men most commonly reported that they lost these connections to their ex-wives (see table 8). The second most common outcome for men was that friends and adult family members were divided between them and their ex-wives. The third group of men reported no significant losses as everyone that they knew remained relatively neutral, and only the smallest group of men stated that friends and adult family members sided with them.

Women, on the other hand, most commonly declared that their friends and adult family members sided with them over their ex-husbands in their gray divorces; this was the sharpest difference with the men. However, a smaller set of women did experience losses; the next most frequent response for women was that friends and adult family members sided with their ex-partners. This response was tied with women not losing any friends or adult family members in the wake of their divorces because most of their networks did not feel compelled to choose sides.

Table 8   Relationships with Friends and Adult Family Members after a Gray Divorce

	40 Men	40 Women
Friends and Adult Family Members' Reactions (Ranked by Order of Mention)	1. Friends and Adult Family Members Sided with Their Ex-Wives 2. Friends and Adult Family Members Were Divided 3. Friends and Adult Family Members Remained Neutral 4. Friends and Adult Family Members Sided with Me	1. Friends and Adult Family Members Sided with Me 2. Friends and Adult Family Members Sided with Their Ex-Husbands (Tie with #3) 3. Friends and Adult Family Members Remained Neutral (Tie with #2) 4. Friends and Adult Family Members Were Divided

Finally, the smallest set of women reported that they split friends and adult family members with their ex-husbands.

Husbands Speak Out: Friends and Adult Family Members Sided with Their Ex-Wives

Many men reported losing friends and adult family members to their ex-wives at the time of their gray divorces. In fact, this was the most prevalent response when men were asked whether or not friends or adult family members took sides during the divorce. For example, Gary was 50 years old, the same age as his ex-wife. They had been married for 29 years when she served him with divorce papers. While he was shocked by this action, he also acknowledged that there were problems in the marriage. He reported feeling verbally and emotionally abused by her during their many years together. What was as disturbing to him as the abuse, however, was his loss of social connections as a result of the divorce. Prior to the divorce, he had been really close to his wife's family, especially his two brothers-in-law and father-in-law. He was also very involved with his church and had many friends there.

After the divorce, however, he felt as if he were a social pariah within his own community. These feelings were strongest when his ex-wife's father died. Gary went to the church for the funeral services of the man whom he had loved for decades. And yet, none of his ex-wife's family, including his ex-brothers-in-law, acknowledged his presence. He said that his ex-wife "never looked at me the entire time." He also felt abandoned by his church friends, people he had known for decades.

> [On that occasion] I got treated about the same way at the church [by its members]. I mean, there was not one single person [who] came up and shook my hand . . . And it's like, how can you go to a church for 30 years and then get treated like that? . . . Not one person . . . not one person even comes up and even asks you your side of the story—not one person.

Gary viewed the loss of his friends at church as a problem that was modeled by the religious leadership there. He stated that the last time he went to services, not one pastor approached him and inquired about his well-being. He hoped that one day, people would understand what happened and what caused his divorce, but for now, he "just walked out the door and never went back."

While Gary lost adult family members and church-based friends with whom he had been very close, Anthony found himself in the position of parting with his best friend as well as his neighborhood friends as a result of his divorce. Anthony was 62 years old and his ex-wife was 63. They had been married for 38 years. Anthony had worked in the computer field, but often struggled with retaining jobs due to the changing economic climate as well as his own struggles with Attention Deficit Hyperactive Disorder (ADHD). His wife was a teacher, and they had two children with health issues; his son had multiple sclerosis and his daughter had several severe psychiatric problems. The combination of frequent job loss with ill children put a significant strain on his marriage. In addition, he and his wife had very different communication styles; he was much more likely to be vocal about contentious issues that emerged in the family, while she was much more restrained.

Anthony had one particular close friend whom he had met in high school. While the two sometimes squabbled, Anthony reported seeing him on a regular basis. This was significant in that although they lived in separate states, they still made time to get together. However, once he learned of Anthony's impending divorce, his best friend did something surprising.

> At the time that we started splitting up, [my best friend] asked me for contact information to get a hold of [my soon-to-be ex-wife] without me. This kind of drove a little bit of a wedge in there because, you know, [I thought], "Hey, you're supposed to be my friend." . . . I don't know if he's talked to her. But we had a little disagreement about it . . . It kind of got ugly . . . So I haven't really seen or heard from him for almost a year now.

In addition to losing his best friend to his wife, since he moved away from the marital home, he lost contact with his close neighbors as well, and had difficulty making new friends. In summing up the demise of these social networks, Anthony sadly remarked that he had "been teaching myself how to live by myself a lot since this whole thing went down."

Husbands Speak Out: Friends and Adult Family Members Were Divided

Not all men experiencing a gray divorce lost friends and adult family members to their ex-wives—and yet, that does not mean that their social networks sided entirely with them. Instead, the most optimistic of these men described their ability to split at least some of these relationships with their former spouses. In this way, their gray divorces did not mean that they were completely alone.

Many men had complicated stories of friends and adult family members being divided as a result of their divorces. As described in a previous chapter, Larry was a 57-year-old man who had discovered that his wife, 51, was cheating on him when he found her communications with another man on her laptop computer. At first he was in complete shock at this news. Then things quickly got worse when he experienced his first significant social loss; this involved a couple with whom they had both spent considerable time. After he found out about his wife's affair, Larry immediately went to the male partner in this couple with his grief.

He was actually my first call, I think, [even] before my brother, [or] anyone [else]. I said, "I just found out." . . . I was hoping that he would help, you know, keep us together as a couple because I thought they liked us as a couple . . . We were their best friends. And I said, "But I need to speak to a lawyer." He said, "Absolutely. My medical school classmate—his wife has been a divorce lawyer up here [for] twenty-five years. I've referred other people to her. You'll love her. But I hope this all works out."

In the beginning, both halves of this couple remained friendly with him. However, as soon as they realized that he and his wife were not getting back together, Larry reported, they dropped him completely from their network of friends. They would not even greet him at the temple where they were all members.

Larry initially said that he had somewhat gotten "over it" in terms of his experience of abandonment by this couple, but upon deeper reflection he admitted that their abandonment still upset him. He remarked that he saw relationships with other couples wither in light of his divorce. However, not all of his social networks were lost. In his own town, there was a group of five coupled friends of which he and his wife were a part. The men got together about once every other month as part of a "guys' night out." After the divorce, two men dropped him as a friend, but the other two remained his friend. Larry was particularly happy with them, especially since their wives remained friends with his ex-wife. After all, he hoped that his divorce did not have to divide everyone into two opposing groups because, "in theory, there's no reason why you have to be mean to one [half of the couple]."

Another man who felt that he was able to at least split some friends and adult family members with his ex-wife was Terry, described in a previous chapter as a 59-year-old man who ultimately divorced his wife after 27 years of marriage. The couple had continuously fought because they had sharp differences regarding how money should be spent. While Terry had concrete goals to save money, his ex-wife valued her freedom to spend money in whatever way she chose. She was also much more permissive in teaching their two sons about the importance of budgets; according to Terry, she allowed them to spend whatever they wanted. Throughout their ups and downs, Terry indicated, he was responsible for bringing many of their friends—both individuals and couples—into their marital network. Terry also acknowledged that his ex-wife had a set of friends that were strictly her own.

In assessing what happened to these groups of friends after the divorce, Terry stated that he remained close to many of them. Indeed, the ones that he lost to his ex-wife, in his view, were not worth the effort anyway. He described one particular case where he and his wife had gone on numerous vacations with another couple over a long period of time. When he and his wife decided to get divorced, he went out to lunch with this couple to discuss the situation. During the lunch, he expressed shock and sadness because he never imagined that he would be getting a divorce. At that moment in time, he was in an extremely emotionally vulnerable state. It was therefore not surprising that after the lunch, he was both mortified and angry when he accidently received an email from the woman in the couple that was intended for his soon-to-be ex-wife. The email described the details of what Terry had said during the lunch, as well as his demeanor. The sender, however, quickly realized that she had made a severe mistake and sent Terry an email of apology. She stated that it was not her intention to "get in the middle of this." But to Terry, she had clearly picked sides in the divorce, and she was not on his side. This "disappointing" event made Terry more aware than ever before that only certain friendships—the ones involving those who unequivocally respected him—should continue after the divorce.

Lastly, it is important to note that sometimes men retained "functional" relationships with male adult family members, but not necessarily personal ones. For example, Ronald, 53 years old, had divorced his wife, 44 years old, after 15 years of marriage. The couple had grown apart after years of raising their two children together. Ronald worked in the construction field, and reported that after the divorce, he "still had all of her family . . . calling me to do all of their general contracting work. I'm still working for her brother. I'm still working for her uncle." The only exception in terms of retaining adult family relationships was with his mother-in-law, whom, he stated, "would make a point of . . . [not] calling [me]." In Ronald's case, then, work- and activity-based relationships could continue with other men, even on his ex-wife's side of the family, but emotionally based relationships with women, especially his ex-wife's mother, could not be sustained over the long run.

Husbands Speak Out: Friends and Adult Family Members Were Neutral

There was also a smaller set of men who experienced a gray divorce but did not report losing friends or adult family members in the process. Randy was 66 years old and had been married to his 66-year-old wife for 41 years. He was a woodwork artist while his wife was employed in the field of college administration, and they had two adult daughters. Randy stated that he felt pressured to get married at a young age to his wife, since he was very close to her father. However, they were incompatible in many ways, and these differences grew more apparent over the course of their marriage. Probably the most important difference was that he needed "a lot of time alone and without any connection, psychic or otherwise," to anyone else. In contrast, his wife was extremely gregarious and desired to constantly be around other people.

Once their children grew up, Randy decided that it was time to start living on his own terms, where he noted that he "found my creative expression just blossoming, so for me, [separating] was just a very wonderful thing to do." He filed for divorce. Possibly because there was no betrayal, cheating, or abuse, Randy did not experience any alienation from those around him. After an initial dispute with one of his ex-wife's siblings that was quickly resolved, he felt very positive about those who remained close to him as well as to his ex-wife.

> For the most part, I think her family was, you know, supportive as they could be under the circumstances. I think they were very kind to me. I think my family was a little bit less so. My family is more conservative [and] traditional. [They were] traditional religiously and I think they thought I was a little bit nutty. (laughing) They've all thought that . . . [The divorce] didn't affect our relationships really; I mean, we disagreed but I'm still on good terms with all [of] the parties.

The strength of these ties was especially notable given that, initially, Randy's wife opposed the divorce. She promised him that she would temper her need to socialize and give him more of the emotional and artistic freedom that he desired. However, after 41 years of marriage, Randy did not want to try any further, and ultimately she had to go along with his plan. In sum, what could have been an explosive divorce that destroyed social networks was a much more moderate experience. The couple parted sadly but relatively amicably, with each half moving forward in a positive direction.

*Husbands Speak Out: Friends and Adult Family
Members Sided with Me*

Finally, the least common response among men experiencing a gray divorce was that their friends and adult family members sided with them. In these cases, this was because their wives had engaged in such bad behavior that the women were clearly marked the "at-fault" party. William told a particularly devastating story of divorce pain. They were both in their late fifties, and he loved his wife dearly during their 38-year marriage. He was a factory worker and she was a schoolteacher. And then one day she developed a shoulder injury requiring that she visit a rehabilitation facility on a regular basis. While there, she met a gentleman 18 years her senior whom the rehab staff told to follow William's wife as she proceeded through her series of exercises, since he, too, had a shoulder injury. They became closer over time, to the point where William found out that they had synchronized their rehabilitation sessions in order to be together. They even started occupying a back room in the facility for periods of time in order "to be alone." Friends started to fill him in on the details of this affair, and William was crushed.

Since this man had been married four times and had a reputation around town, William seriously was worried about catching a sexually transmitted disease from his wife. He finally came out and accused her of the affair, and while she verbally denied it, her actions told a different story.

> She was actually starting to place things of his in the house that he had given her. I said that if she left them out, I was going to throw them away so she had better find someplace else to hide her gifts from him. She dressed differently, more sexual in nature. Then, let me think . . . about a year and a month after they had first originally met, she came home late one day. I knew she hadn't been at school because by then, I was checking to see where she was on a regular basis. She was a schoolteacher. So when she came home late, I said, "You weren't at school? Where were you?" She said, "I've been to see a divorce lawyer and I'm going to divorce you."

By this time, William was not surprised by the announcement. In fact, he remained very calm. He stated that he was mostly angry with the man with whom she was having an affair and not with her. This was because, first, her parents had divorced while she was growing up and, later on, without knowing exactly why, she had developed a serious case of obsessive compulsive disorder (OCD) and needed to be in a germ-free environment. Her OCD in many ways had constrained her development into becoming a happy and fully functional adult. With these serious challenges, he felt bad for her.

Due to these extenuating circumstances, William took a very measured response to her desire to divorce. She moved out but later returned home, and repeated this pattern during the months to follow as her desire to be with her boyfriend waxed and waned. In each case, William took her back, but he also required that she go to couples counseling with him. At one point, the counselor suggested that she needed intensive individual therapy before they could effectively work on their marriage. They agreed to separate while she received this therapy. Soon they signed a six-month lease for her very own apartment. As he was helping her assemble her new bed, she wondered out loud what she was going to do if William no longer wanted her and her boyfriend rejected her, too. At that point, William dejectedly set the bed frame down and told her to call him and ask him if he was still available. He was, and that very night, she jettisoned her plans to work any further on the marriage by returning to her boyfriend's house. Because of her in many ways cruel behavior, William stated that he lost no friends and no adult family members in the process of the divorce. In fact, he noted that "there are family members of hers who email me, talk to me on the phone, . . . and who visit with me who do not talk or deal with her unless they are at a family event like a wedding or something like that . . . They thought that I wasn't such a bad guy and that I shouldn't have been treated that way." Clearly, William went above and beyond the call of duty in trying to salvage his marriage, and he was rewarded with strong social networks of support in the divorce's aftermath.

Wives Speak Out: Friends and Adult Family Members Sided with Me

Unlike the men who experienced a gray divorce, the largest number of women who went through the same process clearly stated that most of their friends and adult family members sided with them. Deborah was 55 years old while her husband was 56 years old. They had been married for 30 years when he filed for divorce. She had an administrative job, while her husband worked more erratically as a truck driver and as a photographer. They had numerous financial problems due to the fact that her husband did not work steadily. Often when she would inquire about how they were going to pay the mortgage each month, he would respond that he was "moving out" because he could not stand her badgering. This situation put incredible stress on the marriage, and at one point, Deborah decided to help him leave by putting his belongings in his car. He grabbed her back, and the police intervened and arrested him.

Of course, this arrest led to the further deterioration of the marriage. When they finally made the decision to split, they had a meeting to hash out the details of the property division. According to Deborah, as they were sitting across the table from each other, he said, "I don't give a shit about you." At that point in time, his only close, nearby relationships were with his aunt and uncle. After they learned about his behavior, which also started to include his "showing off his body" on Craig's List, his aunt became more involved in the divorce process. She told him that she would not support his behavior, and that she would report all of his words and actions to Deborah. She also would not give him any money if he asked for it. However, the couple still needed money to pay for the divorce. It was telling in Deborah's mind that it ultimately was a distant relative of *his* that gave money to *her* to finance the divorce.

Margaret, introduced in an earlier chapter, also had friends and adult family members rally to her side rather than to that of her ex-husband. Recall that Margaret, 56 years old, had been married for 25 years to her husband, 55 years old. They both worked in the restaurant business together, but due in part to his alcoholism, he became a less-than-reliable financial and emotional partner. However, Margaret's ex-husband refused to acknowledge that he had a problem and receive the help that he needed. As they were going through the divorce process, Margaret noted that he continued to be in complete denial about his addiction. She reported that "He doesn't know why I divorced him; he still doesn't understand. In his heart of hearts, as he told me as he was driving out the driveway [recently], 'I love you and I'll remarry you some day.'"

Margaret knew that a remarriage was impossible, and she also recognized the depth of the support that surrounded her when she parted ways with him. She retained the strong infrastructure of social relationship networks while he lost them. Yet because he was in a state of denial, Margaret struggled to get him to accept this new reality.

> [My ex-husband] doesn't have many friends and he actually has commented to me in the last couple of months that he feels very sad that none of my friends have contacted him . . . I tried to explain . . . I mean, these are [my] high school friends; these are, like, 30- and 40-year-old friends and they got to know [my husband] through our marriage . . . They liked him in the beginning and then . . . they didn't like him at the end . . . They weren't going out of their way to call him and say, you know, "We're really sorry about the divorce." He thought it was really odd. And it's like, that doesn't happen . . . It's not a situation where it's like [you lose] an Emmy Award . . . and people call you and express their sadness. It doesn't happen. You know, they are my friends [and] they're going to side with me. That's how it happens.

While Deborah felt that friends and adult family members were on her side in the divorce justifiably, Margaret had many more mixed emotions. As described earlier, right before she made the decision to divorce, her sister's husband passed away and her sister moved in with Margaret and her husband. Margaret therefore had her best friend—her sister—to help her through this divorce transition. Because she had this kind of intense support and her husband did not, she experienced a lot of guilt. On one level, she wanted to be his caretaker because "he [was] a lost soul," and she therefore dragged her feet on the divorce. But ultimately she knew that she could not sustain the relationship and be responsible for upholding the social networks of support that he might need going forward on his own.

Wives Speak Out: Friends and Adult Family Members Sided with Their Ex-Husbands

This is not to say that everything went smoothly for women experiencing a gray divorce. The next group of women, like their male counterparts, described losing friends and adult family members to their ex-partners. Elizabeth was a 57-year-old woman with a 46-year-old ex-husband. They had been married for 17 years. Without a doubt, it was an extremely tumultuous union. Soon after they married, Elizabeth discovered that he was gay; he had been hiding his sexual orientation for years before the wedding under the guise that he wanted sex only to happen after their marriage had been blessed by God. By the time she found out the truth, Elizabeth was getting older and she still wanted children. She agreed to be artificially inseminated by him and they had twins. As part of this deal, they also agreed to live separate lives under one roof until the children had grown up, meaning that each was free to date during the marriage.

Elizabeth quickly realized, however, that this was not the life she wanted. Over time, her husband became verbally, emotionally, and physically abusive to the children, who were then under 10 years old. He would call them "stupid," and throw boxes or use his hand to hit them. When this maltreatment got worse, she decided to file for divorce. The problem for her was that her ex-husband was a narcissist who, according to Elizabeth, had put on a wonderful show of being the perfect husband and father to the outside world. One place where he attracted significant support was in his position as choir director at his church, a role that enabled him to form a ring of protectors around him, beginning with the parish priest. It was difficult for her to continue going to church there because her "husband [was] up in the choir loft saying, 'Lord help us and Lord save us,' and all of these beautiful sentiments. And he's a liar and an abuser."

Beyond this church network, some of her other friends left her support system because they sided with him. The loss of one female friend in particular was very troubling to her. This was a person who had been friendly to her and her husband for years. However, when Elizabeth made the allegations of abuse, this friend sided with him because her own parenting style was similar to his. Elizabeth noted that this friend had "bad parenting skills . . . her temper gets the best of her." While not constituting child abuse per se, her friend's angry outbursts, according to Elizabeth, were toxic to all minors around her. Her perspective on appropriate parenting styles therefore made her more empathetic with Elizabeth's husband and his position as a father in the marriage.

Perhaps worst of all, Elizabeth also lost a person whom she described as her best friend. In the past, this was an individual who would come to her house and spend significant time with her children. When she originally talked to this friend about her husband's behavior, he would listen intently.

However, he too had very strong beliefs about how children should be raised. At one point, Elizabeth told him that "I'm listening [to what you are saying about raising children]; I listen to everybody. But I accept only what I find useful." Because her friend was personally insulted that she would not agree with him completely and incorporate his parenting ideas during the divorce process, he formed an alliance with her ex-husband. Her ex-husband was more than willing to accept all of this friend's ideas. Elizabeth described a sense of complete abandonment when this supposed "best friend" started to spend all of his free time with her children, but only when they were with their father. This grave loss continued to cause her significant grief as she attempted to move on with her life.

Janice also lost friends and family members to her ex-husband. As we heard in a previous chapter, Janice, 61 years old, was a director of a nonprofit organization when she divorced her husband, an IT consultant, after 36 years of marriage. They decided to separate because they were moving in different directions in their daily interests. Janice was also worried that her husband was having an affair. Initially, her closest friends supported her; they would come over in the evenings and help her two daughters with their homework. One friend in particular who was contemplating divorce at the same time asked Janice a lot of questions about her separation experience. She asked how Janice felt going through her own divorce, and asked her why she'd chosen to divorce. Through these conversations, Janice believed that she was being helpful to a friend during a difficult time in her own life.

However, she was sad to report that many of these friends dropped her over time, especially those who stayed married to their own husbands. In her view, they either explicitly or implicitly sided with Janice's ex-husband. This turnaround happened about two years after her divorce was finalized. At first, Janice was perplexed by her friends' change in behavior, especially since they had previously supported her so much. She sought therapy with a series of mental health professionals to help her understand why her friends had abandoned her. These therapists suggested that the rejection might have to do with her new, single status. Although at first these friends may have wanted to embrace her and take her under their wings, eventually they may have started to see a single woman with many positive qualities and "they [felt] a threat" to their own marriages. This was very disturbing to Janice as she proceeded with her divorce, since stealing her friends' husbands was the furthest thing from her mind.

Wives Speak Out: Friends and Adult Family Members Were Neutral

Just like the men in the study, there was also a small group of women who reported not losing friends or adult family members during their divorces, and that both they and their ex-husbands had positive relationships with mostly everyone they knew prior to their splits. Karen, 53 years old, divorced her husband, 56 years old, after 21 years of marriage. She worked in the field of telecommunications sales, while her ex-husband was in the commercial cleaning business. She described the divorce as something that she "had thought about, dreamed about, plotted about, schemed about, for at least 15 years. And the simple reason [was] that we were just not compatible." This incompatibility manifested itself in many different ways. He was constantly accusing her of spending too much money on certain grocery store items, when in her view she was buying basic and necessary household goods. They also had two boys, but they had very different parenting styles. For example, he indulged them by buying them phones and a puppy; she staunchly opposed these purchases as excessive but was ignored and overruled by her husband time and time again.

At the time of the divorce, Karen had a strong circle of close girlfriends who rallied around her. They knew what was going on in her marriage and provided her with significant support, and at the same time never set out to demonize her husband. In terms of people who knew them as a couple, Karen said that sometimes they naturally were closer to either her or her ex-husband due to their gender, but that there was no animosity among them as a group after the divorce.

> We were friends with a lot of people in our neighborhood, but it was more like he was friends with the guys and [some of] the women were just along for the ride. So out of that group, there were a couple of women [with] whom I was friends and the rest of them, I really, you know, was neutral toward. So after the divorce, they were all still his friends ... I'm not [unfriendly] with those people [who were more his friends]. I just don't see them anymore. If I run into them somewhere, we talk. As a matter of fact,

just the other day, like yesterday, I ran into one of his good friends. He lives out of state now but I ran into one of his friends, you know. [He was one with whom] he would play poker, and we stopped and chatted for a few minutes, you know, just like we would have [if there were no divorce]. So there is no bad blood anywhere.

In addition, Karen made it a point to tell her husband that she still wanted him to be a part of her family's life.

When we had our divorce talk, I told him, you know, "I'm not trying to cut you out of my family's life. I'm not trying to take you away from the kids [and] from my grandkids. I want you to still have those relationships. Because why shouldn't you?" ... It wasn't like anybody took sides or anything like that; it was just sort of the natural thing.

To Karen, the divorce was only between herself and her husband. There was no need for others to feel burdened into declaring binding loyalties.

Wives Speak Out: Friends and Adult Family Members Were Divided

Finally, the smallest set of women said that friends and adult family members were divided in the wake of their gray divorces. The reasons for the divisions were complex and unique to each situation. Christine described her 31-year-old marriage to a gastroenterologist as one of deteriorating communication. They gradually stopped inquiring about each other's lives and sometimes barely spoke. At the 20-year mark, she also started to suspect that he was having an affair. When she confronted him with her suspicions, he admitted to it. An important detail related to this affair was that it was with a neighbor who lived across the street—a neighbor who was also Christine's best friend! Christine was heartbroken. She had dedicated most of her life to being a stay-at-home mother to their two children before returning to work full-time as a registered nurse. Now her life was falling apart.

She agreed to go to marriage counseling with him, and the therapist advised him to never see his neighbor again. However, since they lived across the street from each other, this was extremely difficult. Christine, too, agonized over having to see her friend go out and get the mail or take her children out to community activities. Although she never confronted her, the two former girlfriends simply stopped speaking. Meanwhile, Christine was still hoping at that point, even against all odds, that her husband would check back into their marriage. At the same time, however, she suspected that his infidelities were continuing. He had a particularly close relationship with one pharmaceutical representative and oftentimes he would go out "dancing" with her on Saturday nights, not coming home until 4:00 AM. After this behavior went on for a while, Christine finally confronted him.

> I said, "Are we going to make this work, or what's going on?" I was just so lonely in the marriage and that's when he said, "I don't love you. I haven't loved you for a long time. And I don't think I'll ever love you." And so my daughter was very upset about this. And she was funny. She said, "I'm calling Dr. Phil; you can't get a divorce until I call Dr. Phil." So for her sake, we decided to go and to try counseling again.

During one therapy session, Christine's husband finally admitted that he was not willing to make the marriage work anymore. He filed for divorce. Christine reported retaining many friends from the marriage, especially since her husband's behavior was so egregious. However, she experienced a more mixed response from his family. One of his brothers did not talk to her at all, but all of his other "brothers and sisters—he comes from a big family—called me to tell me [that] they still loved me, [and that] they will still consider me their sister. [They said that] I will always be their sister [and asked what they could do] to help me." She was still invited to all of their family events, and overall, with the exception of his one brother, she always felt welcomed. She simply had to accept that the one brother, with whom she had been very close, sided with her ex-husband for whatever unknown reason, and she had to move on with her life.

SOCIAL SUPPORT: RELATIONSHIPS WITH CHILDREN AFTER A GRAY DIVORCE

In addition to issues revolving around friends and adult family members, individuals going through a gray divorce may have to reconsider the relationships that they have with their children. For some couples, this is not an issue because they did not have any children in that particular marriage,

Table 9   Relationships with Children after a Gray Divorce

	40 Men	40 Women
Children's Reactions (Ranked by Order of Mention)	1. Depended on Child	1. Depended on Child
	2. Children Supported Their Ex-Wives	2. Children Supported Me

NOTE: The most common response for men was that they did not have children from their gray divorce. For women, this was the second most common response. These responses are excluded from the table because the issue was not applicable to them.

especially if they married later in life. In this study, 22 out of 80 respondents reported having no children from their marriages that ended with a gray divorce. But for those who did have children in this marriage, there remained the possibility of losing ties with their offspring. While there were some respondents (14) with at least one child under the age of 18 at the time of the divorce, the majority of respondents (44) had only adult children when they experienced their own gray divorces.

Overall, there were stark differences in how men and women experienced the quality of their relationships with their children during and after a gray divorce, with men being much more pessimistic. These men most commonly reported that each child reacted differently to the divorce announcement. In these cases, usually at least one child initially opposed them personally. Their second most frequently noted observation was that all of their children sided with their ex-wives. Women also most frequently reported that reactions to their gray divorces depended on the individual child. Unlike in the case of the men, however, these children provided different types of emotional feedback to their mothers, feedback that typically did *not* include at least one child opposing them. Women's next most common observation when they had children in the marriage was that the children developed alliances with them and not their fathers (see table 9).

Husbands Speak Out: Reaction Depended on Child

Men often reported experiencing at least one child initially opposing them and their role in the divorce. Roger, 59 years old, was married for 34 years to his 57-year-old wife. They had two adult children, a boy and a girl. When discussing the cause of his divorce, Roger pointed to two primary issues. First, in his wife's job as a chef, she gained a lot of weight and, in his mind, stopped taking care of herself. She avoided having sex with him as well. Second, he admitted that he played a role in the marriage's demise by engaging in a series of extramarital affairs. He was a state police officer, and in this job he said that women "just threw themselves at him." While he did try couples counseling with his wife, he continued his affairs. His wife finally demanded a divorce.

When they told the children about the divorce, their reactions were extremely painful to him. He said that the children knew about his cheating, but not the number of times he cheated. His son was shocked, but not extremely judgmental. His daughter, on the other hand, drew a line in the sand and told him that he had crossed it. She had already earned her master's degree in social work and had strong opinions about what was right and wrong; she was, in Roger's words, a real "straight shooter." She was extremely angry at Roger, and he thought he knew why.

> [To my daughter,] I was on a pedestal. I was a police officer. I stood for right and wrong; that's what I did. I was a pillar of my church community, and I was a pillar in our community while I served with the State Park Police. I also got an attorney general's waiver to take a second police job and worked as a part-time officer in our little town here . . . and so I was known to every one of her classmates all through school . . . You know, she always defended me when other kids were talking about, "Oh, your dad is a dirty cop." . . . She really put me on a pedestal.

Roger said his daughter thought so highly of him that she only dated men whom she sensed were similar to him: strong, moral, and righteous. When she found out the truth about his actions, he had a long way to fall.

Fortunately for Roger, with the passage of time, he found that he was able to reconcile with his children. His son was divorced from his own wife after five years of marriage, so he came to see that not all relationships work out. In fact, he eventually moved in with his father after his own divorce was settled. His daughter also became involved in a long-term relationship. With this added perspective about the complexities of adult partnerships, she started to see that her father was a flawed, but not a horrible, human being. Once she got married, she began to visit with her father on a more regular basis. Communication among all three of them, while not perfect, was much better than it ever had been in the past.

Raymond also had a son and a daughter from his 39-year marriage. Both of his children were young adults at the time of the divorce. Sadly reflecting upon his past, Raymond, 63 years old, the same age as his wife, argued that he never should have married her. Although they shared the same religion—Catholicism—they had little else in common. Raymond loved cars, both being around them and fixing them. He actually sold tires for a living. His wife, on the other hand, was a registered nurse and wanted nothing to do with cars. An even more alarming problem in their marriage, even at the very beginning, was their lack of physical affection. Raymond stated that there was simply no hugging, handholding, or kissing. Over time, the couple had sex less frequently and effectively became roommates. Raymond suspected that his wife might have had an affair at some point, but he could not prove it.

Toward the end of the marriage, Raymond could not stand the lack of affection anymore. He started having an affair with a woman who lived about three hours away, and they would meet on a regular basis for sex. He did not struggle with the morality of this affair in his head, nor did he go out of his way to hide it from his wife. For example, he acknowledged receiving cards and gifts from his girlfriend that were sent to the marital home in plain view of his wife. This affair ultimately made him feel even more acutely the emptiness of his own marriage, and he decided to file for divorce. In many ways, he hoped that his children would understand. He did not want his children to use his marriage to their mother as a role model for what all unions should look like. Instead, he wanted them to know that intimacy was a fundamental part of all marriages and that they deserved it when they decided to get married themselves.

When he broke the news of the divorce to his son, Raymond was relieved. Raymond's son simply said, "Dad, I will not be judgmental." On the other hand, his daughter for the first "four or five months, she just wasn't very communicative . . . she didn't communicate at all; she was mad at me." But, just as with the case of Roger, Raymond's daughter's attitude shifted with time. The most meaningful breakthrough occurred when he decided to swap cars with her so that she would have a newer one. Raymond was worried about having the interaction involving the actual swap so soon after the divorce announcement, so he planned to bring a friend along with him for support. In advance of the trip, he spoke with his daughter on the phone.

> I said, "You know, if [this is] going to be awkward or whatever, then we'll just work around it and do whatever we need to do [to get you the car]." And it got quiet. [Finally] she said, "No, we're going to have to deal with it at some point, [so] we might as well do it now." . . . We went out and had a great visit.

After this emotional discussion, their relationship steadily improved. Raymond even proudly described having both of his children at his house over Christmas for a short celebration after they spent time with their mother. To him, the most important thing was that they were now "accepting" of him and made an active place for him in their lives.

Husbands Speak Out: Children Supported Their Ex-Wives

The second most common experience men had with their children after a gray divorce was that their sons and daughters allied themselves with their ex-spouses rather than with themselves. In these cases, there was rarely a reconciliation. For example, recall that Gary and his wife, both 50 years old and described earlier in this chapter, had been married for 29 years. At the time of the divorce, they had three adult sons, all in their early twenties. According to Gary, his ex-wife had a reluctance to communicate and work out problems together. One day, Gary came home to find a note stating that she wanted to leave; by the following week, she had served him with formal divorce papers.

The impact of this decision on his relationship with his children was both immediate and stark. Gary believed that over the course of the marriage, she had been telling them false stories that portrayed him in a negative light, so they quickly jumped to her side. For example, according to Gary, she unjustly accused him of abusing her by saying that he had choked her and otherwise physically harmed her on numerous occasions. She repeated these falsehoods once again when she finally demanded that he leave the marital home within 30 days because she stated that she felt threatened. After he left, she returned to the house until it was sold. During all of this time, Gary's sons remained in close contact with their mother. They were trying to be protective, according to Gary, when this was completely unnecessary.

In retrospect, Gary maintained that he should not have let her get away with the multiple accusations of abuse that she made against him. Instead, he should have stood up to her during their fights. However, he still remained ambivalent about what he should have told his sons. On the one hand, he wanted them to hear his side of the story. On the other hand, he struggled with divulging this information to them because he did not feel like it was appropriate for them to know; he did not want to be in the position of vilifying their mother. As a result of this decision to remain silent about her behavior, he barely retained any type of a relationship with his children after the divorce was finalized, and this caused him extreme pain. He also noted that her manipulative nature actively kept them away not only from him, but also from their paternal grandparents. On this point, he continually tried to get them to attend any of his own family's celebratory events, but they steadfastly refused. Yet, because he believed that they were living under the control of their mother, Gary never blamed his sons for their behavior, and only hoped that one day they would seek him out and love him again.

Rather than point to their wives' interference with the relationships that they wanted with their children, other men placed more blame on the children themselves in causing these breaches. Recall that Terry's ex-wife was much more relaxed about spending money and often made secret purchases without her husband's knowledge. She also paid for their two sons' expenses, things that should have been, in his view, their own responsibilities, such as speeding tickets. This was not, however, simply his ex-wife's fault. Terry viewed his sons as equally responsible in forming an alliance against him beginning early in their teenage years, when the family was still together and then continuing through the divorce.

On one day in particular, this alliance proved exceptionally threatening. Terry had discovered that one of his sons had received another traffic ticket in the mail.

> I recall that day like it happened five minutes ago. My wife started yelling and my two grown sons came downstairs in unison and began to berate me as a miserable father. They [said that they] hoped that I would die alone . . .

It was . . . extraordinary. Actually, for the first time in my life, I realized—
and I'm a big guy—that my two adult sons could probably beat the you-
know-what out of me. I sat down on the couch, listened to it, and I was
frightened.

After this rage-filled, inflammatory fight, his wife had demanded a divorce.
At first, he had some contact with his sons, but over time, even that mini-
mal contact gradually dwindled to almost nothing. His youngest son, 25
years old, remained living at home with his mother. This residential
arrangement probably led him to hear more of his mother's complaints
against Terry, such that Terry and his son's relationship only involved tex-
ting every so often. His older son, 28 years old, went to college but was
constantly having financial problems. Terry blamed his ex-wife for this
state of affairs, since she never had instilled in him the importance of
financial responsibility. When Terry denied the older son a loan of $10,000
that he requested, the son stopped communicating with him altogether.
Overall, the family was suffering from multiple layers of toxicity, layers
that even Terry did not seem to fully comprehend. Terry concluded that
"I've reconciled it, as someday I will die. I will die before my children and
unfortunately, they will have to carry this with them [for] the rest of their
lives. Hopefully they will mature at some point." Terry considered it now
up to his sons to reconnect with him.

Wives Speak Out: Reaction Depended on Child

Women experiencing a gray divorce perceived the state of their relationships with their children completely differently than did the men. Wives
most commonly described the nature of their evolving bonds with their
offspring as child-dependent. In other words, they took pains to point out
differences between their children as their sons and daughters made sense
of their parents' divorce. Unlike the men, however, while their children
gave them a wide range of emotional feedback, these women usually did
not face complete opposition from one or more of their children.

Linda was 55 years old and worked in hair care product distribution.
She had been married to a 56-year-old urologist for 34 years. From this
marriage, she had two daughters, ages 30 and 28, and one son, age 24.
Linda described being "madly in love" with her husband, and still held on

to strong feelings for him after the divorce. The breakdown of their marriage involved many factors. Although they both were Jewish, she was much more observant, and over time, this bothered him more and more. He did not want to spend Saturdays in their temple or refrain from certain types of activities on the Sabbath. They also lived with Linda's mother, who had her own section of the house. Over time, Linda's husband expressed a desire to have more privacy, away from the watchful eyes of his mother-in-law. In addition, Linda described her husband as a narcissist whom she could never really satisfy. He was an expert in his subfield of urology and gave lectures all around the country regarding his work. He would be praised and fawned over at these events, so that when he came home to "reality," he would always be frustrated and unhappy. He also was not satisfied with his sex life with Linda—whom, at a size eight, he called fat—which probably contributed to his having an affair with a nurse practitioner he met on the road.

Even with all of her husband's faults, Linda still did not want a divorce. The adult children, however, were very angry with their father. They expressed their feelings in different ways from one another, and they wanted different outcomes. Linda described their reactions in careful detail.

> For example, my older daughter, she is more the one who . . . believes in princesses and fairy tales. (laughing) And she would have liked, just like myself, for him to sort of just drop this woman and come around. [She wanted] to just go back to the old life. My [other] daughter . . . feels that he's been verbally abusive to her since she could practically remember . . . She's very angry at him and she wanted him to go away . . . When I still talk about it, she says, "I can't even listen to you. You know, you've just got to move on with your life." You know, she wanted the divorce. And my son, he just believed that for my own dignity, this is the right thing to do and at the time [of the divorce], he told his father that he lost total respect for him.

Notably, her husband retaliated by threatening his son with withholding his college tuition payments until he decided to "respect" him again. Linda then reined in her son so as to not further upset his dad. Ultimately, she was able to move forward with all three of her children at her side, with varying degrees of positive support.

In a similar way, Carol, 54 years old, had been married to her 56-year-old husband for 25 years. They had two daughters, ages 19 and 22. She thought that she had a very good marriage. However, one day her younger daughter called her on the phone and was extremely upset. She had found substantial material on their home computer that proved that her husband had been active in various online sex chatrooms. When Carol confronted him, he admitted to even meeting one of the women he had met on the Internet. This younger daughter had been extremely close to her father, so this discovery really altered their relationship. She remained distraught, but after a period of time, wanted to work on her relationship with her father once again.

Her other daughter had been away in college when this discovery was made. She had a complete split with her father. In many ways, she could not get beyond the serious damage he had caused to the family.

> I think it was harder for [my older daughter] because she was out of the house so she left one day . . . and then the next thing she knew it wasn't [a solid family] . . . I mean, when they sat down together to talk, she is very cut-and-dried. So she looked at him and just basically said, you're a liar and a hypocrite because things that were important . . . for us as a family, and what you tried to emphasize to [us as] kids, were honesty and trust.

Even with her children's different reactions to the actions of their father, Carol did not completely give up hope on the marriage. She went into therapy with her husband in order to focus on the importance of strengthening their relationship. After he moved out, they continued with the therapy. However, Carol was not content with her husband's efforts. She concluded, "I didn't feel like he was being genuine in therapy. We weren't getting anywhere, so I was done." The nuclear family, as it was previously constituted, was done as well.

Wives Speak Out: Children Supported Me

The second most common response among women experiencing a gray divorce was that all of their children uniformly and unwaveringly supported them and opposed their spouses when their marriages broke down. This was a theme that did not emerge in any substantial way among the men experiencing a gray divorce. For example, Diane, 51 years old, had been married to her husband, 52 years old, for 25 years. She was a nurse while he was a contractor. There were multiple problems in the marriage, including his alcoholism, which ultimately led to Diane leaving 15 years into the marriage. When Diane saw that their house would be going into foreclosure without her financial contributions, however, she moved back home, and for a while the marriage improved.

Yet this upswing did not last forever. They had a son, 22 years old, and a daughter, 20 years old, when Diane discovered that her husband was having an affair. She decided to end the marriage immediately, an action approved by both of her children. Her children had already been alienated from him for a long time, primarily because he never took any interest in their schoolwork or activities. He was a father who had "checked out." Diane remarked, "The kids kind of got distant from him and they were like, 'Oh, just divorce him already, divorce him already.'"

One decision in particular demonstrated the support that she had from her children going forward with the divorce. Because her husband had financial problems, she allowed him to stay in the house and sleep on a cot in the living room. During this time, their son had been asking his father for help in mounting a television on the wall, but his father kept putting the task off. Suspecting that his father was drinking his nights away, their son got so frustrated one night that he threw the cot out of the house. When his father came home, his son yelled that he did not belong there anymore. After that verbal grenade was thrown in his direction, his father grabbed a knife. Diane stood between him, and he ended up stabbing the wall. The police came, and her son received an order of protection against his father. That resulted in Diane's husband finally moving out of the marital home to live with his uncle.

Betty's situation regarding the strong allegiance of her children was similar to that of Diane's. At 64 years old, Betty had been married to her husband, who was five years older, for 33 years. She was an assistant to a school principal, and he was a mechanic. Seven years into the marriage, when her son and her daughter were just entering school, she discovered that her husband had been cheating on her. Because the children were so small, Betty wanted to save the marriage, but he continued his pattern of what would become serial cheating. Although she took pains to shield her children from his actions, they ultimately discovered his bad behavior. At one point when her son was in high school, Betty went to his room and found him crying. When she asked him what was wrong, he asked, "Why doesn't dad love you the way he should?" Betty tried to steer the conversation in another direction by telling her son that his father was just moody and that he did love all of them. Despite these reassurances, however, their children seemed to understand the full dimensions of their father's actions.

As their family dynamics deteriorated, and as both children entered adulthood, they sided with Betty and truly felt grateful for all of the years that she had endured her husband's adulterous behavior. Her son simply said, "Mom, you have sacrificed enough for my sister and me." In his assertion, he was also acknowledging that his mother "just covered everything up all the time and [that she] made it so [they] had a great family life [and] had family trips." In many ways, Betty acknowledged that she had gone to extraordinary lengths to protect her children from their father's actions at all costs. On one occasion, for example, she even caught her ex-husband with another woman at a public auction that she was attending with her daughter. She told her daughter to stay in one location while she confronted them and then asked her daughter to leave with her because she did not want her exposed to any unpleasantness.

After Betty finally made the decision to divorce, both her adult son and daughter expressed their strong anger with their father. Her son completely cut him out of his life, while her daughter tried to express her frustrations with him at one point. She told him that "she was not happy [with] the way things happened but, you know, he could call her if he wanted to talk or something." After this initial conversation, her daughter tried on multiple occasions to call him, but he never reached back to her. Her relationship with her father, just like that of her brother, sadly ended with no further contact. She was and continued to be now firmly allied with her mother.

.   .   .   .   .

Women divorcing in later years are much more likely than men to pay a high economic penalty. This does not mean, however, that men are unscathed when a divorce hits at mid-life. As this discussion has documented, men are much more likely to pay a higher social gray divorce penalty than women. Both men and women admit that friends and adult family members tend to ally themselves with the wives after a marital breakdown. In addition, children—who are mostly young adults at the time of their parents' separation—can have mixed reactions to the news of a divorce. When they do have an opinion, they are also more likely to side with their mothers than their fathers.

While facing economic and social divorce penalties, couples going through these transitions also experience extraordinary personal grief. They are mourning the loss of what could have been the most important partnerships of the later years of their lives. Yet, although these negative feelings are both painful and serious, most individuals do not just stop living. In fact, in the wake of a gray divorce, both men and women have the opportunity to redefine themselves and map out their new futures going forward. It is to these powerful, personal transformations that this discussion now turns.

5 Moving Forward Personally

I think [the worst part about being divorced right now]
would probably be the time that I [am] . . . alone. You
know, when you're with all of your other friends [who have]
husbands and wives . . . or whatever, and then you have to
show up to events alone? That's probably the worst part . . .
[The best part about being divorced right now is] being
able to watch football on Sunday afternoons without anybody telling me [not to].

—Joseph, 63 years old, married for six years

The [worst part about being divorced right now] that came to
my mind is being single. You know, . . . [it is] not having anybody to call on my break at lunch to talk to about my day. [It
also means] not necessarily having somebody to do something with if I have the day off or the weekend off, or an
evening or lunchtime to meet with somebody. I mean, I have a
lot of friends [with whom] I can do that, but it would be nice
to have someone who was [in] a relationship [with me] . . .
[But ironically, the best part of being divorced right now is]
being by myself. Is that funny? . . . When I do think about, oh,
could I fit a man into my life? I'm like, I don't know . . . I really
like the way that I have a lot of flexibility and a lot of freedom
. . . I don't have to ask [anyone], "Do these pillows make you
smile or . . . are these curtains ugly, or do you think I should
spend this money, or do you think I should go here?" I mean, I
don't have to ask anybody any of that stuff. I just do it.

—Lisa, 55 years old, married for 24 years

• • • • •

For most, gray divorce hurts. There is no avoiding that reality. However, it does not have to stay that way forever. Individuals can both experience the pain caused by the separation with their significant others in mid-life *and* start to move on to lead new, fulfilling lives.[1] This perspective on individual adjustment takes into account the reality that human beings can and often do have multiple, simultaneous, and at times conflicting emotions as they progress through important life events, like a gray divorce. In many ways, then, experiencing a gray divorce is a winding, meandering process, around which a series of multifaceted, personal transformations take place.[2]

Take the case of Joseph. He and his wife had been living in Florida during the beginning of their marriage. However, his wife soon inexplicably started to make numerous trips to New York. Joseph suspected she was continuing a relationship with an old boyfriend. In order to, in his words, "make things right" and get their marriage back on course, Joseph moved to New York so that the couple would not be apart. Yet she would not stop seeing this former boyfriend. Joseph knew then that they had to break up. Most troubling to him about the entire divorce was being lonely. Describing himself as a "private" person, he noted that he "never put it out there that I needed help or anything else." He only had "a couple of friends going back . . . to high school that I talk to and stuff, but [can] never really depend on anybody to ask for advice or anything else like that." In another way, however, the divorce was very freeing for him. For the first time in a long time, he could do what he wanted, when he wanted, such as watch football all day long on any given Sunday.

In many ways, Lisa's assessment of her postdivorce life was very similar. Throughout her long marriage, she had worked as a registered nurse while her husband was a teacher. They had two sons together. In the last year of her marriage, Lisa noticed changes in her husband as he grew increasingly distant. One day, out of the blue, he filed for divorce. Lisa later found out that he had rekindled an old high school romance on the Internet. Shocked and angry, she still agreed to couples counseling to process what was happening to her. Quite surprisingly, after his high school girlfriend broke up with him, he approached Lisa in counseling about the possibility of getting back together. Lisa rejected this proposition, but in living out her new life on her own, she still fought strong pangs of loneliness. It was difficult for her to do things by herself. On the other hand, she enjoyed many aspects of her newfound independence. In fact, she felt bad for her married friends, noting that one of them in particular was severely "constrained to do certain things because she's married: where they go to dinner, what she buys, what she puts in her house, what she puts on her bedroom floor, [and] what she hangs on her kitchen wall. I mean, all of that stuff—she's got to run it by him." On balance, Lisa was relieved that she no longer had to get anyone else's approval for her daily life choices.

Throughout this book, we have seen that those directly affected by marital splits have to confront the inevitable gray divorce penalties that come before them. For women, these are primarily economic penalties, and for men, these are chiefly social penalties. These penalties are substantial hurdles to overcome, and both sexes are likely to have setbacks as they move forward. However, while there are roller coasters ahead, after a period of time many people do gain at least somewhat stable footing so that they can begin to evaluate their future lives in all of their complexities. The most important point to note is that the period of time after a mid-life divorce is not static or black and white. It is dynamic and fluid, with the "bad" effects facing squarely off with the "good" effects as each person shapes their new life.

COMING OUT ON THE OTHER END OF A GRAY DIVORCE: THE BAD

To set the stage for understanding how these individuals assess the overall quality of their lives after their marital splits, we must first note that research on how people experience life postdivorce has not focused on the "gray divorce" population. However, study samples have often consisted of at least some individuals who faced a divorce at age 50 or over, such that we can look to this research for at least initial guidance.

We will first consider the bad news. As both men and women reflect on their lives in the wake of a gray divorce, what are the consequences from their breakups that they find most difficult to manage? Perhaps most importantly, divorce can bring about profoundly sad feelings, resulting in severe loneliness. This loss of companionship may be primarily felt by the noninitiators of the divorce, as they are more likely to retain hope about the marriage's long-term durability. In addition, mid-life women experiencing a divorce have reported feeling hurt by being left to fend for themselves against the world, as well as vulnerable to unknown outsiders when they are no longer part of a couple.[3] Divorced individuals also report more significant "single strain" in comparison to never-married people.[4] Single strain embodies all practical and socioemotional stressors that result from the absence of daily intimacy, shared memories, and the anticipation of a bright future with another partner. Echoing these points, the previously described AARP study conducted in 2003 identified these companionship deficits—such as the lack of someone with whom to share affection, conversation, and activities—as extremely disheartening to both men and women going through a gray divorce.[5]

Of course, money concerns generated by a gray divorce are also often paramount.[6] In many cases, a married couple might explicitly or implicitly assign either the husband or the wife with the task of managing the household budget. A divorce necessitates that both partners become immediately aware of their assets and liabilities as a result of the settlement. Each half of the couple now has to decide how money will be allocated toward various goods and services. Beyond basic financial management, a divorce brings into stark relief the lifestyle choices that the couple has made throughout the marriage. As we have seen, divorce can shock women as to the harsh reality of their economic circumstances, including both current debts and potential future shortfalls. Indeed, the AARP study from 2003 demonstrated that women rated financial concerns as their top worry about being divorced at this point in their lives.[7]

Lastly, maintaining a resilient sense of health is a critical challenge for those experiencing a mid-life marital breakdown. In the wake of a gray divorce, individuals may be coping with feelings of insecurity, pain, self-consciousness, and uncertainty about the future.[8] Some may also carry significant guilt because they caused the breakup.[9] These feelings of guilt can be stronger among those who initiated the divorce because they were the ones who actively "pulled the trigger." Guilt is also an important emotion because one of its most important effects is its ability to impair the development of romantic relationships going forward.

Experiencing a gray divorce can produce a decline in various measures of well-being. The first two aspects of well-being involve overall physical and mental health. Both men and women might suffer long-term damage in these areas, especially for those who do not remarry. Notably, women who do not remarry face lingering and more difficult-to-address health effects than men.[10] Key ailments linked to gray divorce among women include weaker immune systems, as well as anxiety and depression.[11] A third aspect of well-being involves personality changes.[12] Some research has indicated that although the magnitude of these changes may be small, they are not negligible. For example, divorced individuals may become more introverted and less dependable than their nondivorced counterparts. If these tendencies exacerbate over time, they can result in severe social isolation.

COMING OUT ON THE OTHER END OF A GRAY DIVORCE: THE GOOD

While gray divorce clearly has negative consequences, it can also present new opportunities for those who become single at this stage in their lives. First, gray divorce might produce positive feelings of independence and freedom. This is really the upside of ending a mid-life relationship: building a new sense of self without dependence on another.[13] For many people, the departure of a partner opens up new possibilities of a life of self-examination, self-renewal, and individual growth.[14] Men and women gain a newfound ability to engage in adventures that perhaps were unattainable or off limits as part of a couple. Individuals experiencing a gray divorce might obtain a renewed sense of self-identity in not having to consider their old partners in making major decisions. And as they make independent choices with increased frequency, they are likely to gain greater confidence. These inner changes are extremely significant for many undergoing a gray divorce, and can in turn generate new roles and even new relationships with others.[15]

Second, after undergoing a gray divorce, men and women can feel a sense of promise about a wide-open future.[16] Becoming single can be experienced as the ability to start over with a completely blank slate.[17] Emotions around these prospects might be stronger among the initiators of a gray divorce. Because they were the ones who more forcefully pursued a change in their marital status, they might be more likely to experience periods of self-focused growth, visions of new opportunities, and an overall deeper sense of optimism.[18] Practically speaking, starting over can mean many different things. Individuals can find new careers and pursue innovative hobbies that might have seemed unrealistic in the past. They can travel or stay closer to home. They can volunteer on behalf of charities or become more religiously engaged. In all of these cases, they can experience a personal rebirth comprising endless possibilities.

Third, good outcomes are also possible if individuals are removing themselves from toxic relationships and affording themselves the opportunity to live without considering their ex-partners' hostile thoughts, words, and actions. For example, we might categorize couples as having a high-quality marriage full of positive interactions, or a low-quality marriage, where interactions are mostly negative. For couples in low-quality marriages, divorce can serve as a welcome release from a damaging relationship. In fact, research has shown that women in low-quality relationships who ultimately divorce raise their assessment of their overall work and family lives.[19] Interestingly, this effect has not been seen for men, so women in particular might benefit in unique ways or more strongly once they leave damaging relationships.

A fourth and final potential positive effect for those who divorce in mid-life has to do with money. As demonstrated earlier, money can be a significant stressor after a divorce, especially for women, who continue to do the majority of unpaid carework in the United States and drop out of the paid labor market at the height of their highest earning potential years. However, divorce can also produce positive financial benefits for both men and women.[20] In other words, it can be a catalyst for individuals to engage in smart, aggressive financial planning, as well as serve as a mechanism for men and women to feel in total control of their budgets in new ways. Indeed, in the AARP study from 2003, both men and women listed the issue of financial control as among the top-five positive benefits emerging from their own gray divorces.[21]

WHAT ARE YOUR LIVES LIKE NOW? THE BAD

So how did the men and women in this study assess their personal, post-divorce lives? Did their assessments reflect or differ from this previous

Table 10   Negative Assessments of Their Gray Divorce

	40 Men	*40 Women*
Worst Part of Being Divorced Right Now (by Order of Mention)	1. Loneliness	1. Loneliness 2. Financial Concerns

research? All respondents in this study were asked to describe the worst parts of being divorced at this point in their lives, as well as the best parts. Let us begin with expanding on the bad news of gray divorce. Here, men and women had some, though not all, of the concerns laid out by the research mentioned earlier. More specifically, men had only one dominant answer about the worst part of gray divorce: loneliness. Women also reported loneliness most frequently, and secondarily added financial concerns as well (see table 10).

Husbands Speak Out: Worst Part of Being
Divorced Is Loneliness

The severity of loneliness was especially stark among the male gray divorced population in this study. Recall from an earlier chapter the case of James, a 53-year-old man who had decided that divorce was his only option, as he and his wife grew apart over time. They also stopped having sex, which was an extremely important part of marriage to him. As he reflected upon his marriage's demise, he became particularly despondent. He painfully and emphatically stated that "being lonely" was the most horrible result of his marital breakdown. He pinpointed these feelings as emerging from being accustomed to the joint decision-making processes that were in place as part of his 27-year-old marriage. Without feedback from his wife on critical life choices, he felt a significant void.

> When you're married, you're part of a machine. [When you are divorced, you have] separated the two halves of the machine and they have to run independently. You're used to having a sounding board, a second opinion, [and] a moral

compass. Each side uses the other, as [when we ask each other,] "Should I do this?" [You get a thoughtful response. Your partner might say,] "You didn't look at this issue." [Then you respond,] "Oh, no. I didn't think of that. Damn, thank you." You know, so . . . you get used to being part of a well-oiled machine and once you take that apart . . . for a while your engine runs a little rough.

James clearly appreciated the give-and-take involved in his marital relationship, which he viewed as keeping him steady and even on proper ethical footing. Without his wife, he became insecure over his abilities to judge the merits of the decisions that came before him.

To address his loneliness after the divorce, James started trying to find people to date, but he had not been very successful. He found the dating websites that he went to—Match.com, POF.com (Plenty of Fish), and JDate.com—to be less than helpful, because, according to James, the women there wanted him to be in top physical shape, and he was overweight. With sadness, he remarked, "I can't tell you how many of the women on the websites say, 'Must be in shape,' or they'll just put 'No fatties.'" James tried not to take these requirements personally, and declared that these women could "kiss my ass." He also mourned the fact that many women on these websites stated that they were looking for partners that "must earn this much or more." Summing up his reaction to these requirements, James stated, "Well, you know what? Stay single the rest of your life. See if I give a shit." Perhaps with some degree of defensiveness, James summarized his current love life by stating, "No, I've had no dates. I'm single. I'm celibate. I'm bored as hell."

Loneliness also consumed Donald, but manifested in a different way: the pain of physical solitude. Donald was 52 years old and, as described in an earlier chapter, had gone through a painful divorce. He acknowledged that he was very grumpy during his marriage due to an undiagnosed case of sleep apnea, and that he was often absent from home due to his nontraditional work hours as a truck driver. His wife ultimately became fed up with his antisocial behavior and had an affair. The loss of her companionship and the devastating loneliness were difficult for him to accept. Both of his children were minors (one preteen and one teenager) around the time of the divorce. In order to interact with them, therefore, he sometimes had to interact with his ex-wife. These were often devastating encounters for him.

I called my 17-year-old son the other night to talk to him about something
. . . that he and I were planning. And he said, "Dad, can I call you back in just
a minute? We're fixing to sit down and eat." And in the background, I heard
my ex-wife, her boyfriend, and my daughter laughing. [They weren't laughing at me.] I'm sure they were just having a good old time and they were
laughing and cutting up. And I said, "Yeah, that's fine; call me back when
you get finished eating." And I sat down at the table, [and] looked at my
food . . . I was sitting there by myself, and I cried.

The saddest part to Donald was that he was able to acknowledge his role
in causing the marital breakdown. He took personal responsibility for the
actions that he believed prompted his wife to seek a divorce. Accordingly,
in many ways, he thought he deserved the high price of loneliness that he
now had to pay.

Like James, Donald tried to combat his loneliness by visiting dating
websites. He tried ChristianMingle.com and eHarmony.com. But after
searching online and chatting with several women, he reported, he had
only been on a couple of unsuccessful dates. He soon decided to change
his strategy and told his brother, "I'm done with the online stuff. I'll meet
[a woman] the 'old fashioned way' or I won't meet one." He said that
although he would prefer someone who did not smoke and was attractive,
there were really only two characteristics that were nonnegotiable. First,
he wanted to meet someone with high morals. She did not have to be a
"Bible-thumper," in his words, or bring up the Bible in every conversation,
but she needed to be strongly spiritual in a Christian way. Second, learning from his own experience, he sadly noted that she must have the "ability
to stay faithful to a truck driver." He simply could not bear to go through
the pain of a divorce again.

Wives Speak Out: Worst Part of Being Divorced Is Loneliness

Wives also most commonly cited loneliness when they described the worst
part of being divorced at this point in their lives. At 56 years old and married to a 53-year-old man for 16 years, Brenda, who was discussed in an
earlier chapter, had struggled with her decision to divorce. This was her
third marriage, and she really wanted it to work. However, her husband

had an Internet pornography addiction and he could not break his habit. After multiple, failed attempts to change his behavior, she decided she had to divorce him. The initial separation, however, was not easy because of the all-consuming loneliness that she felt in its aftermath.

> I think [I am so lonely] because for me, I've always had someone in my life for so many years. And to be totally on my own was exciting for a little while and then scary for a little while, and then just plain lonely. So I think it's just that [it has] definitely been the hardest thing to deal with because whether you're married or not, you always deal with finances. You deal with difficult people in your life. You deal with happiness, children growing up and moving, you know, you deal with those things whether you're married or not. But not being married [means that you do] not have a special someone who only has to check with you before [that person] makes major decisions, you know, or vice versa. You don't have that person anymore in your life who says, "I can't make this decision [because] I have to check with you." It's a very lonely life.

In many ways, then, Brenda was echoing the sentiments of James in that the loneliness she described was one of missing a partner to share in different types of decision-making. In her new life, she had to do this on her own as she lacked someone "to check with" first.

Her approach to handling her loneliness was similar to those of the men in terms of looking at dating websites, specifically Match.com, POF.com (Plenty of Fish), okCupid.com, and eHarmony.com. Brenda said that overall she did not have much luck with these dating websites because she believed that she presented herself much better in person than online. Brenda decided to pursue speed-dating, a style of dating that involves meeting up with a group of other singles in a central location and doing short "meet and greets" with them. Each individual attending then decides whether they want to have further interactions with the people they met that day. Brenda reported that she made an excellent new girlfriend in the parking lot of one of these events, but that her success with meeting men was not as great. "I think [I met] eighteen men and I [said yes] to eight and four said yes to me, and I had two dates . . . that did not go very well." Brenda did indicate, however, that she was not willing to give up, even though the process of connecting with someone new was very slow and sometimes dispiriting.

Brenda's definition of loneliness was very specific in that she focused narrowly on the lack of shared decision-making that resulted after her marital breakdown. Loneliness was defined in a much broader way for Julie, 59 years old, who described it in the context of both a loss of shared responsibilities and a loss of intimacy. Julie had gone through a particularly painful gray divorce with her husband, 61 years old, after 35 years of marriage. She had three children with her former husband—two girls and one boy. She reported a series of devastating family problems that had led to the divorce decision. Her son had a serious drug addiction, and while married, the couple had encouraged him to join the Army in order "to straighten his butt up." Tragically, he came back from Iraq as a full-blown alcoholic. Once at home, he resumed his past drug abuse behaviors as well. Over time, his addictions got worse; the police arrested him on multiple occasions on drug charges as well as driving under the influence of illegal narcotics. He constantly badgered his parents for money, threatening that if he did not receive it, his drug pusher would have him killed. Throughout all of this turmoil, Julie reported, they had him "Baker Acted" (subjected to an involuntary psychiatric evaluation and hold) at least five times. She and her husband then had repeated arguments about what to do with him. Her husband wanted to impose "tough love" rules on him, but Julie rejected this approach. She viewed "tough love" as too harsh and felt that it would be a way of giving up on him.

Making matters worse for the couple, during a difficult financial time their house went into foreclosure. Luckily, Julie's sister bought them a new house. As they struggled to get settled in the house, with her husband working a variety of jobs, including construction, cooking at a restaurant, and then as a lawn care business owner, they faced another challenge. Julie's husband came into contact with his high school sweetheart on Facebook, and told Julie that the sweetheart "was his true soul mate and [that] he never stopped loving her." While he was still living at home with Julie, he started calling this old girlfriend over ten times a day. He then received an inheritance from his mother in the amount of $250,000, but at the time hid the exact number from Julie. Ultimately, he ended up serving her with divorce papers so that he could start a new life with both his huge windfall and his old high school flame.

Julie remarked that the worst part about being divorced was that she was lonely, which she first defined as being without a partner with whom to share everyday tasks.

[I am alone and now I have] to be responsible for five million things that [I never had to think about before. For example, I am now] taking the garbage out on Tuesdays and Saturdays. I never worried about the garbage . . . Simple things like that [that I now need to worry about] . . . And the dogs . . . I never had to bathe the dogs and make sure [they got fed] every day . . . That was always like his thing and the yard now . . . I mean he does cut my yard for free . . . I have a big yard, too, but now I've got . . . the household things. I've got to climb on ladders and change light bulbs that are real high.

In many ways, Julie acknowledged that she was struggling with the reassignment of what she assumed were "male tasks" versus "female tasks." She argued that taking out the garbage, caring for the dogs, and other home maintenance activities were supposed to be done by men and she could not believe that she now had to do it all. But loneliness also had a second important component to her: the loss of intimacy. She sadly remarked that "sometimes I just want to turn and talk to him but he's not there. And sleeping in a king-sized bed all by yourself [is difficult]."

Pointedly, Julie did not feel ready to address her loneliness by seeking new male friendships or dating at this stage in her life. She remarked that she was not a "bad-looking woman," and made an effort to maintain her weight. She also said that she took care of her hair and wore makeup on a daily basis. However, she felt used up and discarded by men in general, and was in no position to meet someone new. She claimed that she simply did not feel "desirable to men." Even worse, the divorce made her feel invisible, with men not really seeing her or wanting her. As a result, she spent most of her time at home, making very little effort to go out and socialize.

Wives Speak Out: Worst Part of Being Divorced Is Financial Concerns

While both men and women reported loneliness as the worst personal part of being divorced, women had a second set of concerns that men lacked. This involved managing their finances and having enough money to get them through the later years of their lives. For example, Sharon's biggest regret was being financially ignorant of her husband's business practices during their marriage. At 72 years old, Sharon had been married to her

68-year-old husband for 39 years. Prior to adopting two sons, Sharon was a teacher. Once the boys arrived, she became a stay-at-home mother. Her husband had his own business involving the sale of railroad equipment. Their marriage ultimately failed first because her husband became involved in illegal business activities, and second because he was a serious alcoholic. Sharon could pinpoint the moment when she decided to seek a divorce. She stated that "when I really snapped, like when the twig snapped [for me, was when] he said to me, 'My business partners are more important than you or the children.' That just did it [and] prompted me to file for divorce."

In thinking about the worst part of her divorce, Sharon said that she was too complicit in putting her signature on her husband's shady business deals when she never really understood what she was signing. These regrets made her worry about her financial future.

> I still have concerns about being able to financially have enough money to the end [of my life] even though I live a fairly [modest], you know, not extravagant at all [life] . . . I'm very careful about my money . . . But, you know, every time I go to my financial advisor, I always say, "Well, now, how many more years can I live?"

Added to her stress level after the divorce was the fact that she had to confront the impending death of her ex-husband. In the context of their final discussions about his last wishes, he asked that she take care of his golden retriever and she agreed. At the same time, he emphasized that he was not going to do anything to financially help her even *after* he passed.

> We had a conversation two weeks before he died in which he said to me . . . "[Well,] you do know that I have provided for the boys and they will get everything divided equally." And I said, "I do know that." And he said, "And you will not get one penny." And I laughed and I said, "Oh, I know that." You know, that was just a given.

While Sharon was able to laugh about his dying wishes at that moment, she also reported fearing that her precarious financial situation might cause her to become economically dependent on her sons one day, a worry that greatly disturbed her.

Another source of concern regarding financial strain had to do with the hidden costs of being a stay-at-home mother. Cheryl, described in an earlier chapter as 68 years old, was married to her husband, 64 years old, for 32 years. Cheryl was in a verbally and emotionally abusive marriage, in which her husband scapegoated her for all of their family's problems. One of the biggest challenges that they faced together was that one of their two children—their daughter—was born with birth defects and needed extra care. In fact, this daughter required multiple surgeries from birth until about four years old. Then she remained stable until middle school, when several other congenital neurological birth defects emerged. Since these birth defects were relatively rare, Cheryl had to take her to large teaching hospitals all over the country to receive the treatments that she needed; Cheryl traveled with her daughter and provided most of her daughter's care at home. Of course, by doing the critically important work of staying at home, Cheryl was forgoing earnings in the paid labor market as well as contributions to any private retirement savings accounts and the social security system. While her husband had amassed income and the retirement security of being an auditor for the federal government, Cheryl had no such safety net.

> [The worst part about being divorced at this point in my life is] finan-
> cially worrying about the money [and] what I'm going to do when the
> little bit of money I have runs out. I don't even know how I would pay
> [for a funeral] . . . I'm really seriously looking into donating my body to
> science so I don't have to have a funeral . . . because I don't have the money
> for that.

Cheryl noted that she purchased only the basics to keep her household afloat. With the small savings that she had, she bought a foreclosed house that she was trying to repair to leave after her death for her disabled daughter. She said she only had "enough money to live. And that's it. [If] anything major happens, I'm up a creek."

WHAT ARE YOUR LIVES LIKE NOW? THE GOOD

Not everything is bad for people undergoing a gray divorce. Indeed, divorcing couples report having much to look forward to as they set upon

Table 11   Positive Assessments of Their Gray Divorce

	40 Men	40 Women
Best Part of Being Divorced Right Now (by Order of Mention)	1. Independence and Freedom	1. Independence and Freedom
	2. Chance to Start Over	2. Liberation from Ex-Husbands
	3. Liberation from Ex-Wives	3. Happier

their new lives. Recall that previous research suggested that the four best parts about being divorced were independence and freedom, a chance to start over, not having to deal with a toxic ex-partner, and financial control. The main difference in this study was that control over finances did not emerge as a key benefit for these respondents at this stage in their lives. There was, however, significant overlap between the sexes with respect to their other answers regarding the best part about being divorced in mid-life (see table 11). They both valued independence and freedom foremost, as well as being liberated from their ex-partners (ranked third for men and second for women). The only difference between the sexes is that men prioritized a chance to start over (ranked second), while women reported simply being happier (ranked third).

Husbands Speak Out: Best Part of Being Divorced Is Independence and Freedom

Men clearly valued the long-term benefits of independence and freedom first when asked about the advantages of being divorced at this point in their lives. For Kenneth, 52 years old, independence and freedom meant more control over his time. Kenneth and his wife, also 52 years old, had been married 31 years when they divorced. Many factors entered into the decision to divorce—a decision made primarily by Kenneth's wife. They had raised three children together, one girl and two boys, while working in the same construction business. When the Great Recession of 2008 hit, they lost everything that they had built financially as a couple.

As the stress between them mounted, his wife had an affair and told Kenneth that she wanted out of the marriage.

At first, Kenneth remained in a state of shock, saying, "It was worse than a death. I mean I can't describe [it] . . . It was devastating." But as he gradually recovered from his own personal wreckage, he began to notice that with the divorce, he received a certain amount of freedom to control his destiny going forward. He optimistically declared that "[the best part of being divorced right now is that] I can do what I want to when I want to do it. If I want to go skydiving tomorrow, I could. Anything that is financially feasible, I can literally do now. I'm training for a triathlon right now." Kenneth remarked that when he was married, he was often tied to social obligations with his wife, like going out to dinners or other family functions. For Kenneth, then, the most important aspect of being divorced was "freedom of time."

Scott, described in an earlier chapter, treasured independence and freedom in another way: the ability to make his own decisions. Scott was 65 years old and his wife was 68; he had only been married to his wife for three years, but that was more than enough for him. The main problem in his marriage was his wife's controlling nature, which he reported as crushing his spirit on a daily basis.

> I don't know what kind of label to put on a person who is always correcting you but I couldn't [do anything without her correcting me] . . . I love to cook but she didn't like me in the kitchen because I "used too many pots" or I "made too much of a mess." [It] spilled over into other issues as well, [such] as "Why are you wearing that suit?" "Why are you driving in this direction?" "Why are you doing this?" "Why are you doing that?" It just got to be that she was so corrective that it just started to make me crazy. I couldn't do anything without her having to comment about [it, like], "Why are you making that for lunch?" "Why are you doing this?" "Why are you doing that?" That's what I lived with for . . . years.

At first, he tried his best to improve the relationship. He wrote a series of letters to her expressing his feelings, and for brief periods of time she would modify her behavior. Yet it never seemed to last.

After numerous attempts to make it work, Scott realized that he simply could not salvage the marriage. To him, it was a devastating situation because there "was love there; there was a relationship." But he knew it had to end because he felt that he was constantly living on the edge. Finally, he said that he used the classic line from the television show "*Shark Tank*, where [potential investors say to entrepreneur contestants to whom they do not want to offer financial backing], 'I'm done . . . I'm out.' That was it exactly and I said to her, 'I'm out. I was all in and now I'm all out.'" By removing himself from his toxic marriage, Scott was finally able to be free and independent. He soon found himself on online dating sites whereby he could meet someone, as he described, on a casual basis, and never have to partner with another controlling personality again.

Husbands Speak Out: Best Part of Being Divorced Is the Chance to Start Over

The next most common response to what was the best part of being divorced, for men, was the chance to start over. Thomas, 63 years old, made this point in a striking manner with his desire to completely "reinvent" himself. He was divorced from his wife of 17 years, who was 56 years old. They had one son together. Thomas said that about three years into the marriage, he feared that there might be a split. His wife was an alcoholic and extremely abusive to him. He also believed that she had borderline personality disorder and had engaged in multiple affairs while they were together. Overall, he said, the marriage had been very weak from almost the beginning, but Thomas really wanted to make it work. He had been married two times before, once for seven years, and once for two years, and he did not want to repeat his divorce pattern again. Over the course of this third marriage, he and his wife had split up three times and repeatedly went back to couples counseling. Yet they could not resolve their differences. Ultimately, he was the one who filed for divorce.

Thomas, then, had experienced the burden of being in an extremely difficult relationship for a long time. When he finally decided to divorce, it was a breakthrough moment for him. He saw for the first time the opportunity to become his own person.

> Oh my God! You know, being free at this time . . . is kind of like being a teenager . . . You know, the kids are gone. The kids are finished; they are

launched and you are kind of free to reinvent yourself. And that's what I'm hoping to do . . . There are a lot of people who are in the same situation, both men and women, so . . . it is like being a teenager again.

As he thought further about his situation, he said that since he made a good living as an attorney, he would only need to work several more years and then he could retire. In the meantime, he hoped to be actively dating, but saw no need to marry again. For now, Thomas was simply looking for a clear beginning, not only in terms of new hobbies and recreational pursuits, but also with respect to meeting new people. Shortly after his divorce, he started dating a work colleague; that relationship lasted for about one year. He later turned to popular online dating websites to meet women, and overall was optimistic about his future prospects.

Frank, described in an earlier chapter, was another man looking for an opportunity to start over; in his case, however, he remained mostly focused on living a life of full authenticity, either by himself or with another. Now in his fifties, Frank had been married to his wife for 22 years. At first, his marriage was very happy. He shared many of the same interests as his wife and they had the common bond of wanting to start a family together. They soon had two young boys, but shortly afterward, Frank noticed that they started to spend more time apart, even within their own home. For example, Frank stated that at the end of the day, he would be watching a ball game in one part of the house, and she would be watching a movie in another part of the house.

Beyond diverging interests was the more serious problem of what Frank called his wife's financial infidelity. In Frank's view, his wife behaved wildly inappropriately with their money. She would spend too much on her credit cards and take money out of their retirement accounts without his knowledge. In many ways, she wanted to lead a life of more affluence than they could afford. While not poor by any measure—Frank worked in the insurance field and his wife in social services—he still wanted to stick to a budget.

As Frank thought about their marriage, he tried to make changes that he could live with and make their partnership grow stronger. For example, when the credit card bills arrived and they were extraordinarily high, he would question her about them. Yet rather than reflect on her own behavior and attempt to modify it, she would lash out at him. Then Frank would attempt to manage her expenses in another way by putting lower limits on the credit cards. Once he did this, however, she simply found new ways to hide and spend money. Over time, the financial stress they were under created such disappointment and frustration that Frank could not continue any longer.

Interestingly, it was only after the marriage was officially over that Frank could see how much of a burdensome weight it had been on him. As he moved forward, he optimistically declared that he had a lot of hope for finding joy once again in leading a fully honest life. He cheerfully noted that he had a fortune cookie message taped onto his office wall with the saying that he had "a lifetime of happiness" in front of him and that he looked at that every day. In many ways, this message signified his desire to begin again—anew—and he summarized this quest by stating, "I rolled the dice on happiness and the dice are still tumbling."

Husbands Speak Out: Best Part of Being
Divorced Is Liberation from Their Ex-Wives

"I don't have to put up with her bullshit." When asked about the best part of being divorced right now, Dennis put it succinctly. Indeed, not having to be with his ex-wife anymore—an immediate benefit—was the third most commonly named benefit of splitting up among men going through a gray divorce. Introduced earlier in the book, Dennis, a 59-year-old accountant, had started with a relatively happy marriage to his stay-at-home wife, who was 55 years old. During their 35-year marriage, they had four children—two boys and two girls. Over the course of their union, however, Dennis's wife became increasingly religious. She wanted Dennis to be the "traditional" male leader of the household, make all important decisions for the family, and help inculcate extreme religious values into the children.

Dennis firmly rejected this role. He wanted to share decision-making power with his wife. And while he did not object to exposing his children to religion, his wife, in his view, was becoming more and more fanatical. Finally, he just got to the point where he could no longer tolerate these unwanted family dynamics. While Dennis was clearly troubled by the changes that a divorce would bring to his family, he felt that the benefits of being away from his wife outweighed all of the costs.

> I don't have to listen to her crap anymore. I don't have to listen to her about, you know, whatever it is that she wants to talk about today. You know, my ex-wife was definitely a talker and, you know, in her defense she did help me through some very, very difficult times in my life. You know, [she helped with] the death of my brother [and] the death of my stepfather . . . [She helped with] my retirement from the county [as a certified public accountant]. She was absolutely there for me. So sometimes she was very invaluable [in giving] me support, but as the marriage grew worse, that happened less and less.

Dennis did not give up on his marriage without trying to solve their problems. Before they officially decided to divorce, the couple went to counseling together. However, his wife insisted that it be religious-based counseling. When the team of counselors told him that he needed to "go home and pray" about his marriage, Dennis "told them [that] they were full of shit and walked out the door." He believed his marriage needed less religion, not more. With the divorce, he finally was able to make a complete escape from his wife's ideas about spirituality.

Like Dennis, Edward also stated that the best part of being divorced at this stage in his life was not having to be with his ex-partner; however, unlike Dennis, he did not point to one specific attribute or characteristic of his wife as the source of his discontent. Instead, he identified multiple personality flaws that, cumulatively, he was unable to tolerate over time. At 56 years old, Edward had been married to his 50-year-old wife for 22 years. She brought a son from a previous marriage into their relationship, and they had two sons together. With some sadness, Edward characterized the first decade of their union together as "average." One problem that he noticed almost immediately was that she had a troubling habit of exaggerating the truth to make herself look better in other people's eyes. For example, she told everyone that she had been enrolled in a prestigious state university when, in fact, she had taken only one semester's worth of classes at a community college. In another instance, she volunteered as a candy striper at a local hospital, but told anyone who would listen that she worked in the operating room. At one point, she claimed that one of her sons tried to push her down the stairs, but Edward stated that he had witnessed the entire interaction and swore that it never happened. With her constant exaggerations growing worse over time, Edward found himself starting to doubt the truth of anything that she said. Their marriage was beginning to crumble in front of his eyes.

Beyond this issue was another serious problem that emerged in the second decade of their marriage. When their three boys reached their teenage years, they started to express new and independent educational, career, and general life aspirations. Yet instead of encouraging them to find their own voices, his wife told them that their ideas were unworkable. In Edward's perspective, his wife lacked the ability to see people beyond their roles in her life. Edward put it this way: "If you're her son, you exist within the context of being her son, not as an individual, not with your own hopes, dreams, fears, desires, and all that good stuff. So, you know, she basically lost the ability to relate to them as adults, for lack of better terminology."

With her exaggerations and her inability to acknowledge the independence of others, Edward recalled never knowing what "level of insanity at some part during the day" he would have to face. He ultimately decided to seek counseling for himself, but she would not attend with him. She lacked, in his view, the "ability to understand [the nature of being] accountable and responsible" for her personal problems. Over time, the accumulation of these interactions took their toll on him, and he eventually realized that he would only be able to personally prosper and flourish without her in his life anymore. After a long series of discussions, they both finally agreed and decided to move forward with a divorce.

Wives Speak Out: Best Part of Being Divorced Is Independence and Freedom

Just like their male counterparts, women most commonly reported that the best part of splitting up involved the long-term benefits of independence and freedom. Recall from an earlier chapter that Patricia, 58 years old, had a five-year marriage to her 37-year-old husband. While they were married, she was a medical lab technician, and he worked in a warehouse.

When the economy worsened, he lost his job. He expressed some interest in starting his own e-commerce business at home, but never seemed to get around to doing much about it. Instead, he spent more and more time at his best friend's house, where he was able to interact with the true subject of his desire: his best friend's wife. Eventually they had an affair, and Patricia's marriage was over.

But all was not lost in Patricia's case. She had the support of her two adult daughters, and although she was tremendously sad about her situation, she recognized that she had a long life ahead of her. She expressed an interest in paying off her debts and remaining out of the dating scene for a while until she could process the entirety of what had happened to her throughout both the marriage and the divorce. When she did become ready to date again at some point in the future, she said, she would look for someone to help her "take care of business," meaning that she was no longer looking for the love of her life, but a more practical partner to help her with the eventual physical and financial demands of the aging process.

Although the demise of her marriage was disheartening, Patricia noted that there were still many benefits to being divorced at this stage in her life, most notably independence and freedom. Describing these advantages, she declared, "There's an actual lot of good stuff there . . . I don't have to put up with the mess. I get up in the morning, my house is my house, my stuff is my stuff, and my money is my money." A fundamental part of this reclaimed control was no longer having to worry about his "insane" lack of intelligence.

> I don't have to worry about him doing something stupid . . . I mean, it's like [his being able to be suckered into schemes and] infomercials. [I would say], "What, are you kidding me? What are you doing?" I remember [this] phone call one time . . . [He said to me], "You can't believe this. You just won two trips, you know, airline tickets to go here. [The man on the phone just wanted] your credit card number and [he said that he would] ship them to you." He did it [and gave the man the credit card number] . . . I'm like, "Are you insane? Are you insane? You need to stop right now and think that through."

Beyond being liberated from this naivety, Patricia laughingly summarized her other positive feelings about his departure. She stated, "If he's moody or bitchy or any of that stuff, I don't have to listen. I don't have to pay attention. I don't have to be nice." With the marriage over, she was free to be herself.

Nancy, introduced in an earlier chapter, also believed that her third divorce provided her with important freedom and independence. Nancy, 54 years old, was excising an abusive man from her life. Her 61-year-old husband was controlling, especially with any behavior that pertained to her two teenage daughters from a previous marriage, both of whom lived with them. His severe gambling addiction, which lost them thousands of dollars, also did not help improve the quality of their relationship. Finally, he was verbally hostile to her, especially during the latter part of their marriage. He frequently would shout at her, "You slut, you whore, blah, blah, blah." Over time, Nancy simply got to the point where she would not take this type of treatment anymore.

Stating that she is "happier now than I have been since my daughters were little kids," Nancy described the positive, simpler ways that her life had changed now that she was on her own and completely liberated. For one thing, she was free from cleaning up his messes, such as the dishes that he would constantly leave in the sink. She also described being rapturous over the fact that she did not have to live with a man who did not care about showering for three days in a row. At this point in her life, now that her children were both grown up, she could return home to her two dogs who were "always happy" to see her. In sum, "[The dogs] don't bitch at me the minute I walk in the door. Nobody bitches at me is the main thing." She concluded that she was now independent and free to live her life on her own terms.

Wives Speak Out: Best Part of Being Divorced Is Liberation from Their Ex-Husbands

"I can come home and I have a soft place to fall." These words, spoken by Rebecca, 56 years old, seemed carefully selected as she discussed her 28-year marriage to her 53-year-old husband. Rebecca did not make the decision to divorce lightly, but, like many other women, once she had chosen to act, she focused on the immediate benefit of not having to be with her ex-husband anymore. Over the course of her marriage,

Rebecca started to believe that she could never make her husband happy. Calling him a narcissist, Rebecca also noted that he was extremely insecure. She claimed that he was "never satisfied with anything." Even though he had a good job as an electrician, he still believed that he deserved more. He was not satisfied with the way things were done in the home either. He would complain about how poorly the house was managed, but never assume responsibility for fixing it. Rebecca tried in numerous ways to address her marital problems. After her three daughters got older, she went to work as a registered nurse, hoping that the extra money would help ease some of the friction in the house. When that didn't work, she suggested couples counseling. He refused to go. Her relationship with her husband just continued to deteriorate over time. "It would get to the point where we didn't want to come home; we didn't want him to come home."

He was also an alcoholic. When he got drunk, he became verbally abusive and mean. Rebecca claimed that sometimes she and her daughters had to leave the house at 2 o'clock in the morning because he was irate over an inane issue.

> So, he just—he was a very unhappy man. And there was not any way to fix that . . . So . . . he would come home from work, sit in the garage and drink beer until, God, 9 or 10 o'clock at night. Meanwhile, [the kids and I] are in the house [and] I [am] cooking dinner. We are doing our thing, watching TV, and he's out there depressed and there was no reaching him.

Once she decided to get divorced, Rebecca's life completely changed. Immediately after they parted ways, she noted, "I can walk through the door and not have to worry about what's in there. Do you know what I'm saying? I don't have to worry about what I'm going to be accused of, what he's going to be mad at." While she was not open to remarriage right away, she declared that down the road she definitely would welcome a new companion into her life. That person, of course, would have to be stable and secure, and definitely not an alcoholic.

Volatility, then, in their partners' behavior and the desire to avoid it going forward were very important to women experiencing a gray divorce. While Rebecca's husband was moody, verbally abusive, and an alcoholic, Joyce faced instability of a very different type. At 64 years old, she had been married to her husband, 67 years old, for three years. This was her second marriage, and she did not have any children. Joyce was now retired, but throughout her career she had worked in the field of medical technology. Her husband had been employed in a variety of occupations, including security, roofing, and plumbing.

About six months after they got married, her husband started acting erratically with respect to his religion. They both belonged to a Christian congregation, and Joyce described the church as moderate in its views. Nonetheless, to her great embarrassment, her husband began to approach random strangers in places like Wal-Mart to tell them about the word of God. He also declared his intention to teach their pastor about the best way to preach. At about this same time, Joyce was woken up on a regular basis "in the middle of the night at 3:00 AM [because] he would be out in the garage screaming at the top of his lungs in tongues."

Joyce believed that many factors could have contributed to his behavior, but that one central cause was mental illness, for which he had been diagnosed and prescribed medication. The problem was that he only took the medication sporadically. When they went in for couples counseling to try to address his outbursts, their pastor advised him to take his medicine more regularly, but he didn't comply. When Joyce found herself hiding the bullets for his gun because she was afraid for her own safety, she knew it was time to file for divorce.

> [The best part of being divorced now is] that I don't have to wake up in the middle of the night and hear somebody screaming in tongues in my house. Or I don't have to come home and walk in . . . and find him in the kitchen screaming in tongues. Or he would monopolize the TV and have all these crazy religious nutcases on. Don't get me wrong. I don't think every religious program on TV is [crazy] . . . Not every minister is a lunatic, but some of these people are and he would use his credit card to make donations to these people.

Joyce summarized her feelings about being grateful to not have to deal with her ex-partner anymore as simply appreciation "to have peace and quiet and not [to] have to hear all this religious fanatical stuff going on." If she ever were to try seriously dating again, she insisted, she first would have that person "professionally investigated."

Wives Speak Out: Best Part of Being Divorced Is
Being Happier

The last theme women articulated about the best part of being divorced at this point in their lives was that they were happier overall. Sharon, described earlier in this chapter as someone who felt victimized by her husband's shady business deals, put her feelings on the matter this way:

> [The best part of being divorced is] just the ability to enjoy my happiness without someone making [my life bad] . . . He was just such a drag on my whole life and it was like a black cloud that was over my head . . . I don't have that black cloud now.

After her divorce, she reported that her life was now filled with joy. She would not even consider dating at this time because of that joy. In fact, when asked whether she would ever get remarried, she stated, "I seriously doubt it. Someone asked me the other day; [she asked me], what would it take [to get remarried]? I said a billionaire who is 99 years old and has a temperature of 105."

Kathy, described in an earlier chapter as a 53-year-old woman married to a 56-year-old man for 25 years, also reported being so much happier as a result of her divorce. She and her ex-husband had one son together. She cited two reasons behind her decision to divorce: her husband's multiple affairs, and his alcohol problem. The affairs were extremely painful to Kathy, and she participated in couples counseling on numerous, unsuccessful occasions to try to stop this behavior. But the more disturbing issue that affected her on a daily basis was his alcoholism.

> I've said . . . the further away from the situation I get, the crazier it looks. I mean, by the time the marriage ended, I was just very much in survival mode. It was the classic elephant in the middle of the living room and no one wants to talk about it. But it was just a really dysfunctional relationship. The only time that we ever had any good conversations was in the morning because I would leave for work at 7:30 [or] 8:00 o'clock. He was usually in the bar by 11:00 AM and by the time I got home at 5:30, 6:00 o'clock at night . . . he was well on his way [to being completely drunk]. And he would pass out most evenings. So we really didn't have much [of a] relationship. We were just roommates living together for quite a long time.

Kathy also noted that her husband often became verbally aggressive during the nighttime hours. She did her best to try to protect her son from her husband, telling him not to drive with his father after a certain hour of the day, and not to take his father's nasty words personally when he was under the influence. But these constant efforts sapped her energy and finally pushed her toward the divorce decision.

As she reflected on the best part of being divorced at this point in her life, Kathy described being elated. She bought a new house and found a new boyfriend whom she indicated deeply cared about her. Her son was thriving in graduate school and pursuing a doctorate in chemistry. She surrounded herself with great family members and friends who loved her, and she set new personal goals for herself. For example, she completed her first half-marathon after being divorced. In summary, she declared that she was so much happier because she no longer had "to go home to that craziness . . . That's right. [The best part of being divorced is that you] don't have to deal with crazy anymore, because you can't cure crazy."

.   .   .   .   .

In many ways, divorce is a true gamble. In thinking about whether to initiate or agree to a divorce action, individuals must weigh the pros of living on their own terms against the cons of being separated from their spouses whom they used to love. It is no wonder that those experiencing a gray divorce have conflicting feelings about their marital breakdowns. Many of these marriages have been of a long duration, usually also producing children to create larger and more complex family units overall. With a divorce, these couples are hoping that the good will outweigh the bad as they construct new lives on their own terms. On this point, while these men and women were able to articulate the worst part of being divorced at this point in their lives, they were also able to describe, many times with wild enthusiasm, their optimism about their futures. In other words, for many, gray divorce was not the end, but rather the beginning of a new life journey.

But those experiencing gray divorce need not go it alone. We now turn to the public supports that can help make the journey upon which many will embark in the upcoming decades as smooth, as self-sustaining, and ultimately even as self-actualizing as possible.

6 Moving Forward Publicly

Imagine a fictional couple in their late sixties. Jasmine grows up in a large Catholic family with three brothers and three sisters. Her parents, both with only high school degrees, work in the same large textile mill in southeastern Massachusetts when they are younger. They want a better life for their daughter, so they help her become the first member of her family to go to college. She attends Boston College and earns her teaching degree.

One summer break, she goes to the beach and meets a handsome lifeguard named Leonard. During the school year, he attends Boston University, with an interest in business. He also happens to come from a strict Catholic family, with two sisters and four brothers. The young couple starts dating and their relationship quickly becomes serious. Like many others in their generation, they marry immediately after graduating college. Jasmine starts her teaching career, and after working for a short time at a local bank, Leonard decides to head back to school to get his master's degree in business administration at Columbia University in New York City. The couple moves to New Jersey and starts their family: while they both are in their mid-twenties, they have two daughters. Jasmine leaves her teaching career to become a full-time, stay-at-home mother. Leonard secures a high-paying stock analyst position on Wall Street.

The couple provides their two daughters with an idyllic childhood, taking them on trips to amusement parks all over the country and making sure that they have the best public education possible. They give their daughters piano, ballet, tap, and swimming lessons and buy them a series of pets to encourage responsibility. A set of goldfish is followed by a cat, which ultimately is followed by a dog. Jasmine continues to have a strong relationship with her parents, and they, in turn, love their grandchildren. They often bring their granddaughters to live with them for entire summers in Massachusetts; while there, the girls frequent the beach and regularly visit many of their extended relatives. Their grandparents encouraged them to learn more about their Portuguese heritage, and take them to Portuguese festivals, cultural clubs, and church events.

Eventually, the couple's daughters grow up and attend college. After graduating, both daughters pursue graduate degrees in education. In the meantime, Jasmine returns to work as an elementary school teacher, which she finds extremely rewarding. In the evenings and on weekends, the couple enjoys the child-free time that they both feel they've earned; they go out to dinner with their friends more frequently and join a local tennis club to play a sport that they both enjoy.

This is not to say that the couple does not have challenges. Their youngest daughter is diagnosed with a rare autoimmune disease in her early forties, limiting her work and recreational aspirations. Jasmine herself develops breast cancer that results in a double mastectomy. Both of the couple's parents die after battling long-term illnesses. These events put incredible stress on them, but they are resilient and move forward in their lives. Later, they both retire and travel all over the world. Even though they have been married for over 40 years, they still hold hands whenever they are together.

This couple, while fictional, still holds strong power in our minds about what a married couple in their late sixties should look like. They fall in love, get married, have children. They raise their children and work hard. They provide their children with a solid education and extracurricular activities. They support their children's loyal relationships with their grandparents, and are steady in the face of adversity. After all of this, in their retirement years they enjoy the fruits of their labors. In essence, they become the epitome of "happily ever after," and are of course expected to stay together for the rest of their lives.

This was the marriage that was visible to the external world. But what if we now found out that both of them had a series of affairs throughout the course of their marriage? What if the husband repeatedly accused his wife of spending too much money or hiding purchases from him over a long period of time? What if the husband claimed that, for decades, his wife refused to get treatment for her mental health problems? Alternatively, what if the wife accused her husband of a long-standing drug addiction? What if she told her closest friends that he was repeatedly emotionally and verbally abusive to her? What if they both asserted that even though they had spent many years together, they had now grown apart?

These questions bring us to the paradox of gray divorce in modern American life. We simply do not expect couples at or over the age of 50—couples that typically have spent years together—to divorce at this stage in the game. These couples embody our national family fairy tale. They have made it so far, so surely they will spend their remaining years together. But reality is often at extreme odds with fairy tales. Marriages do crumble, and they crumble for a wide variety of reasons. In previous decades, even couples with the types of problems outlined earlier often felt a duty to stay together. Now, however, with the major cultural shifts that have made divorce more acceptable, the shackles of strict marital obligations have been broken for the Baby Boomer generation and beyond. Individuals expect to have successful, rewarding marriages with partners who share in their dreams and aspirations. If this is not possible, divorce is now a viable option.

And so, gray divorce—splitting up in mid-life—likewise is an increasingly acceptable choice. With this growing approval of alternative family forms, including gay and lesbian marriages and divorces, the country at large must be ready to provide the supports both halves of these couples will need as they reenter society in mid-life as aging, single adults. As this book has demonstrated, even within a relatively socioeconomically advantaged sample, women are likely to be financially vulnerable after a divorce, and men are likely to confront social support losses. We now consider public strategies for supporting women experiencing this economic gray divorce penalty, before turning toward public strategies for helping men address their social gray divorce penalty.

Table 12   Poverty Status by Age and Sex, 2014

Sex and Age	Total Population in Age Group	Percentage of This Population below the Poverty Line	Percentage of This Population below 125% of the Poverty Line
MEN			
55–61	14,211,000	10.5	13.6
62–64	5,245,000	10.7	14.7
65–69	7,391,000	7.3	10.6
70–74	5,163,000	7.1	10.9
75–79	3,580,000	7.1	11.5
80 or older	4,304,000	7.9	13.5
WOMEN			
55–61	15,223,000	12.6	15.8
62–64	5,738,000	12.2	16.1
65–69	8,337,000	9.8	14.6
70–74	6,046,000	10.5	14.9
75–79	4,422,000	14.3	20.8
80 or older	6,750,000	14.9	24.1

SOURCE: www.ssa.gov/policy/docs/statcomps/income_pop55/2014/sect11.pdf, tables 11.1 and 11.2.

WOMEN AND THE ECONOMIC GRAY DIVORCE PENALTY

Reforming Retirement Income Possibilities

If the more-advantaged women in this study were exposed to financial vulnerabilities in the wake of their gray divorces, we know that the threats to women at the lower ends of the economic spectrum must be even worse. Solutions to this financial instability must therefore address women across all income levels. To begin exploring how public policy might be used to counteract the economic gray divorce penalty, we must understand that poverty in America is still a daunting problem for aging women overall in today's society. More specifically, older women face a high risk for living in poverty, as table 12 demonstrates.[1] For women ages 55–61 in 2014, 12.6% lived in poverty and by ages 80 and older, 14.9% did. In contrast, men's economic condition improved as they aged, with the corresponding statistics at 10.5% and 7.9%, respectively.

When we also include women near the poverty line, at or below 125% of the poverty threshold, things look even worse. Using this measure, 15.8% of women ages 55–61 lived in poverty, escalating to 24.1% of all American women by ages 80 and older. Only 13.6% and 13.5% of men in these age groups experienced this same hardship. Women who are racial minorities fare even worse. As table 13 illustrates, aside from Asian women, older women of color experience much higher poverty rates than white women, with approximately 20%–25% of Black and Hispanic women living under the poverty line across multiple, older age groups. Again, even more striking, about one-third of Black and Hispanic women across multiple age categories lived below 125% of the poverty threshold.

When we examine the aging population by marital status, we see that older divorced women fare much worse than older divorced men (see table 14). Although we do not know if all of the divorces experienced by this group happened after the age of 50, the aggregate poverty rate in 2014 for divorced men ages 55–61 was 18.8% and then dropped to 9.4% for men ages 80 and higher. For divorced women, there was actually an increase in the poverty rate as they got older, with the corresponding statistics of 22.1% and 26.1% for these age groups, respectively. When using the standard of 125% of the poverty line, the divorced male poverty rate declined from 22.8% to 15.3% for these age groups, while the divorced female poverty rate rose from 27.3% to an alarming 36.7%.

Poverty statistics for divorcing couples are important for understanding the most severe financial problems facing men and women as they age, and women clearly do worse than men.[2] But even if they do not experience poverty, women still undoubtedly pay other types of strong economic gray divorce penalties, as demonstrated throughout this book. This occurs for a variety of reasons, but one of the most important relates to their work patterns throughout the life course. Fortunately, women have dramatically increased their labor force participation rates over the past several decades, which should, overall, improve their economic prospects going forward. However, as also emphasized throughout this book, there are other factors that need to be taken into account even as we acknowledge this cautiously optimistic trend.[3]

First, labor force participation statistics count equally all those who are actually working, those who are looking for work, those who are working

Table 13   Poverty Status for Women by Age and Race, 2014

Race and Age	Total Population in Age Group	Percentage of This Population below the Poverty Line	Percentage of This Population below 125% of the Poverty Line
WHITE WOMEN			
55–61	12,208,000	11.2	14.2
62–64	4,652,000	10.4	14.2
65–69	6,876,000	8.7	13.2
70–74	5,097,000	8.5	12.7
75–79	3,708,000	12.8	18.9
80 or older	5,860,000	14.0	22.8
BLACK WOMEN			
55–61	1,904,000	22.2	26.6
62–64	663,000	24.1	30.2
65–69	890,000	17.4	25.1
70–74	577,000	23.3	29.1
75–79	439,000	24.2	36.1
80 or older	575,000	21.4	34.7
HISPANIC WOMEN			
55–61	1,640,000	17.7	23.6
62–64	529,000	20.0	28.2
65–69	779,000	16.3	26.0
70–74	471,000	16.4	25.5
75–79	326,000	21.5	36.9
80 or older	494,000	26.4	38.2
ASIAN WOMEN			
55–61	781,000	7.9	12.1
62–64	293,000	11.9	13.8
65–69	385,000	11.0	15.1
70–74	278,000	20.3	24.2
75–79	194,000	17.3	20.2
80 or older	246,000	18.1	27.0

SOURCE: www.ssa.gov/policy/docs/statcomps/income_pop55/2014/sect11.pdf, tables 11.1 and 11.2.

Table 14   Poverty Status for the Divorced Population by Age and Sex, 2014

Sex and Age	Total Population in Age Group	Percentage of This Population below the Poverty Line	Percentage of This Population below 125% of the Poverty Line
DIVORCED MEN			
55–61	2,206,000	18.8	22.8
62–64	687,000	13.3	25.2
65–69	1,053,000	12.7	19.4
70–74	627,000	13.5	19.5
75–79	302,000	13.9	25.7
80 or older	225,000	9.4	15.3
DIVORCED WOMEN			
55–61	2,853,000	22.1	27.3
62–64	1,068,000	23.5	29.5
65–69	1,485,000	16.5	25.4
70–74	903,000	16.4	24.4
75–79	507,000	19.3	32.7
80 or older	509,000	26.1	36.7

SOURCE: www.ssa.gov/policy/docs/statcomps/income_pop55/2014/sect11.pdf, tables 11.1 and 11.2.

full-time, and those who are working part-time. Women are much less likely to work full-time than men, which means that they are working fewer hours overall. In many instances, these smaller numbers of hours worked are a result of women taking time out of the paid labor market to either raise children or take care of aging parents. Second, the pay gap is real. Women consistently earn less than men. These lower earnings are a result of both the smaller number of hours that they work and the fact that women still receive lower hourly wages.

Moreover, if they have children, they face a "motherhood wage penalty," or a reduction in earnings in comparison to women without children.[4] These penalties can be so strong that they persist even as women age through their fifties.[5] While the causes are not completely clear, some have attributed these inequities to employer stereotypes of mothers' abilities to do their jobs effectively, given the responsibilities that come along with parenthood. In other words, employers see women as less competent once they have children because they believe that their focus is no longer their job. Interestingly, men do not face a fatherhood penalty and may, in fact, receive a wage bonus for having children, as compared to childless men.[6]

Third, women remain segregated in occupations where wages are low, such as in sales and service jobs. This is especially true for Black and Hispanic women.[7] Occupational segregation is also critical in that it has consequences for a specific type of benefit that is critical for women as they age: pensions and other retirement savings vehicles.[8] Women of color are less likely than white women to be employed in jobs where retirement plans are offered, and some research suggests that they are less likely to participate even if they are offered such retirement benefits.[9] But retirement plans are not failsafe. The overall trend of employers moving from defined-benefit to defined-contribution retirement plans puts many women at risk of outliving their savings.[10]

All of these factors lead to circumstances whereby women are financially weaker going into their retirement years, and minority women are particularly affected. When we add in the possible event of a divorce, which negates a spouse's supplementary income coming into the household, women's financial status has the potential to plummet. Without a doubt, judges first must do their best to divide marital assets and debts fairly in cases of gray divorce. Educating themselves about the complex layers of economic inequalities that women face in their daily lives is a starting point and is nonnegotiable. Law schools in particular might assume primary responsibility for teaching their students about these issues. In addition, and fortunately, there are also many other governmental policy levers available that can be used to fight back against these negative impacts. What, then, are the best public supports in our toolbox that can help women economically as they move forward in their post–gray divorce lives?

Recommendations here can be divided into preretirement and postretirement policies. In terms of preretirement policies, the first step is reforming the public education system. Simply put, the education system can do a better job of encouraging girls to study subjects that are currently underrepresented by women, such as science, technology, engineering, and mathematics. Occupations involving strong knowledge foundations in these areas are generally highly paid and very rewarding. The public education system in the United States also must incorporate financial literacy into curricula at all grade levels. Many Americans—not just women—are unaware of basic finance principles.[11] If people had these important analytical tools at their disposal, they could do a better job in both thinking about and planning for their own financial futures.

The second critical preretirement policy that would help women experiencing a gray divorce relates to improving wages. More specifically, this would involve a raise in the minimum wage and guaranteed equal pay for equal work; this is important for all women, but particularly for Black and Hispanic women as they currently lag behind white women in earning power.[12] While the federal minimum wage has stayed constant over the past number of years, minimums have been raised by city and state laws, such as those in Los Angeles and New York State, for the benefit of women working there. In terms of equal pay for equal work, a critical proposal that would help women would be the passage of some version of the Paycheck Fairness Act. Although there are differences in the bills currently being considered in Washington, DC, most include penalties against employers who punish employees for sharing wage information, measures for workers to sue for damages related to wage discrimination, and training sessions for women to improve their negotiation skills to obtain higher salaries.

Third, the federal government must do a better job in terms of helping workers achieve work-family balance, while at the same time encouraging saving. This would involve investing in child care programs, mandating paid maternity and family leave, and implementing paid sick days for workers. These types of initiatives can assist women with caretaking tasks without imposing severe penalties on their lifelong earnings trajectories. In addition, the government could redesign the tax code to incentivize particular types of savings while women are working. For example, tax credits could be offered to encourage greater asset accumulation during women's key working years; this might be especially important for part-time workers who tend to lack institutional savings plans.[13]

In terms of postretirement policies that could help women facing a gray divorce, perhaps most important is social security reform. Social security is the primary public program upon which women rely for a substantial part of their income after the age of 65. Indeed, recall that there are currently several features of the social security program that already assist women. First, the benefit formula is progressive in that it pays a higher rate of return to those with lower earnings over their lifetimes; on average, these lower earners tend to be women. Second, the government adjusts these benefits for inflation, which is not true of many other savings and retirement vehicles, and makes payments as long as an individual lives. This particularly helps women as they live longer on average than their male counterparts. Third, we know that if a couple has been married for ten years or more and then gets divorced, a spouse can tap either her own benefits or one-half of her former partner's benefits, whichever is greater.[14] The rise in women's labor force participation over time means that women overall are developing their own records of employment that can be used in accessing social security. However, since the majority of women earn less than one-third of what their husbands make over their lifetimes, these women still frequently choose the spousal benefit.[15] Having this option available, therefore, is invaluable for women.

Despite these protections, since social security is still highly linked to earnings, women's disadvantaged economic position relative to men means that they still receive a smaller slice of the benefit pie. According to the Social Security Administration, at the end of 2014, the average yearly benefit for men ages 65 and older was $17,106, and for women, only $13,150.[16] Broken down by recipients' marital status, social security serves as 29% of married couples' total income, and 34% of total income for unmarried men. Strikingly, however, it constitutes 47% of older, unmarried women's total income. Simply put, overall, women receive less than men and yet are more dependent than men on social security as an income source as they age.

What, then, are concrete changes that can be made to the social security system to assist women? Can modifications be enacted to reduce the economic gray divorce penalty? Fortunately, the answer is yes. First, the social security benefit formula needs to include "caregiver credits" for the time and effort that women stay out of the paid labor market to take care of their dependents. Recall that the social security benefit formula is based upon a worker's top 35 years of earnings. For each year that a woman stays out of the paid labor market, she receives a zero in this formula, thereby reducing her lifetime benefits overall. Even if she is in the paid labor force, she likely works fewer hours as a result of her caregiving role, thus earning less as total income that is then used in the formula to calculate benefits. Caregiver credits could be assigned for anyone report-ing responsibility for any type of dependent, such as a small child, a disa-bled individual, or a senior citizen. Not only would these credits acknowl-edge the real work being done by these mostly female caregivers, it would strengthen women's work histories in the social security benefit formula and enable them to have more stable retirements.

Second, the time frame under which women can access their spousal benefits should be reduced. Under current law, a marriage must last 10 years before a woman can tap into one-half of her ex-husband's social security benefits upon retirement. Given that the median length of mar-riages in the United States is eight years, many divorcing women must rely on their own work histories to access social security benefits once they retire.[17] Of course, due to women's overall lower levels of earnings, this spousal benefit can be much higher than what they would receive based on their own work histories. By reducing the marriage length require-ments, the social security system would therefore provide a much-needed boost in financial benefits for these divorced women.

Third, the amount allocated for social security benefits needs to be reex-amined. The relatively low average benefit means that many women are living near or below the poverty line. An across-the-board increase in ben-efits, even a small one, would help these women enormously.[18] Black and Hispanic women, with lower lifetime earnings than whites, could be par-ticularly helped with this change.[19] In addition, although social security benefits are adjusted for inflation, the metric that is used for this calcula-tion, the Consumer Price Index for Urban Wage Earners and Clerical Workers (CPI-W), is not the most optimal choice, since it does not reflect senior citizens' spending patterns. For example, it does not take into account the much higher levels of expenditures that older Americans make on health-related goods and services. In recognition of this fact, in 1987 the Bureau of Labor Statistics created a new index called the Consumer Price Index for the Elderly (CPI-E), which places more weight on medical expen-ditures; this index has traditionally grown at a faster rate than the CPI-W. However, the social security program still uses the CPI-W to account for inflation in the economy. By switching to the CPI-E, benefits would more

accurately represent the true cost of living that older Americans, and particularly more vulnerable women, face on a daily basis.

As part of this benefit review process, policy analysts should also reexamine the Special Minimum Benefit part of the program. In 1972, Congress
added an extra component to the social security program designed to help
lower-income Americans; this component was incorporated in 1973. The
Special Minimum Benefit specifies that, first, workers must have a minimum of 10 years earning a certain threshold of income. If workers meet this
requirement, and they would receive higher benefits from the Special
Minimum Benefit than from the traditional social security program, these
workers can tap into this alternative plan when they retire. The major problems with this alternative program are that typical yearly benefits are lower
than the poverty line; the benefit is indexed to the Consumer Price Index
(CPI, prices for goods by urban consumers) instead of wages (CPI-W) or
elderly spending patterns (CPI-E)—which means it has grown more slowly
than traditional social security benefits; and there is no credit granted for
years spent providing caregiving services to dependents. Important reforms
for this program, therefore, would be lowering the yearly threshold of
income necessary to qualify, and raising retirement benefits to be at least
over the poverty line upon retirement. Adjusting benefits to the CPI-W, or
even better the CPI-E, as well as awarding time spent in caregiving as qualifying "work" time, would also do much to help women after a gray divorce.

Reforming Health Care

The economic gray divorce penalty for women also emerges in the arena of
health care. In this study, most women were lucky enough to have health
care insurance, but lacked long-term care protection. Other women in the
general population are not as fortunate in terms of even holding basic
health insurance policies. To help all women across the income spectrum,
we must first recognize that women live longer than men and also tend to
marry men who are older than them. These facts mean that many women
will live alone in their later years of life. Why does this matter? Older
women tend to have health issues that are more debilitating and require
more assistance over longer periods of time than those facing older men.[20]
More specifically, while men tend to face acute health problems, women

are more likely to confront chronic health conditions as they age, such as cognitive problems and dementia. Health care insurance is thus incredibly important for women as they enter their retirement years.

The need for health care policy reforms for women, especially those who have experienced a gray divorce, cannot be overstated. For those women who are still working and are under the age of 65, the Patient Protection and Affordable Care Act (PPACA) has promised to provide more choices with respect to health care and remove them from dependence on their husbands' policies. This is extremely urgent because, as stated earlier, some research suggests that women actually end up putting off a divorce because they do not want to lose their health care coverage.[21] These women could be living in toxic or otherwise abusive relationships. Other research suggests that women who do go forward with their divorce experience gaps in coverage after their marital breakdowns, and those women with the least education often have to either turn to public programs like Medicaid or remain uninsured.[22] Moreover, those who completely lose coverage can remain uninsured not just for the short term but for many years after their divorces.[23]

By establishing new health care markets in the states, the Obama Administration aimed to encourage competition among insurance companies and drive down health care costs. In addition, the PPACA offered tax credits and subsidies to help people without insurance obtain it, and encouraged states to expand their Medicaid income eligibility rules. It is too early to see the true effects of these changes, but for many women, health care costs remain much too high. Tax credits and subsidies must be reexamined to make sure that they are covering the true costs of these private policies. In addition, states that have not expanded their Medicaid programs by raising qualifying income thresholds should do so. This last safety net needs to be firmly in place for the thousands of women whose lives depend on it.

For long-term care, the PPACA set in motion incentives for states to do more to provide home-based and community-based health services rather than expensive institutional care.[24] These more localized initiatives would help women experiencing a gray divorce with more options for affordable care. These options include strengthening the Money Follows the Person Program (MFP), which aims to modify state laws regarding where Medicaid money must be spent. More specifically, the program eliminates Medicaid rules and regulations that permit money only to be used in long-term care institutions, rather than in homes and communities. The Balancing Incentive Program (BIP), introduced with the passage of the PPACA, offers increased financial assistance to those states that reported spending less than 50% of their Medicaid long-term care services and supports on home and community-based care. The central goal here was to encourage states to rebalance their portfolios away from institutional recipients. Also authorized under the PPACA was the Community First Choice program (CFC), which provides states with increased federal financial support to fund direct care professionals aiding those needing health assistance in noninstitutionalized settings. Most notable about this program is the level of power it provides beneficiaries in hiring and retaining attendants for their own care.

Another critical model of health care delivery services created at the same time as the PPACA was the Community Living Assistance Services and Supports program (CLASS Act). Originally designed as a national, voluntary insurance program, CLASS's goal was to provide cash benefits to adults with a variety of functional or cognitive limits. In order to receive benefits, individuals would have to pay into the program for five years and be working for at least three of these five years. Covered services would emphasize independent living, including home care and community-based care. For those whose needs were greater, the benefits could also be accessed to pay for assisted living and nursing home facilities. Because of the contentious nature of the politics surrounding the passage of the PPACA, however, the CLASS Act was never implemented and Congress even later repealed it. However, this program could serve as a viable model for future initiatives in thinking about structuring long-term care services. An important modification for women in general, including those experiencing a gray divorce, is that in determining eligibility, caregiving must be considered as paid work.

MEN AND THE SOCIAL GRAY DIVORCE PENALTY

As this book has demonstrated, it is not just women who suffer from a mid-life marital breakdown. Indeed, men pay a higher social gray divorce penalty than women. The social divorce penalty can be punishing indeed. Men can lose close friends, especially if their wives were responsible for organizing and maintaining social events that brought them all together while they were married. Men who had important, meaningful ties with adult family members also might find these linkages weakened as they move from the separation stage through the final divorce settlement. Perhaps most devastating for these men are the relationships that can become strained with their mostly adult children. For a variety of reasons, including which parent did the most carework during the marriage, as well as socialization and cultural practices, children are more likely to remain closer to their mothers than to their fathers after a gray divorce. When all of these factors are considered together, not only do men experiencing a gray divorce frequently find themselves with fewer people in whom to confide about their emotional upheavals, but they also lose contact with those who are most likely to provide them with material and health-related support at a time when they need it the most.

What can be done to help men retain strong social supports in the wake of a gray divorce? Divorce support groups can be an excellent starting point.[25] Men at this stage in their lives need more effective ways to deal with the isolation that comes with a marital breakdown.[26] Unfortunately, very few divorce support groups are designed specifically for those undergoing a gray divorce.[27] And to the extent that men's needs have been investigated at all, most research has focused on the younger, male or female experience. Still, we can learn much from a variety of religious, nonprofit, union-based, employer, and other organizations that offer these broader-based support groups.

Most of these groups are run at the local level and are shaped by community needs. For example, Visions Anew, located in Georgia, runs ongoing groups and retreats for women only, but also holds educational seminars on the divorce process that are open to both sexes. DivorceCare, rooted in the Christian faith, holds meetings across the country and interweaves biblical teachings into its program.[28] It offers 13-week programs featuring videos focusing on a different topic each week, such as facing loneliness and forgiveness; the rest of each session focuses on personal sharing. Catholic Divorce Ministries is a similar program, grounded in the Roman Catholic faith tradition.[29] With a multistate presence, these groups encourage personal healing and self-forgiveness from the Catholic perspective. Organizations representing other faiths are also offering groups in many cities across the country. In summary, all of these groups promise to be useful for individuals as they grapple with the interpersonal relationship challenges that they face as they begin their new, single lives.

In many cases, these groups are mixed-sex groups run by trained facilitators; however, men-only and women-only groups also do exist. Usually groups are split into those for people whose divorce is still pending and those who are already divorced. Facilitators can bring up multiple topics for discussion.[30] They may ask participants to address the root causes of their divorce, and what effect the divorce has had on their families and friends. Groups also often bring in lawyers to summarize key decisions that couples must make regarding their settlements, and how to address ongoing legal problems after a divorce has been granted. Group participants also often talk to one another about their feelings, including how they are experiencing anger, guilt, and shame. Finally, these groups are important places for men and women to vocalize their concerns about entering new stages in their lives, including expressing their fears and concerns about dating.

Research indicates that many participants find the support group experience useful because it makes them feel less alone at this often-lonely stage in their lives.[31] In many ways, this is the most important advantage over individual therapy. That is, in a group setting participants are constantly giving and receiving feedback from many people rather than just with a therapist. This interactive dynamic can empower participants and improve self-esteem.[32] Other benefits from the group experience can be an enhanced trust of others, forgiveness toward ex-partners, and more self-confidence as participants journey through their daily lives.[33]

The catharsis provided by the group setting may be particularly helpful for men.[34] Catharsis in this context means an ability and place to share one's feelings and be heard. These groups are often so important to men because, while married, men tend to rely on their wives as their primary emotional confidantes. After a separation and a divorce, men have fewer resources upon which to draw for emotional support; this is the critical moment when the support group steps in to provide that service.

Most importantly for the analysis presented throughout this book, some research has suggested that individuals with weak or moderate social networks, and those most likely to be afflicted by isolation after a divorce, experience the most significant benefits from support group participation.[35] Benefits include healthy, postdivorce emotional adjustment, as well as new friendships with other group members. Studies show that if members keep returning to group meetings on a regular basis, and especially if these groups have a smaller set of members, participants will develop more long-standing and deeper friendships within the group than those who are less committed to attending.[36] These groups, therefore, serve an essential function by enlarging networks of support for people who need it the most: more isolated and vulnerable men.[37]

How can divorce support groups best be structured to help men undergoing a gray divorce? First, the number of people in the group might be particularly important. On this point, research has suggested that groups with eight or more men might not be as effective as more limited groups in helping men recover from divorce. Perhaps the most straightforward interpretation of this finding is that men are more comfortable discussing their feelings in smaller groups rather than in larger groups.[38] A second important component of successful support groups for men experiencing a gray divorce is the gender composition of the group. One notable characteristic of divorce support groups is that they tend to disproportionately attract women. This can make the men in the group feel hesitant to share their points of view.[39] Men-only groups might therefore be helpful here. Third, the strength of the groups' leadership is also important.[40] In this context, a strong leader is one who not only manages time effectively for each member's maximum benefit, but also offers appropriate guidance based on the leader's knowledge of the problems being discussed, experience in dealing with these problems, and history of empathizing with members and offering them hope. Due to cultural socialization practices, men in particular might respond more positively to leaders with a direct feedback style, which is a more familiar type of interaction to them in their everyday world.

As mentioned earlier, private and nonprofit organizations offer many divorce support group options. However, few, if any, focus on men undergoing a gray divorce. In order to facilitate this population's journey of healing, there must be louder and more effective messaging statements from strong, public institutions that amplify the need for self-help initiatives among these men. Currently, there are no support group models that exist on the local, state, and federal governmental levels to address potential social network losses—comprising friends, adult family members, and mostly adult children—for men experiencing a gray divorce. Interestingly, however, the federal government *has* been involved in programming related to promoting positive relationships for men under certain other social conditions. For example, within the context of the Department of Health and Human Services (DHHS), the Responsible Fatherhood Demonstration Grants offer money to organizations that help strengthen marriages, teach men the importance of parenting skills, and provide job and career services.[41] In addition, the National Responsible Fatherhood Clearinghouse crafts courses, factsheets, webinars, and information about specific tools that fathers can acquire to be more active, positive role models in their children's lives.[42]

As the descriptions of these mostly parent-child programs suggest, the focus of these initiatives is on fathers who are married, have young children, and face economic disadvantages. However, as this book has documented, mid-life, divorced fathers with older children—including adult children— and more-advantaged fathers also need assistance in the case of a family breakdown. Two additional recommendations, then, are particularly important here. First, DHHS should consider funding new support groups that would focus on helping older, divorcing men, regardless of income, with the skills that they need to prevent all types of social network losses (adult and child) that might emerge after such a life-changing event. Second, the National Responsible Fatherhood Clearinghouse should expand its purview to include providing resources to assist men experiencing a gray divorce in connecting specifically with their older children. Both of these recommendations would involve pooling together the knowledge of psychologists, social workers, and educators about the specific needs of this particular population. Since an established infrastructure for other fathers has already been built within DHHS, this is definitely an attainable goal.

MOVING FORWARD TOGETHER: HELP FOR BOTH MEN AND WOMEN

Finally, it is important to note that although each sex faces its own set of distinctive gray divorce penalties, the policy recommendations offered here for women have the potential to help men, and vice versa. Raising the social security benefit level as well as adjusting it appropriately for inflation can help strengthen the economic well-being of both sexes. Improving health care coverage through an expansion of the Medicaid program across all of the fifty states, as well as liberalizing health care insurance tax credits and subsidies, will assist all older Americans across the board in achieving necessary health care. Major reforms to make the long-term health care insurance market more affordable are also extremely important. Lastly, governmental funding of a variety of support groups and informational resources for men experiencing a gray divorce has the potential to assist both sexes in recovering from and adjusting to their marital splits as men learn to cope more effectively.[43]

One additional governmental resource that could be critical to both sexes experiencing a gray divorce is the Administration on Aging (AoA), which operates under the auspices of the DHHS. This agency began in 1965 with the passage of the Older Americans Act. The primary mission of the AoA is to protect the well-being of older Americans, especially as it pertains to their ability to live independently and with dignity as they age. The agency directly provides funds to states so that they can achieve these goals. While the AoA as it is currently structured does not single out divorcing individuals as a distinct clientele group, it certainly can tailor its infrastructure and programming to harness its unique potential to address the concerns of all individuals going through a gray divorce.

On this point, the AoA is organized into multiple offices designed to provide a well-defined set of services for the aging population. First, the Office of Supportive and Caregiver Services offers a constellation of resources for those needing transportation, day care, and caregiver assistance. Second, the Office of Nutrition and Health Promotion Programs delivers a set of health-related prevention initiatives and other wellness programs for older Americans. Efforts here cover an enormous array of physical and mental health needs, such as chronic disease management programs, diabetes management education, falls prevention programs, nutrition information, behavioral health education, HIV/AIDS education, oral health programs, and other related initiatives. Third, the Office of Elder Justice and Adult Protective Services runs a well-established system for individuals to prevent, report, and respond to adult abuse events.

Fourth, the Long-Term Care Ombudsman Program, begun as a demonstration project in 1972, supports state-based, long-term care officials to help those who need long-term care as well as their loved ones who are trying to locate such care. Fifth, the AoA provides financial support and guidance for state agencies on aging, which in turn fund a whole host of services for older Americans at the local level.

Overall, the AoA has developed a strong safety net of programs that work to protect the well-being and health of older Americans. These initiatives are particularly important to those experiencing a gray divorce because those who do not remarry or repartner, or even those who do and their new spouses die or require medical assistance, often have considerable needs in these areas. Throughout this book, we have demonstrated that women face a severe economic gray divorce penalty in that they are less likely to be as financially secure as their male counterparts. In addition, women live much longer than men. Even if they have the social support of their families, health assistance requires monetary resources, many times over the long term. The AoA in this case might be able to offer a strong package of information and referrals to low-cost service providers that are within the reach of these vulnerable women.

For men, the need for AoA services is no less great. While they are more likely to have stronger financial resources than their female counterparts, as this book has demonstrated, they are less likely to possess solid social supports. Because they face a social gray divorce penalty, men are more likely to encounter a treacherous and lonely road ahead with respect to their own health care needs. Recall that men are much more likely to lose friends and contacts with adult family members after a gray divorce. The most devastating loss for men, however, relates to the diminished connections with their mostly adult children. As parents age, adult children typically provide unpaid caregiving labor or set up paraprofessional or professional care if these needs intensify. If there is a relationship breach, however, these men have to fend for themselves. The AoA can help fill this gap.

Currently, however, the AoA does not specifically address the growing numbers of Americans who have been or will be involved in a gray divorce. Instead, the AoA provides grants and funds to the states and other eligible organizations based on the number of people who are either 60 years of age or older or, in other cases, 70 years old or older. Only using these age-based metrics to allocate resources, however, is not enough. Instead, the AoA should also determine the percentage of these older population groups within each state that have experienced a gray divorce. Knowing these statistics could help in budgeting across program areas. For example, states with a higher percentage of women who have experienced a gray divorce might direct more resources toward caregiver support. Women typically have stronger networks of friends and family willing to offer such personal assistance, but these caregivers will also need respite from these tasks. Moreover, since women who have experienced a gray divorce are more likely to be financially insecure than their male counterparts, ombudsmen programs for long-term care, especially for women receiving Medicaid to cover these costs, might be particularly helpful. Men who have experienced a gray divorce, on the other hand, are more likely to have financial resources to pay for care, but are less likely to have family and friends providing unpaid care. If they are isolated in nursing homes without visitors, or are receiving purchased care at home, they might be more vulnerable to abuse. States with higher percentages of men experiencing a gray divorce, therefore, might direct resources toward these programs.

BEYOND THE GRAY DIVORCE

Of course, policy change does not come easily in American politics, but the reforms described in this chapter might have a greater-than-average chance for success for the Baby Boomer generation and beyond. First of all, the sheer size of the older American population—including those experiencing a gray divorce—makes its members politically powerful. Each individual has a vote and can exert power in electing officials to represent his/her needs. Second, mid-life and older Americans can flex their political muscle through interest groups like the AARP (formerly the American Association of Retired Persons), the National Council of Senior Citizens, and the National Committee to Preserve Social Security and Medicare. While these organizations often avoid taking positions that might alienate part of their membership, the policy reforms suggested here are not extremely controversial. Third, society in general tends to view mid-life adults as deserving of public assistance. They have lived large parts of their lives as contributing members of society, the reasoning goes, and society in turn should now play a role in protecting their futures going forward.

With these types of public supports in place, gray divorce need not represent the devastating end of two people's lives. While we all hope for "happily ever afters" when it comes to older couples, the reality is that this might not be possible. If a couple's marital relationship has irretrievably broken down, they are no longer duty-bound legally or culturally to remain together until death. True, divorcing people must often work through grief, disappointment, and pain. Then women must predominantly reckon with a difficult economic gray divorce penalty, while men must sort through a harsh social divorce penalty. Still, there is every chance that in the not-so-distant future, each can not only put their lives back together again, but also can embark on a promising new road of happiness and self-fulfillment going into the future.

Data Appendix

BY MARC D. WEINER, JD, PHD

for Jocelyn Elise Crowley

The first challenge of this qualitative research project to investigate mid-life divorce (divorce at or over 50 years old) was to recruit a pool of qualified respondents from which to secure 80 interview subjects—40 men and 40 women—from across the United States. Although mid-life divorce is increasingly common—approximately one in four of all divorces now occurs among this age group—the incidence rate of individuals within the general population meeting these criteria is still so small that traditional recruitment methods are cost-prohibitive.

Simply put, the threshold challenge to conducting the personal interviews that inform this work was locating an adequate number of qualified respondents. A respondent "qualified" for participation as an interview subject if she/he met the following criteria:

1. she/he is 50 years of age or older;
2. she/he is divorced, with the divorce (whether a first, second, or later divorce) having taken place at or after the age of 50; and
3. she/he is English-speaking.

In addition, while our sample region was limited by design to the United States, we wanted to assure some geographic diversity within that framework. Because of the relative uniqueness of individual members of the mid-life divorce group in the general population, they are members of a hard-to-sample subpopulation; indeed, given the relative infrequency of a qualifying member, this subpopulation may be further characterized as hard-to-identify.

The traditional approaches to this kind of recruitment involve either advertising and promotions to stimulate potential respondents to contact the researcher and volunteer to participate, or engaging in some sort of survey-like effort—whether by telephone or mail—to reach out on a one-on-one basis, with a screener questionnaire to identify persons "hidden" within the general population who would qualify as respondents.[1] We explored some of these traditional approaches; for example, we investigated posting recruiting notices—in effect, advertising in various magazines, particularly *AARP the Magazine*—but at the national level, that approach was cost-prohibitive. Similarly, the posting—in geographically diverse locations nationally—of recruiting notices involved an extensive protocol of locating appropriate spots in various and diverse regions of the country and coordinating contacts at those locations. This, we concluded, was beyond the cost capacity of the project, as well as beyond the level of recruitment protocol complexity and control with which we felt comfortable. Telephone and mail outreach efforts were also too expensive. Thus, we realized that we would have to move beyond traditional approaches to gather enough qualified respondents to constitute an adequate sample from which to complete 80 personal interviews.

Recent academic research has shown that social networking facilitates new ways of contacting hard-to-reach populations.[2] Facebook provides previously unimaginable cost-effective ways to connect with the hard-to-reach. So, with limited resources and the need for microtargeting, we turned to Facebook, where, within 13 days over four waves, we recruited 178 presumptively qualified respondents at an average cost of $1.18 per respondent, for a total recruitment cost of $210.04. That total cost is calculated as a function of the number of times the recruitment advertisement is clicked multiplied by the cost per click. The cost per click varies based on Facebook's charging criteria for delivering the content; in our case, it ranged from a high of $0.21 per click for the first (and largest) wave, to a low of $0.09 per click, for the third wave of men only. Across all four waves, the advertisement was "served," that is, displayed, to 25,183 Facebook users' pages, who altogether clicked a total of 1,325 times at a mean cost of $0.15852 per click.

We specified the characteristics of Facebook users who would be shown our solicitation, as well as the location, on the page, that the solicitation would appear. The person-characteristics for the group who would be shown our solicitation were basic: persons 50 years of age or older and living within the United States. For page or news feed location, if the user were on a mobile device, we opted to have the solicitation appear on an individual's news feed; if the user were on a desktop, we directed it to appear either in the news feed or in the right column of the page.

The Facebook recruitment notice carried a headline of "Study of Mid-Life Divorce," the logo for The Edward J. Bloustein School of Planning and Public Policy at Rutgers, The State University of New Jersey, and companion text that read, "Rutgers Professor seeks volunteers for study on divorce experienced at age

50 or older." This was matched with a news feed link description that read, "If you had a divorce at or after 50 years old, and would like to participate in this interesting academic study, please click the link to learn more about the project."

Once the potential respondent clicked on the Facebook ad, she/he was redirected to a web survey screener we administered directly. That web-survey screener presented the following introductory text:

> My name is Jocelyn Elise Crowley and I am a Professor of Public Policy at the Edward J. Bloustein School of Planning and Public Policy at Rutgers, The State University of New Jersey. Thank you for your interest in participating in this study. I am studying the experiences of women and men who divorced at or after the age of 50. To do so, I am asking for volunteers, who divorced at or after the age of 50, to participate with me in a one-hour telephone interview. This project is fully confidential, and has been approved by the Rutgers University Institutional Review Board. Confidential means you will not be identified in any resulting publications or reports that come from my research and that no one will ever know that you participated. However, to schedule your interview at a convenient time for you, I will need to contact you. So that I can do so, kindly provide the following information.

At that point, the respondent was asked, "Did you divorce when you were 50 years of age or older?" Those who answered "no" were thanked for their willingness to participate but told that to be eligible for this study, each individual must have had a divorce at or after the age of 50. Those who answered "yes" were then asked for their first and last names, their sex, and their preferred email address and telephone number, along with a request to identify the best day of the week and time of day to have the one-hour interview. Following those few screening questions, the respondent was thanked for agreeing to be part of the study and advised that the principal investigator would contact her/him over the next few weeks to schedule the telephone interview. The interviewee was then invited to contact the researcher by email if she or he had any questions. During this screening review, 11 of the 178 presumptively qualified respondents in the pool either failed one of the screening questions or dropped out, and the original count was winnowed down to 167, from which we successfully selected and conducted one-hour telephone interviews with 80 qualified respondents.

All told, between July 23, 2014, and February 9, 2015, we conducted four waves of Facebook recruitment postings; initially, our intention was to complete a total of 60 interviews, 30 with each sex. Thus, for the first two recruitment events, we accepted both men and women. After completing the thirtieth female interview, however, we realized that we still had more to learn, that is, we had not reached data saturation, defined as a drop-off in "new" content in later interviews.[3] In other words, when approaching our goal of 60 interviews, we realized that the number was too low to learn the full scope of experiences related to midlife divorce. In turn, we expanded the total number of interviews to 80, with 40 for each sex. We then went back to the Facebook recruitment protocol twice

Data Appendix Table
SURVEY RECRUITMENT AND RESULTS

	Wave 1 7/23 to 7/28/14		Wave 2 8/19 to 8/21/14		Wave 3 1/5 to 1/6/15	Wave 4 2/6 to 2/7/15	Totals	
	MEN	WOMEN	MEN	WOMEN	MEN ONLY	WOMEN ONLY	MEN	WOM-EN
Names Collected	21	38	6	34	46	22	73	94
Interviews Completed	12	21	5	9	23	10	40	40
Incomplete: Not Qualified	2		1		2	0	5	
Incomplete: No Response	20		8		13	4	45	
Incomplete: No Show	1		0		1	1	3	
Incomplete: Declined	3		0		0	1	4	
Incomplete: Not Available	0		0		1	0.	1	
Incomplete: Bad Contact Information	0		0		1	0	1	
Incomplete: Set Aside per Initial Goal	0		17 Women		5	6	28	

more, with the third round focusing on men, and the fourth similarly focused on women. More specifically, the detailed disposition of each round is found in the data appendix table.

As a natural function of the pervasiveness of social media in general, and Facebook in particular, we were able to easily capture wide geographic diversity. The data appendix map indicates locations for each of the qualified respondents.

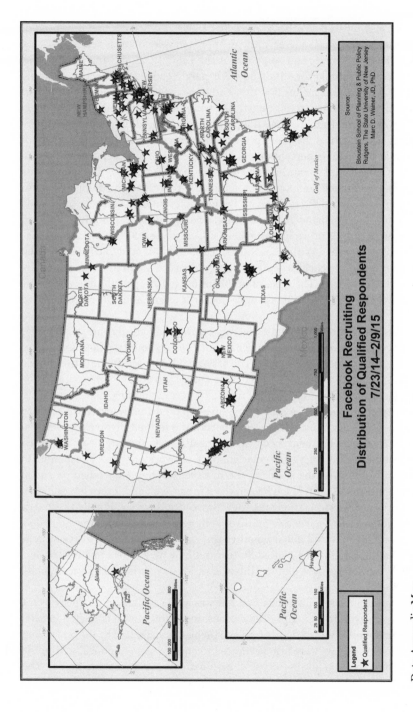

Facebook Recruiting
Distribution of Qualified Respondents
7/23/14–2/9/15

Source:

Bloustein School of Planning & Public Policy
Rutgers, The State University of New Jersey
Marc D. Weiner, JD, PhD

Legend

★ Qualified Respondent

Data Appendix Map

To be sure, compared to other approaches, the cost-efficiency and the speed of completion of the Facebook recruitment approach were impressive.

It is, however, important to point out the limitations of using Facebook in recruiting the sample for this study. All participants self-selected into this research project. This means that they had to be members of Facebook and had to have a strong desire to tell the stories behind their divorces. Perhaps their stories were more dramatic than nonparticipants. In addition, on average, participants had divorced 2.4 years prior to their interviews. With the passage of additional time, their perceptions of their own divorces might be subject to change. Overall, and as outlined in chapter 1 (and in table 4), this sample was relatively advantaged compared to a nationally representative sample of those who have experienced a gray divorce.[4] For example, in terms of race, while in this study over 91% of respondents were white, a nationally representative sample of this population in 2010 would have been 69.4% white, 15.2% Black, 9.7% Hispanic, and 5.8% other. With respect to education, in this study, about 63% of the respondents had a bachelor's degree or more, versus 24.4% in the same nationally representative sample. The types of problems as well as opportunities are therefore likely to be different in this sample than in a more nationally representative one.

In terms of content, beyond collecting basic sociodemographic information from all respondents as described in chapter 1, the one-hour telephone interviews comprised four major topical areas. The first module focused on the cause of their gray divorces. In this module, interviewees were asked about their marital histories, the reasons behind their splits, their efforts at counseling, and their dating and remarriage plans. The second module explored their current and future financial prospects. It asked questions pertaining to their divorce settlements, alimony awards, retirement incomes, and health insurance statuses. The third module inquired about their social support networks. It asked respondents about who supported them during the divorce, whether they relied on social media for assistance, if religion helped them in any way, and if they felt as if they were victims of discrimination once they divorced at their age. Finally, the fourth module focused on their views on divorce in general and their hopes for their future lives. It inquired about whether they believed that the divorce system should be reformed in the United States, and how they were adjusting to their new lives on their own. All of the interviews were recorded and professionally transcribed.

In analyzing these data, each interview was read multiple times. The relevant literature on gray divorce suggested various sensitizing concepts related to each topical module.[5] While anticipating some themes as suggested by the sensitizing concepts, new themes were also permitted to emerge more organically from the data. This is a commonly used type of modified grounded theory analysis.[6] The qualitative software program Atlas.ti was then employed to approach the data with standard open coding procedures and group answers by theme. To count as a significant theme in the tables, over five of the 40 male respondents or over five of the 40 female respondents (over 12.5% of each group) had to identify it as such. Actual quotations are offered from these interviews as embodied by the concept of "thick description"; this allows those undergoing a gray divorce to use their own words to define the importance of this significant transition in their daily lives.[7]

GRAY DIVORCE INTERVIEW PROTOCOL

i. Divorce Summary

1. How many times have you been divorced? Are there any children from any of these marriages or relationships?
2. In what year was your divorce finalized? How many years did that marriage last?
3. How old were you when you got married and how old was your spouse?
4. How many years did you date before you married, and did you live together before getting married?
5. Who initiated the divorce and why? Would your ex-spouse agree with this account of why you got divorced? How did you try to work things out before the divorce was initiated?
6. Did the feelings of your children (and the ones from previous relationships/marriages) influence your decision to divorce or try to work things out? If so, how?
7. After this divorce, were you interested in dating again right away? How did you find people to date? Did you try online dating websites? What type of person were you looking for? [If you were not interested in dating, why not?]
8. Are you currently remarried? If so, what made you want to get married again? [If you are not now currently married, would you consider remarrying again? Why or why not?]

ii. Finances and Health

1. I am interested in your paid employment history around the time of your most recent divorce. Can you tell me what type of job, if any, you had right before the divorce and what you did after the divorce, including possibly retire, retrain, or stay in the same job? At the time of your divorce, what kind of job did your partner have? Did he/she stay in that job?
2. Did you have any concerns about alimony when you were going through your most recent divorce? If so, what were they? If not, why not?
3. Did you have any concerns about property and asset division when you were going through your divorce? If so, what were they? If not, why not?
4. Do you have a pension plan or 401(k) right now? Do you have any concerns about paying for your future retirement? Do you think your ex-spouse has concerns about paying for his/her retirement? Why or why not?
5. Do you currently have health insurance? If so, is it through an employer or

through some other means? [If not, why not?] What about your potential long term health care needs, such as nursing home care? Who will care for you? Do you think your ex-spouse has concerns about his/her health care needs and paying for them? Why or why not?

iii. Networks of Support

1. Who offered you the most emotional support at the time of the divorce? What kind of support did they offer? Did you feel that any friends, adult family members and children "took sides" during the divorce? If so, how so?
2. Did electronic and social media, like email, chatrooms, Facebook, Twitter, or online support groups help you cope in your divorce? If so, how? If not, why not?
3. When you got married, did you believe that your marriage had a religious or spiritual component? If so, how? When the marriage ended, did you become more religious, less religious, or the same? Please explain.
4. Some people say that society looks down on or treats people who divorce at or after the age of 50 in a negative way. Do you feel that people who are divorced at age 50 and over face some type of negative treatment? If so, how so? If so, do you think it is worse for men or for women? Have you ever personally experienced any negative treatment due to your most recent divorce? If so, how?

iv. Public Policy and Future Prospects

1. Do you think divorce should be easier or more difficult to obtain in the United States? Why should it be easier or more difficult?
2. Is there any type of reform regarding the court system—including the behavior/ actions of lawyers and judges—that you would recommend regarding divorce cases?
3. What is the worst part about being divorced this last time? The best part?

Notes

CHAPTER 1

1. Page 735: Brown, Susan L., and I-Fen Lin. "The Gray Divorce Revolution: Rising Divorce among Middle-Aged and Older Adults, 1990–2010." *The Journals of Gerontology Series B: Psychological Sciences and Social Sciences* 67, no. 6 (2012): 731–41.

2. Ibid.; www.pewresearch.org/fact-tank/2017/03/09/led-by-baby-boomers-divorce-rates-climb-for-americas-50-population/.

3. Uhlenberg, Peter, Teresa Cooney, and Robert Boyd. "Divorce for Women after Midlife." *Journal of Gerontology* 45, no. 1 (1990): S3–S11; Uhlenberg, Peter, and Mary Anne P. Myers. "Divorce and the Elderly." *The Gerontologist* 21, no. 3 (1981): 276–82; Wu, Zheng, and Christoph M. Schimmele. "Uncoupling in Late Life." *Generations* 31, no. 3 (2007): 41–46.

4. Whitehead, Barbara Dafoe. *The Divorce Culture.* New York: Knopf, 1997.

5. Wu and Schimmele, "Uncoupling in Late Life."

6. "National Vital Statistics Report (NVSR), Deaths: Final Data for 2014." United States Centers for Disease Control and Prevention, 2016.

7. Of course, living together is another option for these adults. See Brown, Susan L., Jennifer Roebuck Bulanda, and Gary R. Lee. "Transitions into and out of Cohabitation in Later Life." *Journal of Marriage and Family* 74, no. 4 (2012): 774–93; Vespa, Jonathan. "Union Formation in Later Life: Economic Determinants of

Cohabitation and Remarriage among Older Adults." *Demography* 49, no. 3 (2012): 1103–25.

8. Cherlin, Andrew J. *The Marriage-Go-Round: The State of Marriage and the Family in America Today.* New York: Knopf, 2009.

9. Uhlenberg and Myers, "Divorce and the Elderly."

10. Shehan, Constance L., Felix M. Berardo, Erica Owens, and Donna H. Berardo. "Alimony: An Anomaly in Family Social Science." *Family Relations* 51, no. 4 (2002): 308–16.

11. Katz, Sanford N. "Historical Perspective and Current Trends in the Legal Process of Divorce." *The Future of Children* 4, no. 1 (1994): 44–62.

12. Welch, Charles E., III, and Sharon Price-Bonham. "A Decade of No-Fault Divorce Revisited: California, Georgia, and Washington." *Journal of Marriage and Family* 45, no. 2 (1983): 411–18.

13. Table 2: BLS. "Women in the Labor Force: A Databook." Washington, DC: US Bureau of Labor Statistics, 2015.

14. Table 7: ibid.

15. Table 7: ibid.

16. Table 25: ibid.

17. Table 16: ibid.

18. Bair, Deirdre. *Calling It Quits: Late-Life Divorce and Starting Over.* New York: Random House, 2007.

19. Census. *Current Population Survey, March and Annual Social and Economic Supplements, 2014 and Earlier.* 2014.

20. Crowley, Jocelyn Elise. *Mothers Unite! Organizing for Workplace Flexibility and the Transformation of Family Life.* Ithaca: Cornell University Press, 2013.

21. Amato, Paul R. "Research on Divorce: Continuing Trends and New Developments." *Journal of Marriage and Family* 72, no. 3 (2010): 650–66; Teachman, Jay. "Wives' Economic Resources and Risk of Divorce." *Journal of Family Issues* 31, no. 10 (2010): 1305–23.

22. Medicare has four parts. Part A covers the cost of hospital stays, while Part B offers outpatient medical coverage for an additional premium. Part C (Medicare Advantage) combines and adds to the coverage of Parts A and B, and can be packaged at times with Part D, which provides prescription drug coverage for a designated premium. In other words, Medicare Advantage plans contract with the government to offer traditional Medicare services. Medicare Advantage plans can be run by health maintenance organizations (HMOs) and preferred provider organizations (PPOs), for example. For those who can afford them, there are also supplementary policies that can be carried over through employment or bought in the health insurance market. Those that can be purchased are called Medigap policies; for a monthly premium, the policies pick up some of these costs that traditional Medicare does not cover under Parts A and B.

Medigap policies, however, do not cover prescription drugs. Moreover, individuals cannot hold Medigap and Medicare Advantage plan coverage at the same time; in addition, in both types of plans, individuals must still pay monthly premiums for Medicare Part B.

23. Sohn, Heeju. "Health Insurance and Risk of Divorce: Does Having Your Own Insurance Matter?" *Journal of Marriage and Family* 77, no. 4 (2015): 982–95.

24. Peters, Elizabeth H., Kosali Simon, and Jamie Rubenstein Taber. "Marital Disruption and Health Insurance." *Demography* 51, no. 4 (2014): 1397–421.

25. Lavelle, Bridget, and Pamela J. Smock. "Divorce and Women's Risk of Health Insurance Loss." *Journal of Health and Social Behavior* 53, no. 4 (2012): 413–31.

26. Brown, Jeffrey R., and Amy Finkelstein. "The Private Market for Long-Term Care Insurance in the United States: A Review of the Evidence." *Journal of Risk and Insurance* 76, no. 1 (2009): 5–29.

27. Brown, Jeffrey R., and Amy Finkelstein. "Why Is the Market for Long-Term Care Insurance So Small?" *Journal of Public Economics* 91, no. 10 (2007): 1967–91.

28. Curry, Leslie A., Julie Robison, Noreen Shugrue, Patricia Keenan, and Marshall B. Kapp. "Individual Decision Making in the Non-Purchase of Long-Term Care Insurance." *The Gerontologist* 49, no. 4 (2009): 560–69.

29. Page 10 on data from 2000: Brown and Finkelstein, "The Private Market for Long-Term Care."

30. Levy, Donald P. "Hegemonic Complicity, Friendship, and Comradeship: Validation and Causal Processes among White, Middle-Class, Middle-Aged Men." *The Journal of Men's Studies* 13, no. 2 (2005): 199–224.

31. Cooney, Teresa M., and Kathleen Dunne. "Intimate Relationships in Later Life Current Realities, Future Prospects." *Journal of Family Issues* 22, no. 7 (2001): 838–58.

32. Damaske, Sarah. *For the Family? How Class and Gender Shape Women's Work.* Oxford: Oxford University Press, 2011; Crowley, *Mothers Unite!;* Stone, Pamela. *Opting Out? Why Women Really Quit Careers and Head Home.* Berkeley: University of California Press, 2007.

33. Troilo, Jessica, and Marilyn Coleman. "Full-Time, Part-Time Full-Time, and Part-Time Fathers: Father Identities Following Divorce." *Family Relations* 61, no. 4 (2012): 601–14; Amato, Paul R., Catherine E. Meyers, and Robert E. Emery. "Changes in Nonresident Father-Child Contact from 1976 to 2002." *Family Relations* 58, no. 1 (2009): 41–53.

34. Brown and Lin, "The Gray Divorce Revolution."

35. See ibid.

36. Burstein, Nancy R. "Economic Influences on Marriage and Divorce." *Journal of Policy Analysis and Management* 26, no. 2 (2007): 387–429.

CHAPTER 2

1. Amato, Paul R. "Research on Divorce: Continuing Trends and New Developments." *Journal of Marriage and Family* 72, no. 3 (2010): 650–66; Amato, Paul R., and Danelle D. DeBoer. "The Transmission of Marital Instability across Generations: Relationship Skills or Commitment to Marriage?" *Journal of Marriage and Family* 63, no. 4 (2001): 1038–51; Teachman, Jay D. "Stability across Cohorts in Divorce Risk Factors." *Demography* 39, no. 2 (2002): 331–51; Martin, Steven P. "Trends in Marital Dissolution by Women's Education in the United States." *Demographic Research* 15, no. 20 (2006): 537–60.

2. Teachman, "Stability across Cohorts in Divorce Risk Factors"; Sweeney, Megan M., and Julie A. Phillips. "Understanding Racial Differences in Marital Disruption: Recent Trends and Explanations." *Journal of Marriage and Family* 66, no. 3 (2004): 639–50.

3. Amato, "Research on Divorce."

4. Ibid.

5. Kalmijn, Matthijs, and Anne-Rigt Poortman. "His or Her Divorce? The Gendered Nature of Divorce and Its Determinants." *European Sociological Review* 22, no. 2 (2006): 201–14; Sayer, Liana C., and Suzanne M. Bianchi. "Women's Economic Independence and the Probability of Divorce: A Review and Reexamination." *Journal of Family Issues* 21, no. 7 (2000): 906–43.

6. Rogers, Stacy J. "Dollars, Dependency, and Divorce: Four Perspectives on the Role of Wives' Income." *Journal of Marriage and Family* 66, no. 1 (2004): 59–74; Oppenheimer, Valerie Kincade. "Women's Employment and the Gain to Marriage: The Specialization and Trading Model." *Annual Review of Sociology* 23 (1997): 431–53; Ono, Hiromi. "Husbands' and Wives' Resources and Marital Dissolution." *Journal of Marriage and the Family* 60, no. 3 (1998): 674–89.

7. Teachman, Jay. "Wives' Economic Resources and Risk of Divorce." *Journal of Family Issues* 31, no. 10 (2010): 1305–23; Schoen, Robert, Stacy J. Rogers, and Paul R. Amato. "Wives' Employment and Spouses' Marital Happiness: Assessing the Direction of Influence Using Longitudinal Couple Data." *Journal of Family Issues* 27, no. 4 (2006): 506–28.

8. Sayer, Liana C., Paula England, Paul Allison, and Nicole Kangas. "She Left, He Left: How Employment and Satisfaction Affect Men's and Women's Decisions to Leave Marriages." *American Journal of Sociology* 116, no. 6 (2011): 1982–2018; Sayer and Bianchi, "Women's Economic Independence and the Probability of Divorce."

9. Özcan, Berkay, and Richard Breen. "Marital Instability and Female Labor Supply." *Annual Review of Sociology* 38 (2012): 463–81.

10. Amato, "Research on Divorce"; Bratter, Jenifer L., and Rosalind B. King. "'But Will It Last?': Marital Instability among Interracial and Same-Race

Couples." *Family Relations* 57, no. 2 (2008): 160–71; Teachman, "Stability across Cohorts in Divorce Risk Factors."

11. Clements, Mari L., Scott M. Stanley, and Howard J. Markman. "Before They Said 'I Do': Discriminating among Marital Outcomes over 13 Years." *Journal of Marriage and Family* 66, no. 3 (2004): 613–26; Orbuch, Terri L., Joseph Veroff, Halimah Hassan, and Julie Horrocks. "Who Will Divorce: A 14-Year Longitudinal Study of Black Couples and White Couples." *Journal of Social and Personal Relationships* 19, no. 2 (2002): 179–202.

12. Fincham, Frank D., Scott M. Stanley, and Steven R. H. Beach. "Transformative Processes in Marriage: An Analysis of Emerging Trends." *Journal of Marriage and Family* 69, no. 2 (2007): 275–92.

13. Amato, Paul R., and Bryndl Hohmann-Marriott. "A Comparison of High- and Low-Distress Marriages That End in Divorce." *Journal of Marriage and Family* 69, no. 3 (2007): 621–38; DeMaris, Alfred. "Till Discord Do Us Part: The Role of Physical and Verbal Conflict in Union Disruption." *Journal of Marriage and Family* 62, no. 3 (2000): 683–92.

14. Gottman, John Mordechai, and Robert Wayne Levenson. "The Timing of Divorce: Predicting When a Couple Will Divorce over a 14-Year Period." *Journal of Marriage and Family* 62, no. 3 (2000): 737–45.

15. Previti, Denise, and Paul R. Amato. "Is Infidelity a Cause or a Consequence of Poor Marital Quality?" *Journal of Social and Personal Relationships* 21, no. 2 (2004): 217–30.

16. The studies discussed in this section primarily focus on young couples; however, several of them include as part of their overall samples individuals both under and over the age of 50.

17. Cherlin, Andrew J. *The Marriage-Go-Round: The State of Marriage and the Family in America Today.* New York: Knopf, 2009.

18. Goode, William J. *Women in Divorce.* New York: Free, 1956.

19. Levinger, George. "Sources of Marital Dissatisfaction among Applicants for Divorce." *American Journal of Orthopsychiatry* 36, no. 5 (1966): 803–7.

20. Kitson, Gay C., and Marvin B. Sussman. "Marital Complaints, Demographic Characteristics, and Symptoms of Mental Distress in Divorce." *Journal of Marriage and the Family* 44, no. 1 (1982): 87–101.

21. Cleek, Margaret Guminski, and T. Allan Pearson. "Perceived Causes of Divorce: An Analysis of Interrelationships." *Journal of Marriage and the Family* 47, no. 1 (1985): 179–83; Thurnher, Majda, Cathy Birtley Fenn, Joseph Melichar, and David A. Chiriboga. "Sociodemographic Perspectives on Reasons for Divorce." *Journal of Divorce* 6, no. 4 (1983): 25–35.

22. Amato, Paul R., and Denise Previti. "People's Reasons for Divorcing Gender, Social Class, the Life Course, and Adjustment." *Journal of Family Issues* 24, no. 5 (2003): 602–26.

23. Hawkins, Alan J., Brian J. Willoughby, and William J. Doherty. "Reasons for Divorce and Openness to Marital Reconciliation." *Journal of Divorce & Remarriage* 53, no. 6 (2012): 453–63. ·

24. Canham, Sarah L., Atiya Mahmood, Sarah Stott, Judith Sixsmith, and Norm O'Rourke. "'Til Divorce Do Us Part: Marriage Dissolution in Later Life." *Journal of Divorce & Remarriage* 55, no. 8 (2014): 591–612.

25. Rokach, Rachel, Orna Cohen, and Solly Dreman. "Triggers and Fuses in Late Divorce: The Role of Short Term Crises vs. Ongoing Frustration on Marital Break-Up." *Journal of Divorce & Remarriage* 40, no. 3–4 (2004): 41–60.

26. Montenegro, Xenia P. *The Divorce Experience: A Study of Divorce at Midlife and Beyond.* Washington, DC: AARP, 2004.

27. The AARP study does break down whether each reason is applicable "mostly to me (the respondent)," "mostly to spouse," or "applied equally to both of us." This somewhat vague wording makes attribution difficult.

CHAPTER 3

1. Kemp, Candace L., Carolyn J. Rosenthal, and Margaret Denton. "Financial Planning for Later Life: Subjective Understandings of Catalysts and Constraints." *Journal of Aging Studies* 19, no. 3 (2005): 273–90.

2. Green, Janice. *Divorce after 50.* Berkeley, CA: Nolo, 2010.

3. Ibid.

4. Ibid.

5. Sharma, Andy. "Divorce/Separation in Later-Life: A Fixed Effects Analysis of Economic Effects by Gender." *Journal of Family and Economic Issues* 36, no. 2 (2015): 299–306; Uhlenberg, Peter, Teresa Cooney, and Robert Boyd. "Divorce for Women after Midlife." *Journal of Gerontology* 45, no. 1 (1990): S3–S11.

6. Espenshade, Thomas J. "The Economic Consequences of Divorce." *Journal of Marriage and Family* 41, no. 3 (1979): 615–25; Hoffman, Saul. "Marital Instability and the Economic Status of Women." *Demography* 14, no. 1 (1977): 67–76.

7. Oster, Sharon M. "A Note on the Determinants of Alimony." *Journal of Marriage and Family* 49, no. 1 (1987): 81–86; Katz, Sanford N. "Historical Perspective and Current Trends in the Legal Process of Divorce." *The Future of Children* 4, no. 1 (1994): 44–62.

8. Shehan, Constance L., Felix M. Berardo, Erica Owens, and Donna H. Berardo. "Alimony: An Anomaly in Family Social Science." *Family Relations* 51, no. 4 (2002): 308–16.

9. Ibid.; Katz, "Historical Perspective and Current Trends in the Legal Process of Divorce."

10. Crowley, Jocelyn Elise. "Ambiguous Financial Responsibilities: Second Wives and Alimony Reform Activism in the United States." *Journal of Family Issues* (Forthcoming).

11. Van Oorschot, Marlo. *How to Survive Grey Divorce*. Los Angeles: Law Offices of Marlo Van Oorschot, 2012.

12. Hartmann, Heidi, and Ashley English. "Older Women's Retirement Security: A Primer." *Journal of Women, Politics & Policy* 30, nos. 2–3 (2009): 109–40.

13. Table 2: BLS. "Women in the Labor Force: A Databook." Washington, DC: US Bureau of Labor Statistics, 2015.

14. Table 16: ibid.

15. Tang, Fengyan, Eunhee Choi, and Rachel Goode. "Older Americans Employment and Retirement." *Ageing International* 38, no. 1 (2013): 82–94.

16. O'Rand, Angela M., and Kim M. Shuey. "Gender and the Devolution of Pension Risks in the US." *Current Sociology* 55, no. 2 (2007): 287–304.

17. http://laborcenter.berkeley.edu/pdf/2016/NIRS-Women-In-Retirement.pdf.

18. O'Rand and Shuey, "Gender and the Devolution of Pension Risks in the US."

19. Agnew, Julie, Pierluigi Balduzzi, and Annika Sunden. "Portfolio Choice and Trading in a Large 401 (K) Plan." *American Economic Review* 93, no. 1 (2003): 193–215.

20. Pleau, Robin L. "Gender Differences in Postretirement Employment." *Research on Aging* 32, no. 3 (2010): 267–303.

21. Anderson, Keith A., Virginia E. Richardson, Noelle L. Fields, and Robert A. Harootyan. "Inclusion or Exclusion? Exploring Barriers to Employment for Low-Income Older Adults." *Journal of Gerontological Social Work* 56, no. 4 (2013): 318–34.

22. Roscigno, Vincent J., Sherry Mong, Reginald Byron, and Griff Tester. "Age Discrimination, Social Closure and Employment." *Social Forces* 86, no. 1 (2007): 313–34; Gee, Gilbert C., Eliza K. Pavalko, and J. Scott Long. "Age, Cohort and Perceived Age Discrimination: Using the Life Course to Assess Self-Reported Age Discrimination." *Social Forces* 86, no. 1 (2007): 265–90.

23. All data in this paragraph are from the Henry J. Kaiser Family Foundation. http://kff.org/womens-health-policy/fact-sheet/womens-health-insurance-coverage-fact-sheet/.

24. The PPACA required that the states expand coverage to Americans at 138% or below of the poverty line. However, in 2012, the Supreme Court struck this provision down. States now have the option of expanding Medicaid coverage, but are not required to do so.

25. http://kff.org/uninsured/state-indicator/rate-by-gender/.

26. Medicare also provides health care coverage for younger individuals with certain disabilities and health conditions.

27. Pages 3 and 5: Cubanski, Juliette, Christina Swoope, Cristina Boccuti, Gretchen Jacobson, Giselle Casillas, Shannon Griffin, and Tricia Neuman. *A Primer on Medicare: Key Facts about the Medicare Program and the People It Covers.* Henry J. Kaiser Family Foundation, 2015.

28. Salganicoff, Alina. "Women and Medicare: An Unfinished Agenda." *Generations* 39, no. 2 (2015): 43.

29. www.medicare.gov/your-medicare-costs/costs-at-a-glance/costs-at-glance.html Document15 and https://www.medicare.gov/part-d/costs/deductible/drug-plan-deductibles.html.

30. Most Medicare Part D prescription plans have a coverage gap (commonly known as the donut hole) whereby individuals have to pay significantly more for their drugs up to a certain limit.

31. www.cms.gov/Research-Statistics-Data-and-Systems/Statistics-Trends-and-Reports/NationalHealthExpendData/Age-and-Gender.html.

32. http://kff.org/report-section/what-could-a-medicaid-per-capita-cap-mean-for-low-income-people-on-medicare-appendix-update/.

33. Brown, Jeffrey R., and Amy Finkelstein. "The Private Market for Long-Term Care Insurance in the United States: A Review of the Evidence." *Journal of Risk and Insurance* 76, no. 1 (2009): 5–29; Brown, Jeffrey R., and Amy Finkelstein. "Why Is the Market for Long-Term Care Insurance So Small?" *Journal of Public Economics* 91, no. 10 (2007): 1967–91.

34. https://attorney.elderlawanswers.com/uploads/media/documents/2017_price_index_ltc.pdf. Note that this index is calculated by the American Association for Long-Term Care Insurance and is based on a typical resident in Tennessee. Rates vary significantly by state.

35. www.genworth.com/about-us/industry-expertise/cost-of-care.html.

36. Montenegro, Xenia P. *The Divorce Experience: A Study of Divorce at Midlife and Beyond.* Washington, DC: AARP, 2004.

CHAPTER 4

1. Cooney, Teresa M., and Kathleen Dunne. "Intimate Relationships in Later Life: Current Realities, Future Prospects." *Journal of Family Issues* 22, no. 7 (2001): 838–58; Milardo, Robert M. "Changes in Social Networks of Women and Men Following Divorce: A Review." *Journal of Family Issues* 8, no. 1 (1987): 78–96.

2. Dare, Julie, and Lelia Green. "Rethinking Social Support in Women's Midlife Years: Women's Experiences of Social Support in Online Environments." *European Journal of Cultural Studies* 14, no. 5 (2011): 473–90.

3. McLaughlin, Deirdre, Dimitrios Vagenas, Nancy A. Pachana, Nelufa Begum, and Annette Dobson. "Gender Differences in Social Network Size and Satisfaction in Adults in Their 70s." *Journal of Health Psychology* 15, no. 5 (2010): 671–79; Milardo, "Changes in Social Networks of Women and Men Following Divorce."

4. Messner, Michael. "Boyhood, Organized Sports, and the Construction of Masculinities." *Journal of Contemporary Ethnography* 18, no. 4 (1990): 416–44; Strikwerda, Robert A., and Larry May. "Male Friendship and Intimacy." *Hypatia* 7, no. 3 (1992): 110–25.

5. Levy, Donald P. "Hegemonic Complicity, Friendship, and Comradeship: Validation and Causal Processes among White, Middle-Class, Middle-Aged Men." *The Journal of Men's Studies* 13, no. 2 (2005): 199–224.

6. Shaw, Rhonda, Judith Gullifer, and Rebecca Shaw. "'I Think It's a Communal Thing': Men's Friendships in Later Life." *The Journal of Men's Studies* 22, no. 1 (2014): 34–52.

7. Kearns, Jill N., and Kenneth E. Leonard. "Social Networks, Structural Interdependence, and Marital Quality over the Transition to Marriage: A Prospective Analysis." *Journal of Family Psychology* 18, no. 2 (2004): 383.

8. Ibid.

9. Kramrei, Elizabeth, Carissa Coit, Sarah Martin, Wendy Fogo, and Annette Mahoney. "Post-Divorce Adjustment and Social Relationships: A Meta-Analytic Review." *Journal of Divorce & Remarriage* 46, nos. 3–4 (2007): 145–66.

10. Miller, Nancy B., Virginia L. Smerglia, D. Scott Gaudet, and Gay C. Kitson. "Stressful Life Events, Social Support, and the Distress of Widowed and Divorced Women: A Counteractive Model." *Journal of Family Issues* 19, no. 2 (1998): 181–203.

11. Greif, Geoffrey L., and Kathleen Holtz Deal. "The Impact of Divorce on Friendships with Couples and Individuals." *Journal of Divorce & Remarriage* 53, no. 6 (2012): 421–35; Cooney and Dunne, "Intimate Relationships in Later Life."

12. McLaughlin et al., "Gender Differences in Social Network Size and Satisfaction in Adults in Their 70s."

13. Miller et al., "Stressful Life Events, Social Support, and the Distress of Widowed and Divorced Women."

14. Milardo, "Changes in Social Networks of Women and Men Following Divorce."

15. Greif and Deal, "The Impact of Divorce on Friendships with Couples and Individuals."

16. Ibid.

17. The studies discussed in this section generally include adult children whose parents divorced after they had reached the age of 18, but do not necessarily imply that all parents divorced after the age of 50, the definition of gray

divorce used in this book. Some include younger parents of these adult children (parents in their forties) and some do not indicate at what ages the parents divorced when they describe the effects of marital breakdowns that occur after the children turn 18. However, the inclusion of children ages 18 and over when their parents divorced is a good proxy for those parents experiencing a gray divorce.

18. Cooper Sumner, Christa. "Adult Children of Divorce: Awareness and Intervention." *Journal of Divorce & Remarriage* 54, no. 4 (2013): 271–81.

19. Campbell, Marjory. "Divorce at Mid-Life: Intergenerational Issues." *Journal of Divorce & Remarriage* 23, nos. 1–2 (1995): 185–202.

20. Duran-Aydintug, Candan. "Adult Children of Divorce Revisited: When They Speak Up." *Journal of Divorce & Remarriage* 27, nos. 1–2 (1997): 71–83; Cooney, Teresa M. "Young Adults' Relations with Parents: The Influence of Recent Parental Divorce." *Journal of Marriage and the Family* 56, no. 1 (1994): 45–56.

21. Campbell, "Divorce at Mid-Life"; Cooper Sumner, "Adult Children of Divorce"; Greenwood, Joleen Loucks. "Parent–Child Relationships in the Context of a Mid- to Late-Life Parental Divorce." *Journal of Divorce & Remarriage* 53, no. 1 (2012): 1–17.

22. Aquilino, William S. "Later Life Parental Divorce and Widowhood: Impact on Young Adults' Assessment of Parent-Child Relations." *Journal of Marriage and the Family* 56, no. 4 (1994): 908–22.

23. Montenegro, Xenia P. *The Divorce Experience: A Study of Divorce at Midlife and Beyond.* Washington, DC: AARP, 2004.

24. Brown, Susan L., and I-Fen Lin. "The Gray Divorce Revolution: Rising Divorce among Middle-Aged and Older Adults, 1990–2010." *The Journals of Gerontology Series B: Psychological Sciences and Social Sciences* 67, no. 6 (2012): 731–41.

25. Jensen, Todd M., and Gary L. Bowen. "Mid- and Late-Life Divorce and Parents' Perceptions of Emerging Adult Children's Emotional Reactions." *Journal of Divorce & Remarriage* 56, no. 5 (2015): 409–27.

26. Crowley, Jocelyn Elise. *Mothers Unite! Organizing for Workplace Flexibility and the Transformation of Family Life.* Ithaca: Cornell University Press, 2013.

27. Shapiro, Adam. "Later-Life Divorce and Parent-Adult Child Contact and Proximity: A Longitudinal Analysis." *Journal of Family Issues* 24, no. 2 (2003): 264–85.

28. Kalmijn, Matthijs. "Relationships between Fathers and Adult Children: The Cumulative Effects of Divorce and Repartnering." *Journal of Family Issues* 36, no. 6 (2015): 737–59; Kalmijn. "Adult Children's Relationships with Married Parents, Divorced Parents, and Stepparents: Biology, Marriage, or Residence?" *Journal of Marriage and Family* 75, no. 5 (2013): 1181–93.

29. Cooney, "Young Adults' Relations with Parents."

30. Aquilino, "Later Life Parental Divorce and Widowhood"; Shapiro, "Later-Life Divorce and Parent-Adult Child Contact and Proximity."

31. Kalmijn, Matthijs. "Gender Differences in the Effects of Divorce, Widowhood and Remarriage on Intergenerational Support: Does Marriage Protect Fathers?" *Social Forces* 85, no. 3 (2007): 1079–104.

32. Ibid.; Bulcroft, Kris A., and Richard A. Bulcroft. "The Timing of Divorce Effects on Parent-Child Relationships in Later Life." *Research on Aging* 13, no. 2 (1991): 226–43; Shapiro, "Later-Life Divorce and Parent-Adult Child Contact and Proximity"; Cooney, Teresa M., and Peter Uhlenberg. "The Role of Divorce in Men's Relations with Their Adult Children after Mid-Life." *Journal of Marriage and the Family* 52, no. 3 (1990): 677–88.

33. Brown and Lin, "The Gray Divorce Revolution."

CHAPTER 5

1. Bohannan, Paul. "The Six Stations of Divorce." In *Divorce and After: An Analysis of the Emotional and Social Problems of Divorce*, edited by Paul Bohannan, 33–62. Garden City, NY: Doubleday Anchor, 1971.

2. Mezirow, Jack. *Learning as Transformation: Critical Perspectives on a Theory in Progress.* San Francisco: Jossey-Bass, 2000; Thomas, Cindy, and Marilyn Ryan. "Women's Perception of the Divorce Experience: A Qualitative Study." *Journal of Divorce & Remarriage* 49, nos. 3–4 (2008): 210–24.

3. Sakraida, Teresa J. "Divorce Transition Differences of Midlife Women." *Issues in Mental Health Nursing* 26, no. 2 (2005): 225–49.

4. Pudrovska, Tetyana, Scott Schieman, and Deborah Carr. "Strains of Singlehood in Later Life: Do Race and Gender Matter?" *The Journals of Gerontology Series B: Psychological Sciences and Social Sciences* 61, no. 6 (2006): S315–22.

5. Montenegro, Xenia P. *The Divorce Experience: A Study of Divorce at Midlife and Beyond.* Washington, DC: AARP, 2004.

6. Kemp, Candace L., Carolyn J. Rosenthal, and Margaret Denton. "Financial Planning for Later Life: Subjective Understandings of Catalysts and Constraints." *Journal of Aging Studies* 19, no. 3 (2005): 273–90.

7. Montenegro, "The Divorce Experience."

8. Määttä, Kaarina. "The Throes and Relief of Divorce." *Journal of Divorce & Remarriage* 52, no. 6 (2011): 415–34; Lloyd, Griselda M., Joanni L. Sailor, and William Carney. "A Phenomenological Study of Postdivorce Adjustment in Midlife." *Journal of Divorce & Remarriage* 55, no. 6 (2014): 441–50; Montenegro, "The Divorce Experience."

9. Baum, Nehami. "'Separation Guilt' in Women Who Initiate Divorce." *Clinical Social Work Journal* 35, no. 1 (2007): 47–55; Kiiski, Jouko, Kaarina Määttä,

and Satu Uusiautti. "'For Better and for Worse, or until . . . ': On Divorce and Guilt." *Journal of Divorce & Remarriage* 54, no. 7 (2013): 519–36.

10. Gray, Matthew, David de Vaus, Lixia Qu, and David Stanton. "Divorce and the Wellbeing of Older Australians." *Ageing and Society* 31, no. 3 (2011): 475–98.

11. Sakraida, Teresa J. "Common Themes in the Divorce Transition Experience of Midlife Women." *Journal of Divorce & Remarriage* 43, nos. 1–2 (2005): 69–88.

12. Allemand, Mathias, Patrick L. Hill, and Regula Lehmann. "Divorce and Personality Development across Middle Adulthood." *Personal Relationships* 22, no. 1 (2015): 122–37.

13. Montenegro, "The Divorce Experience"; Määttä, "The Throes and Relief of Divorce."

14. Thomas and Ryan, "Women's Perception of the Divorce Experience."

15. Sakraida, "Common Themes in the Divorce Transition Experience of Midlife Women."

16. Määttä, "The Throes and Relief of Divorce."

17. Lloyd, Sailor, and Carney, "A Phenomenological Study of Postdivorce Adjustment in Midlife."

18. Sakraida, "Divorce Transition Differences of Midlife Women."

19. Bourassa, Kyle J., David A. Sbarra, and Mark A. Whisman. "Women in Very Low Quality Marriages Gain Life Satisfaction Following Divorce." *Journal of Family Psychology* 29, no. 3 (2015): 490–99.

20. Kemp, Rosenthal, and Denton, "Financial Planning for Later Life."

21. Montenegro, "The Divorce Experience."

CHAPTER 6

1. Data for this entire paragraph come from www.socialsecurity.gov/policy/docs/statcomps/income_pop55/2012/sect11.html#table11.1.

2. Lee, Sunhwa. "Racial and Ethnic Differences in Women's Retirement Security." *Journal of Women, Politics & Policy* 30, nos. 2–3 (2009): 141–72.

3. Hartmann, Heidi, and Ashley English. "Older Women's Retirement Security: A Primer." *Journal of Women, Politics & Policy* 30, nos. 2–3 (2009): 109–40.

4. Budig, Michelle J., and Paula England. "The Wage Penalty for Motherhood." *American Sociological Review* 66, no. 2 (2001): 204–25.

5. Kahn, Joan R., Javier García-Manglano, and Suzanne M. Bianchi. "The Motherhood Penalty at Midlife: Long-Term Effects of Children on Women's Careers." *Journal of Marriage and Family* 76, no. 1 (2014): 56–72.

6. Hodges, Melissa J., and Michelle J. Budig. "Who Gets the Daddy Bonus? Organizational Hegemonic Masculinity and the Impact of Fatherhood on Earnings." *Gender & Society* 24, no. 6 (2010): 717–45.

7. Lee, "Racial and Ethnic Differences in Women's Retirement Security."

8. Purcell, Patrick. "Pension Sponsorship and Participation: Summary of Recent Trends." Congressional Research Service, 2009.

9. Ibid.; Holden, Karen C., and Angela Fontes. "Economic Security in Retirement: How Changes in Employment and Marriage Have Altered Retirement-Related Economic Risks for Women." *Journal of Women, Politics & Policy* 30, nos. 2–3 (2009): 173–97.

10. Holden and Fontes, "Economic Security in Retirement."

11. Sharma, Andy. "Divorce/Separation in Later-Life: A Fixed Effects Analysis of Economic Effects by Gender." *Journal of Family and Economic Issues* 36, no. 2 (2015): 299–306.

12. Table 16: BLS. "Women in the Labor Force: A Databook." Washington, DC: US Bureau of Labor Statistics, 2015.

13. Cleek, Margaret Guminski, and T. Allan Pearson. "Perceived Causes of Divorce: An Analysis of Interrelationships." *Journal of Marriage and the Family* 47, no. 1 (1985): 179–83.

14. Tamborini, Christopher R., and Kevin Whitman. "Lowering Social Security's Duration-of-Marriage Requirement: Distributional Effects for Future Female Retirees." *Journal of Women & Aging* 22, no. 3 (2010): 184–203.

15. Page 129: Hartmann and English, "Older Women's Retirement Security."

16. All data in this paragraph are from www.ssa.gov/news/press/factsheets/ss-customer/women-ret.pdf.

17. Table 8: Kreider, Rose Marie, and Renee Ellis. "Number, Timing, and Duration of Marriages and Divorces, 2009." US Department of Commerce, Economics and Statistics Administration, US Census Bureau, 2011.

18. Herd, Pamela. "Women, Public Pensions, and Poverty: What Can the United States Learn from Other Countries?" *Journal of Women, Politics & Policy* 30, nos. 2–3 (2009): 301–34.

19. Lee, "Racial and Ethnic Differences in Women's Retirement Security."

20. Hartmann and English, "Older Women's Retirement Security"; Salganicoff, Alina. "Women and Medicare: An Unfinished Agenda." *Generations* 39, no. 2 (2015): 43.

21. Sohn, Heeju. "Health Insurance and Risk of Divorce: Does Having Your Own Insurance Matter?" *Journal of Marriage and Family* 77, no. 4 (2015): 982–95.

22. Peters, Elizabeth H., Kosali Simon, and Jamie Rubenstein Taber. "Marital Disruption and Health Insurance." *Demography* 51, no. 4 (2014): 1397–421.

23. Lavelle, Bridget, and Pamela J. Smock. "Divorce and Women's Risk of Health Insurance Loss." *Journal of Health and Social Behavior* 53, no. 4 (2012): 413–31.

24. http://kff.org/medicaid/report/medicaid-and-long-term-services-and-supports-a-primer/; Howes, Candace. "Who Will Care for the Women?" *Journal of Women, Politics & Policy* 30, nos. 2–3 (2009): 248–71.

25. Vukalovich, Dragica, and Nerina Caltabiano. "The Effectiveness of a Community Group Intervention Program on Adjustment to Separation and Divorce." *Journal of Divorce & Remarriage* 48, nos. 3–4 (2008): 145–68.

26. Rae, Judith, Jamia Jasper-Jacobsen, and Carol J. Blatter. "Support Groups for Persons Experiencing Divorce in Later Life." *Behavioral Sciences & the Law* 9, no. 4 (1991): 477–86.

27. For information on support groups for younger men with children, see Frieman, Barry B. "Challenges Faced by Fathers in a Divorce Support Group." *Journal of Divorce & Remarriage* 37, nos. 1–2 (2002): 163–73.

28. "National Vital Statistics Report (NVSR), Deaths: Final Data for 2014." United States Centers for Disease Control and Prevention, 2016.

29. Jenkins, Kathleen E. "In Concert and Alone: Divorce and Congregational Experience." *Journal for the Scientific Study of Religion* 49, no. 2 (2010): 278–92.

30. Molina, Olga. "Members' Satisfaction with Union-Based Divorce Support Groups." *Journal of Divorce & Remarriage* 42, nos. 1–2 (2004): 145–57.

31. Øygard, Lisbet, and Stein Hardeng. "Divorce Support Groups—How Do Group Characteristics Influence Adjustment to Divorce?" *Social Work with Groups* 24, no. 1 (2002): 69–87.

32. Molina, "Members' Satisfaction with Union-Based Divorce Support Groups."

33. Øygard, Lisbet. "Divorce Support Groups: What Is the Role of the Participants' Personal Capital Regarding Adjustment to Divorce?" *Journal of Divorce & Remarriage* 40, nos. 3–4 (2004): 103–19; Saunders, Magon M., Denice C. Curtis, Jeffrey L. Alexander, and Emanuel L. Williams. "Can Christian Divorce Support Groups Influence Forgiveness and Health Outcomes in Black Divorcees? A Phenomenological Investigation." *Journal of Divorce & Remarriage* 54, no. 7 (2013): 550–75.

34. Øygard, Lisbet. "Therapeutic Factors in Divorce Support Groups." *Journal of Divorce & Remarriage* 36, nos. 1–2 (2001): 141–58.

35. Øygard, "Divorce Support Groups: What Is the Role of the Participants' Personal Capital Regarding Adjustment to Divorce?"; Øygard, "Divorce Support Groups: What Factors Are of Importance Regarding Friendship Development in the Groups?" *Social Work with Groups* 26, no. 4 (2004): 59–77.

36. Øygard, "Divorce Support Groups: What Factors Are of Importance Regarding Friendship Development in the Groups?"

37. Vera, Maria I. "Effects of Divorce Groups on Individual Adjustment: A Multiple Methodology Approach." Paper presented at the Social Work Research and Abstracts, 1990; Øygard, "Divorce Support Groups: What Is the Role of the Participants' Personal Capital Regarding Adjustment to Divorce?"

38. Øygard and Hardeng, "Divorce Support Groups."

39. Saunders et al., "Can Christian Divorce Support Groups Influence Forgiveness and Health Outcomes in Black Divorcees?"; Molina, "Members' Satisfaction with Union-Based Divorce Support Groups."

40. Øygard and Hardeng, "Divorce Support Groups."

41. www.acf.hhs.gov/programs/ofa/programs/healthy-marriage/responsible-fatherhood.

42. www.fatherhood.gov.

43. For some evidence of how a support group has helped older women experiencing a gray divorce, see Blatter, Carol Wechsler, and Jamia Jasper Jacobsen. "Older Women Coping with Divorce: Peer Support Groups." *Women & Therapy* 14, nos. 1–2 (1993): 141–55; Norberry, Laura Portz. "Divorce over 50: A Program of Support." *The Journal for Specialists in Group Work* 11, no. 3 (1986): 157–62.

DATA APPENDIX

1. Tourangeau, Roger. "Defining Hard-to-Survey Populations." In *Hard-to-Survey Populations,* edited by Roger Tourangeau, Brad Edwards, Timothy P. Johnson, Kirk M. Wolter, and Nancy Bates, 3–20. Cambridge: Cambridge University Press, 2014; Teitler, Julien O., Nancy E. Reichman, and Susan Sprachman. "Costs and Benefits of Improving Response Rates for a Hard-to-Reach Population." *Public Opinion Quarterly* 67, no. 1 (2003): 126–38.

2. Rife, Sean C., Kelly L. Cate, Michal Kosinski, and David Stillwell. "Participant Recruitment and Data Collection through Facebook: The Role of Personality Factors." *International Journal of Social Research Methodology* 19, no. 1 (2016): 69–83; Schneider, Sid, Amelia Burke-Garcia, and Gail Thomas. "Facebook as a Tool for Respondent Tracing." *Survey Practice* 8, no. 1 (2015): 1–6; Bhutta, Christine Brickman. "Not by the Book: Facebook as a Sampling Frame." *Sociological Methods and Research* 41, no. 1 (2012): 57–88.

3. Hennink, Monique, Inge Hutter, and Ajay Bailey. *Qualitative Research Methods.* Thousand Oaks, CA: Sage, 2011.

4. All of these statistics from a nationally representative sample are drawn from Table 2: Brown, Susan L., and I-Fen Lin. "The Gray Divorce Revolution: Rising Divorce among Middle-Aged and Older Adults, 1990–2010." *The Journals of Gerontology Series B: Psychological Sciences and Social Sciences* 67, no. 6 (2012): 731–41.

5. Blumer, Herbert. "What Is Wrong with Social Theory?" *American Sociological Review* 19, no. 1 (1954): 3–10; Blumer. *Symbolic Interactionism: Perspective and Method.* Berkeley: University of California Press, 1986.

6. Strauss, Anselm, and Juliet Corbin. *Basics of Grounded Theory: Grounded Theory Procedures and Techniques.* Newbury Park, CA: Sage, 1990.

7. Geertz, Clifford. *The Interpretation of Cultures.* New York: Basic, 1973.

Index